BLOWBACK

The Untold Story of the FBI and the Oklahoma City Bombing

MARGARET ROBERTS

RESEARCH BY RICHARD BOOTH

Published by Bombardier Books
An Imprint of Post Hill Press
ISBN: 979-8-88845-842-6
ISBN (eBook): 979-8-88845-843-3

Blowback:
The Untold Story of the FBI and the Oklahoma City Bombing

Cover Design by Jim Villaflores

Post Hill Press
New York • Nashville
posthillpress.com

Published in the United States of America

2 3 4 5 6 7 8 9 10

For Kenneth Michael Trentadue

Kenneth with older brother Jesse in 1950s West Virginia

TABLE OF CONTENTS

CHAPTER 1

TRAIL OF DEATH

Kenneth Trentadue was no saint. He robbed banks to feed a heroin habit that followed him home from the Army during the Vietnam War. Then, after serving prison time for the robberies, Kenneth skipped out on his parole over a no-drinking rule, violating what he saw as a working man's right to a beer at the end of the day. No one looked very hard for him for years. By 1995, Kenneth had turned his life around at the age of forty-four. He was happily married with his first child on the way, working construction in Southern California. Life was good until June 10 of that year, two months after the Oklahoma City bombing that killed 168 men, women, and children on April 19, 1995, in what still stands as America's deadliest domestic terror attack.

While Kenneth was crossing back into California that day after visiting his wife Carmen's family in Mexico, border officials arrested him for the old parole violation. Two months later, in August, authorities suddenly moved Kenneth 1300 miles away to Oklahoma City for a hearing that would likely result in a few months of prison time. The move struck the Trentadue family as suspicious. Kenneth's arrest, crimes, and parole officer were all in California. "It's that jet age thing," he told his sister-in-law by phone, downplaying the family's concern and referring to the US Marshals Service "Con Air" flight that transported him to Oklahoma City.

But something was wrong. Three days later, on August 21, 1995, Kenneth Trentadue was dead in cell 709A of the Bureau of Prisons' Federal Transfer Center (FTC) in Oklahoma City. The prison's call to Kenneth's mother, Wilma Trentadue, in California raised an immediate red flag. Associate Warden Marie Carter said that Wilma's son, Vance Paul Brockway, had committed suicide. This death made no sense. Kenneth's mother told the warden that she did not have a son by that name, but she did have a son at the Federal Transfer Center named Kenneth Michael Trentadue. Brockway was an alias Kenneth had used in his bank robbery days in the 1980s. As implausible as it seems, the Federal Bureau of Prisons (BOP), FBI, and Justice Department never knew Kenneth's actual name until his mother informed the warden.

Still, Wilma Trentadue could not believe that her son had killed himself. She had spoken to Kenneth by phone the day before. He was in good spirits and looking forward to coming home to his wife and newborn son. Another red flag went up when Carter offered free cremation for the dead prisoner. Kenneth's mother said she would need to consult his wife about that. But the warden corrected her from prison records: Brockway had no wife. Oh yes, he certainly did, Mrs. Trentadue advised, and a brother, too, who was a lawyer. "He will know what to do," she told the warden.

By that afternoon, Kenneth's older brother, lawyer Jesse Trentadue, was on the phone with Carter, straightening out what he could about the tragedy, a complicated challenge. For reasons no one would ever explain, all of Kenneth's 1995 prison records listed him not by his actual name but by his alias, Vance Paul Brockway.

In Jesse's call to the prison, Associate Warden Carter confirmed from medical records that Kenneth had no injuries when he entered the special housing unit cell, where he supposedly committed suicide despite the prison's claim its maximum-security cells were suicide-proof. As for the strange cremation offer, Jesse rejected it and ordered the warden to return his brother's body to California for burial.

For three decades, Jesse has engaged in a guerrilla war for the truth that began with those two confounding phone calls with the prison the day Kenneth Trentadue died. But before he could figure out what to do, Jesse would have to find out why most of the puzzle pieces went missing.

Kenneth was headed home to California in a wooden coffin. His family had no reason to connect his death to his move to Oklahoma City, mythologized as "the Heartland" since the bombing. Even more remote was any connection to the global FBI manhunt in search of the escaped terrorist bomber, known only as John Doe 2, who rode next to the Oklahoma City bomber, Timothy McVeigh, in the now infamous yellow Ryder truck—then vanished into thin air.

The FBI never captured or even identified John Doe 2. He eventually evolved into the mystery man of the bombing case, out there somewhere or nowhere with D. B. Cooper and other fugitive legends of American crime. Unknown to the Trentadue family, Kenneth was a perfect match to the John Doe 2 profile the FBI was circulating nationwide, including the dragon tattoo on his left arm, the brown pickup truck he drove, and his profile as a former bank robber.

The search for John Doe 2, with its $2 million reward, was briefly the biggest, most expensive manhunt in US history. In the bombing's aftermath, dozens of eyewitnesses swore they saw a bombing suspect with a bodybuilder's physique, dark hair, and dark complexion accompanying McVeigh in Kansas or on the bombing run in Oklahoma City. Journalists reported that the FBI had surveillance videotape of the escaped bomber at the crime scene with McVeigh.[1]

The massive manhunt was surprisingly short-lived, however. By mid-June 1995, right around the time of Kenneth's arrest, federal authorities began floating the idea that John Doe 2 existed only in witnesses' imaginations. Sorry, they said, the search for John Doe 2 was all a mistake. However, as this investigation will reveal, that message was Justice Department spin for public consumption. The FBI did not wind down its John Doe 2 manhunt. Instead, about a month after the bombing, the bureau simply confined the search to FBI professionals only. They continued to hunt for John Doe 2, refocusing on a developing lead tying Timothy McVeigh to a domestic terror group that was robbing banks to finance a neo-Nazi insurrection in America.

In FBI teletypes on April 27 and May 1, 1995, that were part of the bombing investigation, the bureau pressed its field offices nationwide to search for bank robbers fitting a profile that included using hoax explosives and other behavioral markers "used by subject McVeigh and his associates."[2] On April 26, 1995, the FBI's crime lab began an investigation to check Timothy McVeigh's fingerprints against those from unsolved bank robbery scenes across the Midwest. While that investigation produced no fingerprint matches, it marked the start of the FBI's sustained focus on a bank robbery connection to the bombing. On April 28,

1995, the *Los Angeles Times,* with deep law enforcement sources on the bombing investigation, reported on its front page that the FBI believed the bombing was the work of four to five people and mentioned a possible bank robbery link.

The FBI's private theory was that John Doe 2 might be one of Timothy McVeigh's associates in a fugitive neo-Nazi bank robbery gang calling itself the "Aryan Republican Army," or the "ARA," as the FBI frequently called it. The FBI didn't know the whereabouts of the ARA gang, but suspected they were professional revolutionaries and a threat to public safety.

In 1994–95, the Aryan Republican Army gang robbed $250,000 (double that today, adjusting for inflation) from twenty-two banks around the Midwest, donating generously to white power causes from the proceeds. Authorities never recovered any of the money, which, in the aftermath of the Oklahoma City bombing, the FBI secretly believed Timothy McVeigh had helped steal.

Kenneth Trentadue knew nothing of this. Tragically, the FBI knew nothing about Kenneth either, not even his true name. The man known to the FBI only by his bygone bank robbery alias, Vance Paul Brockway, had no connection to the bombing. His fatal misfortune was being in the wrong place at the wrong time, crossing the Mexican border, and driving his brown truck with a dragon tattoo visible on his arm while still owing a small debt to society for an old parole violation. This book exposes a cover-up reaching deep inside the US Justice Department. It drove the urgency of the manhunt for John Doe 2 and tragically may have caught Kenneth Trentadue in its web, taking his life.

To this day, the Department of Justice (DOJ) resists telling the whole story of the Oklahoma City bomb plot, which would identify and reveal the roles of law enforcement insiders in the tragedy. Through a rogue undercover informant operation, evidence suggests that DOJ insiders helped incite and somehow failed to prevent the catastrophic terror attack in Oklahoma. Then, operating behind a smoke screen of official secrecy, they used the Justice Department's considerable resources to cover their tracks.

Like the rest of the American public in late August 1995, the Trentadue family knew nothing about the secret FBI manhunt that was underway for a tattooed bank robber believed to be Timothy McVeigh's accomplice. They were in Southern California, waiting in suspense for Kenneth's body to arrive home, hoping it would bring some tangible clarification to the heartbreaking mystery of his death in Oklahoma. Nothing could have prepared them for what was coming when the train bearing his coffin arrived.

At the funeral home in Westminster, California, Kenneth's wife, mother, and sister had the staff remove heavy makeup applied by the prison to Kenneth's body. Underneath, they discovered bruises, his cracked skull, possible stun gun burns, and an incision indicating that someone had cut Kenneth's throat.[3] Knowing they needed to preserve the evidence of torture, Jesse Trentadue and Kenneth's sister, Donna, undertook the agonizing task of photographing and videotaping their brother's battered body.

After the memorial service, Jesse let down his lawyer's guard and gave voice to raw fury: "My brother had been so badly beaten that I personally saw several mourners leave the viewing to vomit in the parking lot!" Jesse wrote in a letter to federal Bureau of Prisons officials. "Anyone seeing my brother's body with his bruised and lacerated forehead, throat cut, and blue-black knuckles would not have concluded that his death was either easy or a 'suicide'!"

With his letter and copies of the family's photos documenting Kenneth's injuries, Jesse flew to Dallas and Oklahoma City, delivering these materials to prison officials, the FBI, the state medical examiner who was investigating the cause of death, and reporters. None of the evidence made any difference to federal authorities, however. Eleven days after Kenneth Trentadue died, the prison issued its only press release, calling his death a suicide by hanging. The state medical examiner, Dr. Fred Jordan, was furious when he saw that press release. He had not made any such determination as to how Kenneth died, and the call was his, not the prison's.

The press release attempted to explain that the "cuts and abrasions" on Kenneth's body were "self-inflicted" with "permissible items found in the cell," presumably referring to a toothbrush, a tube of toothpaste, a deck of cards, and three combs. This flimsy piece of disinformation wouldn't settle the matter. But it did have one powerful thing going for it. It was the official story.

Toward the end of 1995, Jesse received a phone call at his law office in Salt Lake City that gave him pause. An anonymous tipster on the line claimed that the FBI killed Kenneth in an interrogation gone wrong. The tipster said that Kenneth "fit a profile." The caller mentioned "bank robberies" and soon hung up. To Jesse, the message sounded far-fetched. Jumping into conspiracy theories was not going to bring his brother back. Jesse set the call aside. He needed tangible leads to pursue. The lawyer dug in for what he knew would be a marathon investigation.

Around the same time as that phone call from the anonymous tipster in late 1995, an Arkansas family vanished from their home. Gun dealer William Mueller; his wife, Nancy; and her eight-year-old daughter, Sarah, remained missing for half a year until June 1996. A woman fishing spotted a pair of tennis shoes and a leg bobbing in the water of an Arkansas bayou. The missing couple and the little girl, their heads sealed inside plastic bags with duct tape, had been suffocated and weighted down with heavy rocks.

Two radical neo-Nazi gang members, Chevie Kehoe and Daniel Lee, were tried on federal racketeering charges, including the murders of the Mueller family, and for their roles in a Kehoe-led domestic terror group modeled, like the Aryan Republican Army, on Robert Mathews's notorious 1980s gang, "The Order."

Kehoe's mother, Gloria Kehoe, testified that her son confessed while driving her to the grocery store, saying he put the Muellers "on a liquid diet." According to her, Lee also later confessed. Both defendants were convicted, though rumors swirled about the malignant Kehoe family dynamic that might have led a mother and a brother, who also testified against Kehoe, to accuse him.[4]

Meanwhile, authorities never questioned two men William Mueller told a reporter he was "especially concerned about" a month before the family disappeared. The gun dealer, a Special Forces veteran and militia member, said he believed he might be a target for assassination because of his conflict with the federal Bureau of Alcohol, Tobacco and Firearms (ATF) over products he was selling at gun shows. A worried Mueller pulled out a spiral notebook and showed the reporter the page where he had written down the names of two men he believed were ATF agents who had given him trouble at a gun show: Andreas Strassmeir and Michael Brescia.[5]

Before the Oklahoma City bombing, these two men were roommates in Elohim City, a reclusive white separatist compound and reputed white power way station with a heavy anti-government vibe in rural eastern Oklahoma. Strassmeir, Elohim City's paramilitary trainer and, some said, its security chief, was in the US illegally on an expired visa. In the two weeks before the April 1995 bombing, Timothy McVeigh placed two phone calls to Elohim City asking to speak to Strassmeir.

Strassmeir's roommate, Michael Brescia, was a member of the Aryan Republican Army gang, several of whom lived or stayed in Elohim City in 1994-95. The Kehoe family also lived in Elohim City before the bombing.

Afterward, Strassmeir and Brescia both left Elohim City. Under a cloud of questions about his ties to Timothy McVeigh and with the help of a former CIA operative, Strassmeir slipped across the Mexican border in January 1996, the same month the Mueller family disappeared in Arkansas. As for Brescia, he moved randomly around the country, dogged by blogger Mike Vanderboegh's campaign in *The John Doe Times* portraying Brescia as a likely John Doe 2 suspect, until his arrest in early 1997 for his role in the bank robberies. Through their lawyers, both men denied any role in the bombing.

In a perplexing 2006 footnote to the Mueller family murder mystery, a Justice Department–funded academic terrorism study uncovered fresh connections between the Muellers, the Aryan Republican Army, Chevie Kehoe, and the bombing. According to the report, the Mueller killings were murders for hire, ordered by the Aryan Republican Army to be carried out by Chevie Kehoe, whose neo-Nazi gang was a cell of the ARA.

Quoting from the report: "The ARA contracted Kehoe to murder the Mueller family, brief residents of Elohim City, who were privy to information dealing with the ARA's supposed involvement in the Oklahoma City bombing. The Muellers reportedly left Elohim City in fear they would be assassinated by Andreas Strassmeir and Michael Brescia, the latter a known member of the ARA."[6]

⅄

Back in Oklahoma City in May 1996, a month before the Muellers' bodies surfaced in the Arkansas bayou, another mysterious death occurred with never-explained links to the bombing. Police Sergeant Terrance Yeakey was a hero cop who arrived on the scene of the blast within a few minutes and carried at least four victims from the rubble of the Alfred P. Murrah Federal Building. A year later, just before he was to receive the Oklahoma City Police Department's Medal of Valor, Yeakey died a gruesome death in a field close to the federal prison in nearby El Reno. Like Kenneth Trentadue, Officer Yeakey supposedly committed suicide. But it was only possible to draw that conclusion by ignoring compelling evidence of murder.

Police found Yeakey's blood-soaked car, then his body a mile and a half away with his wrists, neck, and throat slashed and a gunshot wound to his head from a small-caliber weapon. Author Craig Roberts, a former Tulsa police officer who has written about the case, revealed irregularities in the crime-scene investigation in a 1998 radio interview with Yeakey's ex-wife, Tonia Rivera-Yeakey.

From cuts, bruises, and clumps of dirt and grass in his wounds, it appeared that Yeakey had wrestled on the ground with his killer after a chase from the location where his car was found. At first, a police team found no gun—a red flag to the suicide theory. Sometime after the FBI arrived on the scene, a nine-millimeter semiautomatic pistol was recovered. However, that weapon has never been publicly seen, described, or matched to one that might have belonged to Yeakey.

His body was taken to the Oklahoma City Medical Examiner's Office, then dispatched, without an autopsy, to a funeral parlor, where deep cuts were sewn up and makeup applied. As CNN's Thomas Lake reported in a 2023 story, Yeakey's mother insisted on viewing the body and saw injuries the medical examiner did not report: ligature marks and disfiguring head wounds.[7]

"Mama, they executed him," Yeakey's sister remembered saying. The family theorized that someone tortured the police officer in his car and then handcuffed him, eventually forcing him to kneel in the desolate field and murdering him with a shot to the head.

Author Craig Roberts reached the same conclusion based on ballistics in his book *Medusa File II*. From the downward angle of the bullet wound, Roberts theorized that someone shot Yeakey as he knelt on the ground.[8] Large circular indentations in the skin around the wound led Roberts to conclude the killer used a silencer. But why murder this police officer? Yeakey's family believes that as one of the first responders at the bomb site, he saw shocking evidence of a cover-up in progress to conceal a bombing scenario very different from the one reported to the American public.

"They're not telling the truth," Yeakey told his ex-wife, Tonia. "They're lying about what's going on down there," he said when she picked him up at a hospital after he underwent treatment for injuries he suffered during the rescue mission.[9]

Associates of Yeakey's told CNN's Thomas Lake that Yeakey was "surprised to see so many federal agents, apparently dressed in riot gear, on the scene moments after the blast," as if they had foreknowledge of the mass disaster.[10] If Yeakey had witnessed such a mobilization, that knowledge might have jeopardized him. If federal law enforcement knew what was coming, why didn't someone warn the victims?

Yeakey's sister gave Lake another compelling clue, which supports another persistent outlier theory about the bombing: that explosive charges planted inside the building contributed to the massive damage it sustained. "You know how they said the truck bomb blew in?" Yeakey's sister asked. "He saw evidence of blowing out." Could that evidence have been surveillance videotapes stored at the Oklahoma City Police Department, to which Yeakey might have had access?

Tonia Yeakey claimed in the radio interview that Yeakey's department lost or suppressed his nine-page report on the rescue operation and then ordered him to write a different account. In the following months, she said Yeakey became despondent, secretive, and even paranoid about a private investigation he was conducting.

The day he died, sources told the family that Yeakey left his apartment with boxes of files and videos for a meeting with a federal task force on the bombing investigation. But he changed his mind and reportedly drove to a storage locker he kept in the nearby town of Kingfisher. According to family sources, Yeakey told a friend that federal agents were following him in an unmarked car as he drove to the storage locker, but those reports are unconfirmed.

Craig Roberts speculated that Yeakey's killer or killers beat and threatened him at gunpoint to learn the whereabouts of his briefcase and documents relating to his investigation. "No one knows if he told them or not, but none of it ever surfaced later," Roberts told me.

The Oklahoma City Police Department has refused to make Terrance Yeakey's suicide report public or reopen the case as Roberts has requested multiple times.

⅄

In July 1996, two months after Terrance Yeakey's death, Richard "Wild Bill" Guthrie, coleader of the Aryan Republican Army gang, was found hanging in his jail cell in Coventry, Kentucky. Six months earlier, the FBI's capture of Guthrie and his ARA coleader, Peter Langan, had crushed the gang. The captures ended the ARA bank robbery spree and set the stage for the arrests of the rest of the gang. Within months, Guthrie made a plea deal to testify against them, including Langan and Michael Brescia. Guthrie's jail cell hanging followed soon after that plea deal.

Guthrie and Langan, friends and ardent anti-government radicals, formed the ARA in 1993 at the peak of public outrage over the deadly FBI siege at Waco. Guthrie had washed out of US Navy SEAL training, and the Navy discharged him for painting a swastika on the side of a ship. Langan, son of a CIA officer, had been paroled from a Florida prison after serving five years for a strong-arm robbery at age sixteen. In October 1992, the two robbed a Pizza Hut in Georgia, which led to Langan's arrest and Guthrie's pursuit by the Secret Service for threatening the life of President George H. W. Bush. However, through an extraordinary twist, the partners in crime were soon back together.

In a highly unusual move, the Secret Service obtained Langan's release from jail, where he was awaiting trial for the robbery, to help locate Guthrie. However, the Secret Service almost immediately lost track of its newly minted informant, who joined up with Guthrie instead and formed the ARA. The Secret Service reported to a Georgia district attorney that Langan would not be returning to jail because he was dead. But that wasn't true. Langan was very much alive and helping to run a domestic terror organization.

According to one version of Guthrie's 1996 jail cell demise, the FBI double-crossed Guthrie and threatened to try him for his suspected role in the Oklahoma City bombing.[11] Instead, Wild Bill chose to take his secrets to the grave. However, not everyone believed Guthrie committed suicide.

His good friend and fellow neo-Nazi Dennis Mahon theorized that a guard may have killed Guthrie. "He was helped," Mahon told the *Village Voice*, chuckling: "Let me tell you something. Even some of these prison guards are on our side."[12]

In his final days, Guthrie gave reporters interviews, claimed he was writing a tell-all book, and told his family he was looking forward to the future. "I got a lot to do in the next few weeks," he told the *Los Angeles Times* two days before his death, adding, "I've got a couple of grand juries to present to."

Richard Guthrie was indeed a high-value potential witness with deep knowledge of a terror group that had plotted to overthrow the US government. As part of his plea deal, he had promised to lay out that insurrection plot for federal authorities. Until he honored that pledge, he would be kept in solitary confinement under the watch of the US Marshals Service. How could they possibly lose track of him in his jail cell?

On July 12, 1996, Guthrie was reportedly alive at 5:30 a.m., then dead an hour later. It wasn't as short a timeline as Kenneth Trentadue's virtually impossible official death scenario, but it was still tight. Guthrie wasn't known to be on any medication, yet his blood reportedly tested positive for at least trace amounts of drugs. Still, after an open-and-shut investigation lasting all of one day, federal prisoner Richard Guthrie, like Kenneth Trentadue a year earlier, was declared a suicide by hanging.

⅄

Back in Oklahoma, two months later, Shawn-Tea Farrens, a twenty-three-year-old topless nightclub dancer, died suddenly in Tulsa. Just like police Sergeant Yeakey, the Mueller family, and Richard Guthrie, Farrens had a mysterious brush with the bombing case.

On April 8, 1995, eleven days before the blast in Oklahoma City, a dressing room surveillance camera at the Lady Godiva nightclub in Tulsa captured an exchange involving two dancers. But it wasn't stolen glimpses of strippers backstage that prompted the club's owner to save the camera's videotape. What was truly valuable was evidence that Timothy McVeigh was in the house at Lady Godiva's that night.

The videotaped exchange occurred when a dancer entered the dressing room and claimed she had been drinking with three guys. She said one of them, a man believed to be McVeigh, bragged, "I'm a very smart man, and on April 19, 1995, you're gonna remember me for the rest of your life." As she exited the dressing room, the dancer turned to the camera lens and summed up the braggart in one word: "Weirdo!"

Soon, she returned to invite another dancer, Shawn-Tea Farrens, to party with these men, now hunting for a girl to "fool around with." At first, Farrens said no, but after a mention of money, she changed her mind and declared that she would figure out a way to "scam 'em."

A year and a half later, in September 1996, Oklahoma newspaper reporter J.D. Cash heard about this video and traveled to Lady Godiva's, eager to interview the dancer who partied with the men. But the reporter's pursuit took a fatal turn. The day he arrived in Tulsa, Farrens was found dead alone in her apartment. Police concluded it was a drug overdose, perhaps suicide. Author Craig Roberts, the former Tulsa police officer, disagrees. He told me that when he reviewed death scene photos, he saw a bloody handprint on the wall of Farrens's apartment next to its sliding glass patio doors.

"That was clear across the room from where her nude body was found on the floor, sitting up and leaning on her side against the couch," Roberts said. "An open bottle of pills was on the end table next to her, but it was obvious to me she was 'suicided.' The whole scene was staged."

"She knew too much," Roberts told me. "What she saw, and who she saw and talked to at the table at Godiva's and what she told the other girls in the dressing room got her killed."

Reporter J.D. Cash understood what it might signify to place Timothy McVeigh in Tulsa eleven days before the bombing. Covering the case exclusively for his tiny newspaper, the *McCurtain Daily Gazette* in southeastern Oklahoma, Cash was chasing a lead pointing to a broader bombing conspiracy when he landed at Lady Godiva's in September 1996, six months before McVeigh's trial began.

According to the government's developing case against McVeigh, on April 8, 1995, he was still in Kingman, Arizona. He would not arrive in Kansas to rent the yellow Ryder bomb truck for another week. Yet Cash had now picked up McVeigh's trail in Tulsa on April 8, and not alone, but with two other men at a time when the FBI believed McVeigh had been trying to recruit an accomplice.

In the *Gazette*'s October 23, 1996, edition, Cash reported that dancers at the club identified McVeigh's companions as Elohim City roommates Andreas Strassmeir and Michael Brescia, based on interviews by Canadian TV journalists. However, an FBI agent recorded a different story after interviewing club owner Floyd Ratcliff. He reported that three club staffers identified not Michael Brescia but Michael Fortier—McVeigh's former Army buddy turned star witness against him by way of a lenient plea deal—as McVeigh's companion that night at Lady Godiva's.[13]

Ratcliff's FBI interview report did not mention Strassmeir, but it contained another startling disclosure. Ratcliff said Lady Godiva's doorman reported that two Ryder trucks were parked in the club's lot that night. The doorman remembered this because he had watched a distraught dancer run through the parking lot, tear off her clothes, and urinate on one of the Ryder trucks.[14]

Aside from the local color, this detail bore significant evidentiary weight. As Cash had reported to his readers in the *Gazette*, multiple witnesses in Kansas saw a yellow Ryder truck at Geary Lake State Park a week before McVeigh supposedly even arrived in the area. Witnesses at the Dreamland motel had reported seeing McVeigh driving a Ryder truck there the weekend before the bomb truck's rental.[15]

In a nutshell, the eyewitness reports from Lady Godiva's placed McVeigh in Tulsa with companions and at least one Ryder truck eleven days before the bombing. That was hard to square with the official story of lone-wolf terror. Soon, the FBI dropped the incendiary matter of McVeigh's night at Lady Godiva's like the proverbial hot potato it was.

In six months, the government would try Timothy McVeigh as the lone-wolf terrorist. But as of September 1996, the truth of who traveled through Tulsa with him on April 8, 1995, was clouded in contradictions. As the witness who may have spent the most time with McVeigh and his two companions, Shawn-Tea Farrens was the best source to sort it out. But with a reporter in hot pursuit, the twenty-three-year-old witness was suddenly dead. No one would ever hear her story.

In hindsight, this trail of mystery deaths in and around Oklahoma while federal prosecutors were developing their lone-wolf terror case raises troubling questions. All the victims except Kenneth Trentadue had puzzling but known intersections with the bombing case. The nightclub dancer had encountered McVeigh with two possible accomplices and a yellow truck shortly before the blast. The dead police officer was investigating his own department, which he believed was hiding a damaging secret about the case. The neo-Nazi terror leader was reportedly under threat of being charged in the bombing. Before disappearing, the gun dealer had suspected two men in the terror leader's circle might be a threat to his life.

Still, no alarms sounded. Most of the seven victims were obscure figures, their deaths easily dismissed and forgotten except by their loved ones. Even the hero cop was marginalized once the Oklahoma City Police Department leaned into mental health issues on his record. Almost no one paid any attention to these mysteries, much less the possibility that they might be somehow linked. But one more unexplained fatality was still to come. For

Jesse Trentadue, this one would mark the point of no return in his solitary pursuit of his brother's killers.

In August 2000, five years after the bombing, Jesse was preparing for his day in court in his family's wrongful death lawsuit against the federal government, Jesse's answer to the official story that Kenneth had killed himself. But to make his case, Jesse would have to navigate a nearly impenetrable cover-up at Oklahoma City's Federal Transfer Center that went into motion on the day Kenneth died there in August 1995.

Against protocol and state law, prison authorities blocked Medical Examiner Dr. Fred Jordan's staff from entering the death cell. Before a forensic team could arrive that afternoon to conduct a federally mandated death reconstruction, prison officials sealed cell 709A and cleaned it, destroying any crime scene evidence. Dr. Jordan's chief investigator was so furious that he called the FBI, advising it to investigate Kenneth Trentadue's death as a murder. The medical examiner, who personally conducted Kenneth's autopsy that same morning, pointedly listed the cause of death as "undetermined," pending further information.

Evidence and logbooks disappeared. Guards lied. Prison staff tampered with records, including the transcript of Kenneth's phone call from the FTC with Jesse's wife, Rita, the day before he died. In support of a false theory that Kenneth killed himself because he was a homosexual suffering from AIDS, the call's transcript altered his words from "that jet-age stuff," referring to the Con Air flight to Oklahoma, to "that AIDS stuff."[16] Kenneth wasn't gay, nor was he HIV-positive, as the medical examiner confirmed from his autopsy.

The FBI agent assigned to the case locked blood-stained evidence, including Kenneth's bedding, in the trunk of his car, accidentally leaving it there in the summer sun for two weeks and rendering it worthless for laboratory testing. "What do I do?" the distraught FBI agent asked the medical examiner's staff. "My car smells like a decomposed body."[17]

When Dr. Jordan's investigator visited the death cell in November 1995, he instructed an FBI agent to preserve cryptic words scrawled on the wall: "My mind is no longer its friend / love ya familia," supposedly Kenneth's suicide note. The prison ignored the instructions and painted over the wall, leaving the FBI's crime lab with only poor-quality photographs, which it claimed could not identify the handwriting.

A month later, when Dr. Jordan finally got access to the death cell, he sprayed the blood-sensitive chemical luminol on the walls and floor of the cell. "It lit up like a Christmas tree," he said, reinforcing a profoundly troubling question: Since hangings are relatively bloodless acts, why was there so much blood in Kenneth's cell?

By the time Jesse Trentadue's wrongful death lawsuit went to trial in November 2000, the Oklahoma County District Attorney's Office was the authority of record on Kenneth's death scenario, based on its July 1998 finding backing up the prison's suicide determination.[18]

With support from the Bureau of Prisons, a TV reconstruction was videotaped on location in cell 709A of the Federal Transfer Center by the ABC newsmagazine *Nightline* and distributed to news outlets nationally. However, E. Paul France, a biomechanics expert hired by the Trentadue family, judged the frantic scenario envisioned by the district attorney's investigation "highly improbable." He concluded "to a reasonable degree of scientific certainty" that Kenneth's death "did not happen as proposed" in the hanging reenactment.[19] Still, with such a loud media drumroll, it was easy to miss that the official scenario of Kenneth's final moments bordered on physical impossibility, not just the hanging analyzed by France.

All of Kenneth's grievous injuries had to occur within a tight twenty-four-minute time frame between the last time he was seen alive and the discovery of his body at 3:02 a.m. on August 21, 1995. Even if Kenneth could have executed the acrobatics attributed to him, trying and failing to hang himself from a ceiling vent, falling and splitting open his skull, slitting his own throat on his bunk, then climbing back up to the ceiling and this time completing the suicide—even somehow accepting all of that, the district attorney's scenario still left huge forensic questions unanswered.

Why would Kenneth sign someone else's name to the cryptic suicide note he supposedly wrote on the wall? Why didn't he leave fingerprints on the surfaces as he staggered around the cell? Who inflicted the fingerprint bruises on his upper arms and the stun gun–like marks on his feet? Why did he not bleed on the cot where he supposedly slashed his throat? What happened to the missing pieces of bedsheet used to make the hanging rope? And for that matter, what happened to Kenneth's blood-stained clothes, which vanished without a trace from his locked cell? Why, why, and why again? No answers were ever forthcoming to these questions and many others.

Up against the wall of the suicide theory, first issued by the prison in 1995, Jesse took a step he would repeat in years to come with remarkable results. He partnered with investigative journalist Mary A. Fischer of *GQ* magazine. Their two-year probe in 1996–97 uncovered stunning evidence of murder, perjury, and cover-up at the prison: paramedic and police witnesses turned away from the crime scene, missing photos, the blood evidence discovered by the medical examiner, and several critical inmate eyewitness accounts.

The inmate orderly tasked with cleaning the death cell told Fischer he believed Kenneth "was killed" and described the cell not as the scene of a hanging but as "a bloodbath." "There was blood on the floor and splattered all over the walls," the orderly said, recalling so much blood "that it had to be cleaned up with a mop." Of the bloody fingerprints he saw around the cell's panic button, the orderly said: "It seemed to me as though he had been trying to reach the alarm button when he was killed."[20]

Another inmate witness interviewed by Jesse and Fischer branded as "a lie" the FBI report that he heard Kenneth shouting, banging on walls, or jumping off the sink in his cell.[21]

Some years later, I had lunch with Mary Fischer in Los Angeles. Across the table sat a reporter who had struck like a tigress. Yet, in person, what stood out was the gentle demeanor of this slight woman, almost fragile in appearance. She had coaxed truth that exposed a cover-up from vulnerable prisoner witnesses and even the prison's ex-warden, whom she tracked down in retirement in Texas.

In 1998, one more prisoner on the cellblock where Kenneth died stepped forward and offered Jesse an eyewitness account that catapulted Alden Gillis Baker into a star witness in the coming civil trial. Baker told Jesse that he saw and heard parts of Kenneth's murder by three men dressed in riot gear. Afterward, Baker claimed, the prison dosed him with heavy psychotropic drugs and transferred him away from the FTC to another prison. "Diesel therapy" (sudden relocations in prison parlance) moved

Baker far from the heat of any investigation at the FTC that might draw him into its net.

Alden Baker was a bank robber, a psychopath, and a suspected serial killer. He had been in the federal prison system for eight years when he briefly met Kenneth Trentadue in the prison yard at the FTC in Oklahoma City the morning Kenneth arrived there. Baker gave his account of witnessing Kenneth's murder in a sworn deposition at the federal prison in Florence, Colorado, on November 13, 1998.[22]

Sometime on the night of August 20, 1995, Baker said he overheard an angry Kenneth Trentadue demanding to make a phone call to his wife. A guard refused. Sometime later, Baker saw three men dressed in riot helmets and dark vests enter Kenneth's cell. For the next half hour, Baker heard loud sounds of a fight, pleading and moaning, and then nothing. Finally, the squad left Kenneth's silent cell.

Around midnight, Baker said he witnessed a second visit to the cell. He could hear what sounded like someone tearing bedsheets. Then, two men emerged from the cell, one removing gloves. Baker interpreted this second visit as covert preparation for a guard on the next shift to discover Kenneth's body hanging.

A few hours later, amid chaos on the cellblock, guards noticed Baker watching them from his cell and moved him out of view. Baker told lawyers at the deposition that his decision to go public jeopardized his life. He explained. "And that is because no one is exempt here in this prison, or any prison for that matter, to where if something wants to be done to you, it can be done."

At times, Baker sounded fatalistic about the consequences of his testimony. "You know, I just hope if they do it, that they do it the first time, and, you know, it's over with," he testified. Later, after another move to the federal prison at Lompoc, California, Baker told Jesse and a federal prosecutor that inmates were threatening him. Jesse filed a motion for a protective order with the trial judge in the lawsuit. Nothing happened for ten months. Then, on August 3, 2000, three months before the wrongful death trial began, federal prisoner Alden Baker, like Kenneth Trentadue and Richard Guthrie before him, was found dead in his cell and declared a suicide by hanging without even an autopsy.

The loss of this witness put the trial's outcome in jeopardy, as did another setback when Oklahoma's medical examiner, Dr. Fred Jordan, flip-flopped on his critical opinion that Kenneth was an assault victim in his cell. Jesse never knew what triggered Dr. Jordan's eleventh-hour turnabout. He openly despised the federal officials he believed had bungled Kenneth's death investigation or, worse, covered up a murder and pressured him to call it a suicide. Now, Dr. Jordan was signing off the struggle.

Despite those devastating reversals, the Trentadue family won the lawsuit, which Jesse directed from the wings since his role as a critical witness barred him from acting as an attorney for his family. The court awarded the family a million-dollar judgment against the federal government, but the victory was bitter. The family had sued for wrongful death. However, so much evidence had been lost, perjured, or tampered with that the judge stopped short of declaring Kenneth's death a murder. Instead, the judge awarded damages to the family for intentional emotional distress inflicted on them in the aftermath of Kenneth's death. That meant the suicide ruling would stand.

Under an extraordinary protective order sought by the government and granted by the judge, Jesse wouldn't even be able to refer to congressional committees or federal prosecutors the perjury and destruction of evidence exposed by the trial.[23] Under normal circumstances, such referrals could lead to criminal charges, but nothing about this case was routine. What happened in cell 709A would stay there.

At this juncture, the strange anonymous phone call Jesse had received back at the end of 1995 no longer seemed so far-fetched. The tipster who said the FBI killed Kenneth and that he fit a profile had not offered any way to verify or refute his information. But could that tip be accurate? Was the FBI the hidden hand Jesse thought he kept glimpsing during his investigation?

He had now exhausted virtually every avenue the US justice system offered, with only the judgment in the civil case to show for his effort. But Jesse hadn't come to this fight for the million dollars. He came for the truth, and he wasn't done searching.

CHAPTER 2

THE PHANTOM

In the blink of an eye, at 9:02 a.m. on April 19, 1995, the bomb transformed Oklahoma City into a hellscape. The sound was so loud that a federal judge in the courthouse across the street from the Murrah Federal Building thought his eardrums had burst. Nine floors of the building pancaked into a pit of death and destruction at ground level. Vicious shards of glass flew through the air. A man riding a bus nearby said the explosion lifted the vehicle and nearly tipped it over. A motorist said his car swung like a hammock tied between two trees. The blast pushed him and his car into the side of a building. Cars in the parking lot across the street from the Murrah Building ignited into a field of flame. Two columns of inky black smoke rose toward the sky, concealing the full horror from view. The apocalypse ended seconds after it hit, when a 250-pound missile of twisted metal, which had been the axle of the Ryder truck bomb, fell from the sky a half block away. It crash-landed onto the hood of a Ford Festiva parked in front of the Regency Tower apartment building, somehow miraculously not killing or injuring the occupants. Doomsday had arrived.

Author Michele Marie Moore captured the haunting details of the scene in her history, *Oklahoma City: Day One*.[24] Sirens wailed.

Ambulances appeared. Victims began to emerge from the Murrah Building. Hundreds of them would walk, crawl, or be carried out dead and alive. Some were bloody, missing limbs, their clothes torn off, dazed, confused, and lost. A man who dropped four stories from his office to the ground floor walked out of the building in shock. Another man who didn't realize he had no arms was seen walking on the street. Victims were so bloody that emergency medical technicians had to ask them to describe injuries they couldn't see. One critically wounded patient waiting for an ambulance had part of a file cabinet impaled in her chest.

In one of the myriad acts of kindness that day that would become known as "the Oklahoma Standard," the federal judge who cleared his courtroom after the ear-splitting explosion rushed outside and was seen wrapping an injured victim in his judicial robes. On the upper floors of the Murrah Building, rescuers would find office workers still seated at their desks, eyes open, pieces of metal stuck in their dead bodies. Again and again, survivors registered amazement at the surreal experience of looking around after the blast to find people and whole offices missing, gone into the abyss. Husbands lost wives. Families lost brothers, sisters, mothers, and most heartbreaking of all, little children.

Beyond the adult horror were the tiny victims from the daycare center on the second floor that took a direct hit. Jannie Coverdale's grandsons Aaron and Elijah, Kathy and Glenn Wilburn's grandsons Chase and Colton, and eleven other children under the age of six were slaughtered when the bomb destroyed the nursery that was supposed to keep them safe while their parents were at work. Only six children in the America's Kids daycare center survived. The firefighter holding mortally injured one-year-old Baylee Almon in his arms would become the photographic icon of the tragedy.

As it unfolded, the wails of grief-stricken mothers who rushed to the scene gave voice to the unthinkable. Recovery workers placed the dead children's bodies in the playground where they would never play again. Parents and grandparents huddled together in churches for days, waiting for rescue workers to bring out their children's remains so authorities could identify them. A merciful funeral director persuaded at least one child's mother that it was better not to view the body.

What in the world had happened? The catastrophe struck so fast that people didn't know what hit them. In some real sense, by 9:03 a.m., "America's Heartland," the phrase intended to celebrate the region's wholesome midwestern normalcy, was already history. The Age of Terror had claimed Oklahoma City. Searching questions about the attack, the terrorists, and their weapon of mass destruction would spiral into a baffling mass-murder mystery over the next thirty years.

When the bomb exploded, I knew criminal manhunts as well as any journalist. As news director of *America's Most Wanted*, based in Washington, DC, I had worked alongside the FBI on some of the nation's most prominent cases. But I had moved on to Los Angeles to produce other genres, away from crime TV, and became just another horrified witness among millions to what happened that terrible day.

I watched Oklahoma City's nightmare images live on TV in disbelief. The explosion had scooped out the front of the nine-story Murrah Federal Building like ice cream. Its carcass was now a heap of collapsed concrete, broken glass, and black smoke. Some watching the news coverage might say this terror attack blew a gaping hole not just in the building and the city but in the nation's soul. What leaped out at me was a question: Who could have done this?

I wished I was back at *America's Most Wanted* for one more manhunt. I wanted to hear what my best law enforcement sources knew. I wanted to urge my reporters to find and debrief the survivors. I wanted to rally viewers with a call to action, telling the FBI what they saw and knew about the perpetrators, still unidentified and very much at large.

Eight years earlier, when I was a print journalist covering the buttoned-down arena of Washington politics and policies, being hired by *America's Most Wanted* became an adventure beyond thrilling. Sandwiched in a borrowed conference room of the local Fox TV station, my tight-knit staff and I learned the new true-crime genre of TV manhunt stories on the fly as we invented it. Using case files and interviews, we investigated crimes committed by perpetrators now at large. We shared the intense human drama of victims seeking justice, the twisted reality of the fugitives we pursued, the tireless dedication of the cops, and the courage of tipsters. Most of all, we were moved by the emotions felt by victims' families watching arrest videos of now-handcuffed murderers who'd taken the lives of their loved ones.

As the show's frontline contact for crime victims, I met desperate people who'd endured unthinkable tragedies. Now, they lived in a twilight-zone reality, searching for answers. This memory never fades: A parent phoned me one day to beg *America's Most Wanted* to profile the senseless murder of their teenage daughter. The killer had mutilated the girl and then gone for a joyride along Virginia's scenic Skyline Drive, tossing parts of her body from his car's window. "Who could do such a thing to our daughter?" the parent asked me. "Please help us."

I had no answer. The case was too cold. The killer was unidentified. A father's desperate plea for justice would remain unanswered, possibly forever.

Other cases sometimes ended in almost miraculous arrests. Our first episode in February 1988 led to the capture of one of the FBI's 10 Most Wanted fugitives. Prison escapee David James Roberts had carjacked a young Indiana mother, raped her, locked her in the trunk of her car, and left her baby on the side of a road to die of exposure.

That first episode made *America's Most Wanted* a breakout TV hit and crime-solving phenomenon. By the time I moved on to Los Angeles in 1992, *America's Most Wanted* had captured scores of dangerous criminals. Those memories came flooding back as I watched coverage of the bombing in Oklahoma City from Venice, California. The body count was climbing. An intense FBI manhunt was mobilizing to track down the unknown terrorists. It was tough to watch, but I couldn't miss any beat of the unfolding news story.

⅄

Oliver "Buck" Revell, former FBI counterterrorism chief and one of the bureau executives I remember best from the launch of *America's Most Wanted,* told CBS News: "I think it's most likely a Middle East terrorist. I think the modus operandi is similar. They have used this approach."[25]

An eyewitness on the ground in Oklahoma City told the FBI he saw two Middle Eastern–looking men racing to get in a brown

Chevy or GMC pickup truck in front of the Murrah Building at 8:55 on the morning of the bombing. Based on this witness and others, at 11:15 a.m., the FBI issued an all-points bulletin for a brown pickup truck that the bombers might have used.[26] Five hours later, however, at 4:15 p.m., the FBI canceled its APB for the brown truck without explanation. When journalist David Hoffman drilled into this mystery, all he could learn was that an FBI agent named Webster had reportedly given the order.[27]

The course reversal by the FBI did not deter Oklahoma City's KFOR-TV, an NBC affiliate. The station launched an aggressive pursuit of the brown truck story and a possible Middle Eastern connection to the attack. KFOR's sometimes controversial local news coverage of the investigation set it apart, mainly for its independence from the Justice Department's steering of the story. Outside Oklahoma City, though, the station's coverage was barely noticed.

The early hints of a Middle Eastern connection disappeared quickly, replaced by the real-life horror story of an all-American lone-wolf terrorist fresh from the Gulf War. The FBI's lightning-fast takedown of Timothy McVeigh—the nomadic twenty-something gun show groupie with a Bronze Star for his Army service in Iraq—was so smooth and challenge-free it almost seemed made for television. By late in the day of the bombing, the FBI had already made a breakthrough. In the chaotic rubble near the destroyed building, the bureau located the axle from the presumed bomb vehicle's wreckage and quickly traced its vehicle identification number to a Ryder truck rental agency in Junction City, Kansas, 275 miles north. The next day, the FBI flew forensic sketch artist Raymond Rozycki to Kansas, where he interviewed rental shop staffers and produced composite sketches of two suspects, images that would generate 15,664 leads, according to Oklahoma City's National Memorial Museum.

The first suspect, John Doe 1, appeared to be a young white man with a military-style crewcut using the alias Robert Kling to sign the truck rental contract. The second suspect, John Doe 2, was Doe 1's stocky, dark-complexioned companion at the truck rental agency. He was depicted with a square jaw, piercing dark eyes, a tattoo on his left bicep, and a baseball cap with a wing motif on the sides.

The day after the blast, armed with these sketches, FBI agents fanned out into Junction City, Kansas, and hit paydirt within hours. Amazingly, a lookalike for the John Doe 1 suspect had rented a room at the city's Dreamland motel, driving a Ryder truck and using his real name, Timothy McVeigh. This identification would lead the FBI to McVeigh himself in one more day and in the nick of time. McVeigh was already in custody in Perry, Oklahoma, and about to be released on bond. He had been arrested about ninety minutes after the bombing by Oklahoma Highway Patrol Trooper Charles Hanger for driving without a license plate and carrying a concealed weapon.

Trooper Hanger's peaceful, by-the-book arrest of a desperate anti-government terror suspect on the run would go down as law enforcement at its best, methodical, lowkey, and without a trace of the overreach that had the country on edge after Waco and Ruby Ridge. When the details of Trooper Hanger's takedown came out, America savored them.

"I have a gun," Timothy McVeigh said when the trooper inspected a suspicious bulge in McVeigh's jacket.

"My weapon is loaded," McVeigh advised. Hanger, who now had a gun to McVeigh's head, didn't miss a beat. "So is mine."

Along with a .45-caliber Glock and Black Talon rounds in his jacket, McVeigh also had an ammo clip and a knife in a pouch on his belt. He claimed he needed to be armed for his protection. He'd even memorized the handgun's serial number. Hanger phoned his dispatcher and requested an ID check of the now-handcuffed McVeigh. The dispatcher advised that this individual's record was not entered as wanted, and he had no criminal history. The yellow Mercury was not reported as stolen. It all sounded routine.

With twenty/twenty hindsight, it might seem curious that the trooper took no notice of Timothy McVeigh's T-shirt on full display when he opened his jacket to reveal the gun. President Lincoln's image and his assassin's words were printed on the front. McVeigh was carrying something else, too, a pair of earplugs he would surrender at the courthouse when he emptied his pockets. Still, in the sea of visual data the trooper was surveying, nothing jumped out to signal this was more than a routine arrest.

A short time later, as McVeigh waited to be booked in the Perry, Oklahoma, courthouse, Hanger and jailer Marsha Moritz watched TV coverage of the frantic search for victims buried deep in the Murrah Building's rubble as paramedics triaged survivors. As the preliminary death toll rose, McVeigh stood beside the trooper and jailer, watching in stone-cold silence. "There was no reaction," Hanger testified at the federal trial of McVeigh's coconspirator, Terry Nichols.[28]

That Friday afternoon, April 21, live on TV, the prime suspect appeared for his perp walk, face-to-face with a sea of journalists and outraged citizens shouting, "baby killer." I knew from *America's Most Wanted* how highly orchestrated these sequences were—the perp walk for television. In his orange jumpsuit, with a thousand-yard stare and no bulletproof vest, Timothy McVeigh looked the part of the young criminal mastermind prosecutors would portray at his trial.

It was a bravura FBI performance. The bureau had collared its prime suspect in this horror in only three days. Yet disturbing cracks in the evidence would soon emerge as news coverage of the bombing case pivoted from a global manhunt for multiple terrorists to a monstrous act of terror by the unlikeliest of perpetrators: a boy next door who was also a decorated war veteran.

⅄

I wish I could say that *America's Most Wanted* gave me special powers to see into the bombing investigation. Mostly I followed the story like any other news junkie in 1995, absorbing the captivating mystery with part of my brain while pursuing work and life with the other. I was on television's up escalator that year. It was thrilling and all-consuming, doing something you weren't supposed to be able to do as a rookie independent television producer: pitch and sell a nationally syndicated show.

I read newspapers and watched TV, relying on professional journalists to report the bombing story. In hindsight, that was problematic. They repeated what the Department of Justice in Washington, DC, told them, but there was much more to the story. America's news junkies got disturbing inklings of this by doing what we couldn't help doing: reading between the lines as a story filled with unanswered questions and red flags evolved.

From national news coverage, we learned how a phone card and multiple storage lockers containing explosives tied Timothy McVeigh and his accused coconspirator, Terry Nichols, to preparations for the bombing. We learned how a McVeigh fingerprint tied him to explosives in Nichols's home. We learned how another former Army buddy, Michael Fortier, flipped and became the star witness against McVeigh, serving up incriminating details of his plot.

Fortier was a major red flag, a disconnect for any news junkie following the story with a critical mind. He started out pledging that his friend Timothy McVeigh couldn't have done this but then buried him after the FBI exerted maximum pressure.[29] Fortier's grand jury testimony on August 8, 1995, sealed the case. Two days later, the grand jury handed down indictments of McVeigh and Nichols. Thanks to Fortier's plea deal, he only faced charges of transporting weapons illegally and failing to notify authorities about the deadly terror plot.

With Fortier on their side, prosecutors had their storyline, except for one glaringly missing piece: Who was McVeigh's unidentified accomplice in the ball cap with the wings on the sides? Who was the man who helped rent the bomb truck and rode shotgun with McVeigh when he delivered his deadly payload to the Murrah Building? Who was John Doe 2? And where was he? The grand jury was left wondering too. In a pointed nod to John Doe 2, the elephant in the room, the grand jury also indicted "Others Unknown."

No one has ever answered the question of who those others were.

I admit that I brought an unorthodox point of view to this riddle, along with my newshound's curiosity. When the bomb ignited in Oklahoma City, I was deep into researching *The X-Files* as a cultural phenomenon. After immersing myself in crime TV at *America's Most Wanted*, I pivoted from murder mysteries to paranormal ones. From research into alien abduction, ghostly hauntings, miracle healings, and mind control, I was developing a new reality television series called *Strange Universe*.

In 1995, my producing partner and I pitched our new show as a reality TV version of *The X-Files*. It was a nod to the Fox hit drama series following FBI agents Mulder and Scully as they investigated paranormal mysteries. Along their way, the agents often encountered a shadowy and powerful government conspiracy dedicated to keeping secrets from the public. Their paranormal adventures were fantasy, of course. But for millions of viewers, the show tapped into a dark political menace that might be all too true. The show's ratings and cult following revealed that much of America embraced a deep skepticism about the powers that be in government.

These viewers were the audience for my new show, too, and I wanted to understand them. But to my surprise, as I juggled researching *The X-Files* and devouring news coverage of the bombing investigation, the lines between reality and fiction began to blur to an uncanny degree. Over the rest of 1995, the oddities and contradictions in the bombing investigation spiraled into disturbing discrepancies, all seemingly related to the mystery of John Doe 2.

First, there was the on-again, off-again FBI manhunt. This global search targeted a criminal monster who had helped slaughter 168 victims, including 15 children in their daycare center. The Justice Department played for the highest stakes, announcing a $2 million reward for the capture of John Doe 2. And early indications were that the FBI was going to get its man.

Dozens of eyewitnesses in Kansas and Oklahoma swore they saw John Doe 2 with McVeigh in the days and hours leading up to the bombing. Top journalists quoted unnamed federal officials with an explosive revelation: Surveillance cameras had captured the crime of the century on videotape. Federal law enforcement officials were leaking clues about who and what the tapes featured to their favorite reporters and producers. These would be prize news gets, but the recordings remained hidden, though not, perhaps, for lack of trying by an enterprising FBI agent. Almost a decade and a half later, lawyer Jesse Trentadue would discover FBI documents revealing that the bureau investigated one of its agents for attempting to sell a videotape containing some of the bombing surveillance footage to NBC's newsmagazine *Dateline* for $1 million.[30]

The search for John Doe 2 continued to build, and then, within weeks, it appeared that the FBI might have its suspect in custody. According to news reports, authorities had identified McVeigh associate Steven Colbern—a university-trained chemist with bomb-making expertise—through his brown pickup truck.

The dashboard surveillance camera in Trooper Hanger's patrol car had reportedly captured Colbern's truck and license plate by chance during Timothy McVeigh's arrest when the brown truck stopped up ahead, waited briefly, and then drove off.

A front-page news story in the *Houston Chronicle* on May 12, 1995, reporting on Colbern's arrest in Arizona, credited his identification to state-of-the-art video enhancement techniques allowing investigators to read his license plate number. According to the story, the brown truck, registered to Colbern, contained traces of ammonium nitrate, believed to be the main explosive ingredient used in the bomb.[31]

Less than a month after the crime, this intriguing account of Steven Colbern's arrest seemed to tease the possible grand finale of the global manhunt for John Doe 2. The truck, its license plate, the ammonium nitrate, and Colbern's chemistry degree were compelling clues. Sometime later, it would also turn out that Colbern had reportedly picked up mail for McVeigh in Kingman, Arizona,[32] and that Colbern had no credible alibi for April 19.

Before disappearing for two weeks around the time of the bombing, he said he was going to visit his mother in Southern California. However, when interviewed afterward by a reporter, his father said the family last saw Colbern at a wedding in September 1994 in Oxnard, California. Meanwhile, back in Oatman, Arizona, where Colbern worked as a cook, a good friend volunteered that Colbern had been there with him the day of the bombing, "sitting right here, watching television."[33]

None of this boded well for Colbern, a fugitive from illegal weapons charges in California who had been hiding out for more than a year in Arizona, living in a messy trailer where neighbors said he kept snakes and sometimes camping out in caves where he practiced his survival skills. Now in federal custody, Colbern faced enhanced pressure to tell authorities anything he knew about the bombing. But then the investigation made a dramatic U-turn, never fully explained.

Within days, US Attorney Janet Napolitano made a heavyweight appearance at Colbern's arraignment on the weapons charges. She declined to comment when asked if Colbern's arrest related to the bombing. However, she requested no bail for the prisoner, and the judge agreed. Whatever Napolitano and federal law enforcement may have learned from Colbern about the bombing was about to become a state secret that the government would not share with the public.

Steven Colbern's suspect status as John Doe 2 vaporized almost instantly, with few questions asked. The suspicious brown pickup truck parked outside his Arizona trailer was said to be covered in cobwebs, indicating no one had driven it recently. The traces of ammonium nitrate vanished from the story. Stranger still, it turned out that the report of those suspicious chemical traces in the truck had been published a day before Colbern's arrest. No one asked how or why until researcher Richard Booth spotted the contradiction decades later.[34]

But what about the surveillance videotape of Colbern's license plate that led authorities to him in the first place? It was simply never mentioned again in news media coverage. Some years later, when I began my deep dive into the case, I called Peter Copeland, one of the two byline reporters on the *Houston Chronicle* wire service story, to ask him about the dashcam video from Trooper Hanger's squad car and his federal law enforcement source.[35]

"I've been wondering when someone would call up and look into this," Copeland said, to my surprise. He referred me to the other byline reporter on the story, who did not reply to my email.

As for Steven Colbern, the non-suspect made a plea agreement, served a few years in prison, reinvented himself as a UFO researcher, and never spoke publicly about his connection to Timothy McVeigh or their mailbox service in Kingman. Agent Mulder would have shaken his head at all the secrets hiding behind the elaborate smoke screen of Colbern's ties to the case, as I did.

But if Stephen Colbern wasn't John Doe 2, who was? The FBI soon had an answer that raised yet another red flag. A month after Colbern's arrest, in mid-June 1995, the Justice Department announced that its global manhunt had only been an expensive mistake. The FBI was canceling it, claiming the escaped terrorist was a phantom in the imaginations of the dozens of eyewitnesses. He had never really existed.

In a new, far-fetched theory, the DOJ now explained that Timothy McVeigh had rented the bomb truck alone. In this rendition, mechanic Tom Kessinger at Elliott's Body Shop in Junction City, Kansas, the primary source for the FBI's John Doe 2 wanted poster, had been mistaken in his memory of a McVeigh companion.

In support of this idea, the FBI had located a soldier resembling John Doe 2 at nearby Fort Riley. Private Todd Bunting had visited Elliott's with a friend the day after the bomb truck rental. Even more helpful to this new theory, Bunting wore a ball cap similar to John Doe 2's and had a tattoo on his left arm. According to the DOJ, Kessinger had somehow time-traveled Bunting into a false memory of a McVeigh companion who was never there.

This theory was supremely awkward, even when cloaked in fancy psychological transference jargon. When local Oklahoma reporter J.D. Cash asked about the notion for a *Gazette* story on June 30, 1996, mechanic Kessinger doubled down, declaring: "I know McVeigh was there with another person.... I watched him standing there for a long time.... He had his arms crossed and never said a word while one of our employees filled out the rental papers for McVeigh."

I still remember a whiplash sensation when I read about the U-turn in the John Doe 2 case. A spellbinding manhunt story had developed from the dozens of eyewitnesses to the videotapes and the dragnet around Colbern. Suddenly, the story vanished into thin air. At this juncture, I realized something troubling: I had parted company with the official story of the bombing. Taking their lead from the Justice Department in Washington, DC, the national news media were chronicling the story of justice in the making for a lone-wolf terrorist. But if you were using common sense, you knew that story didn't add up.

⅄

That summer of 1995 brought another head-scratcher, this one so outlandishly graphic it could have anchored an entire episode of *The X-Files*. The story broke in the national media on August 8, 1995. It turned out that, while removing the last bodies from the rubble of the bombed federal building in late May, recovery workers had unearthed a disembodied human leg, severed above the knee. Whose leg was this? Inexplicably, two and a half months later, the office of the Oklahoma medical examiner had to admit they deliberately kept this bombshell discovery secret from the sitting grand jury and the public. The story only came out because an Oklahoma Highway Patrol trooper close to the recovery operation tipped off McVeigh's lawyer, Stephen Jones, who alerted the media.

More intrigue ensued. The severed leg was dressed in a black military-style boot and blousing strap of the type soldiers use to keep their fatigue pants tucked in. Paramilitary attire was also a style favored by Timothy McVeigh. Based on anthropological analysis, the medical examiner's forensic experts reported a 75 percent probability that the mystery leg belonged to a man who was "light skinned," under the age of thirty with dark hair, and who stood five feet six to five feet nine inches tall. The profile was all the more intriguing because it closely matched the FBI's forensic profile of John Doe 2.

Could this leg belong to the unidentified terrorist? Had he not escaped after all but died in the explosion of his bomb? When a *New York Times* reporter asked why the ME had not disclosed this astounding discovery sooner, a spokesman for Medical Examiner Dr. Fred Jordan's office blew off the question. "Why should we?" the official retorted. John Doe 2's mystery was back in play with a vengeance. In due course, it would become a highlight of Timothy McVeigh's defense at trial.

Nine days later, on August 17, *The New York Times* interviewed Dr. Jordan again. "We have no idea who it is," he said of the mystery leg. He added that his office was now sure the limb did not belong to any known bombing victim, which would require raising the official death toll by one victim. There was a sobering unintended consequence of this new development: The official death count for the bombing might now include the terrorist who helped deliver it, a person whose identity was still unknown.

According to Dr. Jordan, the FBI was in the process of running DNA tests to double-check his exclusion of the seven bombing victims buried without their left legs. Dr. Jordan described those FBI tests as due diligence. Meanwhile, the mystery of the severed leg created a furor of activity in the medical examiner's office as it struggled to respond to media inquiries and FBI pressure to resolve the question: Did this leg belong to one of the bombers, perhaps John Doe 2?

Four days after the *Times* interview, the ME's office confronted another emergency. With the office stretched to its limits by the John Doe 2 uproar, Kenneth Trentadue was found dead in his cell at Oklahoma City's Federal Transfer Center on August 21, 1995. That same day, while the ME's head investigator alerted the FBI to investigate the case as a homicide, Dr. Jordan personally conducted Kenneth's autopsy.

At the time, no one imagined that the reanimation of the John Doe 2 mystery by way of the severed leg might somehow relate to Kenneth Trentadue's death. Yet there was this coincidence: Kenneth was an uncanny match to the FBI's physical profile of John Doe 2, from his height, weight, and build, right down to the tattoo on his left arm.

Would it be paranoid to think there might be a sinister connection here between the manhunt and this brutalized prisoner? It was a mystery worthy of Agent Mulder. Ten days later, on August 31, when the ME issued a second press release on the matter, the bombing case took another hairpin turn.

Based on DNA testing by the FBI, Dr. Jordan explained that he was reversing his original opinion on the gender of the leg's owner. In a new press release, Dr. Jordan reported that the mystery limb belonged not to a white male but to a Black female. The FBI must have welcomed this finding because it seemingly ruled out the possibility of John Doe 2.[36]

Just in case anyone might still be pondering that line of thought, though, a *New York Times* story helpfully quoted federal law enforcement officials pointing out that no one had seen either McVeigh or Nichols in the company of a Black woman. And just to further reassure the public that no stone would go unturned to solve the leg mystery, the *Times*'s law enforcement sources offered that investigators were scouring homeless shelters proactively at that very moment in search of a Black woman who might have gone missing the day of the bombing. No such woman ever turned up.

McVeigh's attorney, Stephen Jones, quipped that the government's forensic evidence "appears to be moving in different directions like a weathervane in an Oklahoma stormy spring." Jones was already looking ahead to trial, seeking to use the mystery leg as evidence to shift suspicion from McVeigh onto John Doe 2.

Attorney Jones was right about his observation. The government's case was spinning like a crazy weathervane. From the Colbern manhunt to the Private Bunting mistaken-identity theory to the severed leg, the pattern of secrecy and deception about John Doe 2 was anything but reassuring. A titanic tug-of-war between prosecutors and McVeigh's defense team was just getting started. As it played out, the public's right to know what happened on April 19, 1995, would be far from the top priority in this high-stakes contest.

⅄

Another controversy unfolding that summer of 1995 was also cloaked in secrecy. It was a local Oklahoma City story that failed to get the national spotlight it deserved. In hindsight, it's another striking clue to an investigation that needed investigating.

Hoppy Heidelberg was a fifty-five-year-old Oklahoma horse rancher and respected state Breeders' Association president. In the summer of 1995, he was also a sitting member of the federal grand jury that would bring the indictments in the bombing case. Heidelberg was a strong-minded, cantankerous man. He took seriously his civic duty as a grand juror and knew its rules. He often carried a well-thumbed copy of a slim blue government-issued juror's handbook.

Heidelberg understood the magnitude of the grand jury's constitutional right to search out evidence and witnesses independent of prosecutors managing the proceedings. He was ready to stand his ground on principle—and would have to. Heidelberg's collision with prosecutors over investigating John Doe 2 would soon break through the curtain of secrecy that seals all federal grand jury proceedings and go loudly public.

Based on the evidence prosecutors presented, this grand juror had no qualms about sending Timothy McVeigh and Terry Nichols to face trial. It was the other suspects who troubled Heidelberg. Who were they? He wanted to interview the FBI sketch artist who produced the composite drawing of John Doe 2 and the soldier who supposedly resembled the fugitive suspect in the drawing. But prosecutors controlled the grand jury's witness list. "They kept promising and promising to answer all my questions, but ultimately, they stalled me," Heidelberg told a journalist. "I was had."[37]

From news coverage, the grand juror knew about the surveillance videotapes allegedly showing at least one McVeigh accomplice at the scene of the bombing. He wanted to see those tapes, but prosecutors also controlled the flow of evidence. "We were never allowed to see the photo evidence from the cameras on the Murrah Building that would have shown the truck being parked and the people who got out of the truck," Heidelberg said in an interview. "That's all on tape, and we were authorized to see all of that, but we weren't allowed to see it...and in fact, nobody has been allowed to see it."[38]

Prosecutors' conflict with their rogue grand juror continued to build during the summer and fall of 1995. Once, when Heidelberg broke grand jury rules by taking his notes home overnight, two FBI agents showed up at his ranch to forcibly take custody of the paperwork. As he recalled the scene, one agent wore his suit jacket open, pointedly displaying a pistol in his belt. The armed lawmen used an official FBI evidence pouch to secure the juror's notebook.[39] By mid-July, Heidelberg was confidentially airing his claims of prosecutorial misconduct to his congressman and leaking information about the jury's proceedings in violation of grand jury rules. The *Daily Oklahoman* cited Heidelberg as an unnamed source until the grand jury handed down its indictments in August 1995.

The story of the compromised McVeigh grand jury, pitting prosecutors who allegedly muzzled its investigation against a rogue juror who leaked its secrets, broke open in October 1995, two months after the bombing indictments. When the story broke, the media spotlight turned once again to the mystery of John Doe 2. The alternative Indiana-based monthly magazine *Media Bypass* was the little-known publication that scooped everyone else. Headlined "OKC Bombing Grand Jurors Claim 'Cover-up,'" the story by Lawrence W. Myers did not identify Heidelberg by name but only as "a juror." It detailed his concern that the federal government had concealed evidence from the grand jury that could prove the elusive John Doe 2 was one of the bombers.

In the magazine's account, the Private Bunting theory of the Fort Riley soldier the staff at the body shop supposedly mistook for John Doe 2 had triggered skepticism on the part of several grand jurors. The magazine reported: "'The story did not fit,' a juror said. 'When the media ran photographs comparing the soldier to the composite drawing of John Doe No. 2, it was a huge red flag that something wrong was going on.'"

Another red flag: None of the dozens of eyewitnesses who saw John Doe 2 appeared to testify before the grand jury. Heidelberg said: "The media was a lot more inquisitive and concerned about the John Doe Number 2 angle than the prosecution. It was never brought up by the government during the proceeding."

Still another flag, according to Heidelberg: Reports that cameras in front of and around the Murrah Building had captured the Ryder truck and two occupants on tape moments before the blast. "All they showed us were a series of video still photographs showing the Ryder truck, but no one in or around the vehicle," the juror said.

To be sure, the *Media Bypass* spotlight had a low wattage by national media standards. However, the magazine ensured that it would have an impact beyond its subscriber list by sharing transcripts of its interview of Hoppy Heidelberg with Timothy McVeigh's media-savvy defense attorney, Stephen Jones. He packaged the eye-popping Heidelberg material from *Media Bypass* as a motion to dismiss the McVeigh indictment and attached a digest of highlights from the interview transcripts. Though the judge dismissed the motion, Heidelberg's leaks of grand jury secrets and his charges of prosecutorial misconduct would now go on the record—including this exchange between Heidelberg and interviewer Lawrence J. Myers:

> LM: What was the most...significant news even[t] during the grand jury proceeding, that you think that influenced you or the grand jury? The John Doe #2 being identified as a Fort Riley, Kansas, soldier?
>
> HH: Yeah, that's the most significant aspect of this whole thing.
>
> LM: Okay. So, that would be a media influence that didn't work? How about John Doe...
>
> HH: Not only did it not work. It had the exact opposite effect intended.
>
> LM: Okay.
>
> HH: It was a bombshell, in my opinion.

LM: Okay. That created suspicion?

HH: That's what, oh, my God, that's the thing that got me, got my attention. They went to a hell of a lot of trouble to try and make John Doe 2 go away.

Hoppy Heidelberg went a step further. On October 4, 1995, in a letter to US District Court Judge David L. Russell, he laid out his charge of prosecutorial misconduct in detail. The juror recommended that the judge impanel a new grand jury to keep investigating. "The families of the victims deserve to know who all was involved in the bombing, and there appears to be an attempt to protect the identity of certain suspects, namely John Doe II...," Heidelberg wrote. He called out the government's failure to bring critical witnesses to John Doe 2 or subpoena videotape depicting John Doe 2—and called the government's mistaken identity theory a "hoax."[40]

Three weeks later, on October 24, 1995, Judge Russell fired back a terse four-sentence letter of his own. The judge expelled Heidelberg from the grand jury, threatened him with jail if he violated his continuing "obligation of secrecy," and did not acknowledge Heidelberg's charge of jury rigging by prosecutors.

The grand juror's contest with the powers that be was over. After his expulsion, Heidelberg pushed back, calling it unfair. "You don't fire a man for trying to do his job," he told the *Daily Oklahoman* in a story published on October 27, 1995. "You fire him because he's not doing his job. This is the exact opposite of what needs to be done."

Hoppy Heidelberg broke grand jury rules, and the judge had grounds to expel him. But how could the judge ignore the detailed charges of prosecutorial misconduct laid out by this grand juror?

Who was looking out for the rights of the jury, and, by extension, the public, to see and hear the evidence relating to John Doe 2? It was another *X-Files* moment.

The national media mostly dismissed Hoppy Heidelberg as a wild-eyed conspiracy theorist. However, to the *McCurtain Daily Gazette,* the rural Oklahoma newspaper that published J.D. Cash's coverage of the bombing case, the booted grand juror was a trusted source. On record in the *Gazette,* Hoppy Heidelberg now repeated a provocative opinion he had first offered to *Media Bypass* as to why the government might be engaged in a cover-up.

In a story published on January 21, 1996, Heidelberg told Cash: "It is likely John Doe No. 2 is a government agent or informant. And if this is true, then the government wouldn't want that to come out."

Was this a crazy conspiracy theory or a dark prophecy? Only time would tell. I had to leave this infinitely fascinating mystery in the hands of others now. It wasn't my story. I was just a visiting news junkie. In January 1996, Rysher Entertainment greenlighted my show *Strange Universe* for broadcast. Other mysteries would consume my attention for years until my fateful encounter with Jesse Trentadue again lit a fuse to the bombing story.

CHAPTER 3

THE CALL

WHO KNOWS WHAT RIDDLES live deep in our subconscious mind, waiting to fuel future obsessions? Long after my television series *Strange Universe* ran its course for two seasons and I moved on to develop new TV projects, Oklahoma's bombing resurfaced in the news, sparking intrigue all over again.

In the spring of 2001, a month before Timothy McVeigh's scheduled execution, the FBI suddenly "found" thousands of documents that it should have turned over to defense lawyers—many related to the mystery man in the bombing case, John Doe 2. The FBI found those documents as the result of an audit by its Oklahoma City field office for evidence that disappeared without explanation from Kenneth Trentadue's official case file.[41]

If ever there was an execution the federal government wanted to go forward, it was this one. But the FBI disclosure was so extraordinary that Attorney General John Ashcroft delayed McVeigh's execution for a month. When the day arrived, I was in the Grand Canyon, hiking down to the Colorado River with my brother. I thought I was unhooking from the Timothy McVeigh death spectacle, but I was wrong. Out here on an empty stage in what seemed like infinite space, a surreal reminder awaited me of the tragedy that would reach some measure of closure on this day.

We descended into the canyon in the predawn darkness so the fireball sun wouldn't overtake us on the way back. As we headed into the vast empty canyon bowl, our flashlights suddenly lit up a solemn procession of a half dozen children marching toward us in a row as if out of nowhere.

The youngest child, a solemn boy, maybe five years old, was out front, proudly bearing an American flag and gazing straight ahead, a toy version of Timothy McVeigh and his thousand-yard stare. There are ghosts in this story, boys, including this one, whom I have come to think of as messengers. Timothy McVeigh was back inside my head. He was about to die and, with him, a precious piece of the strange truth about the bombing.

Lethal injection terminated Timothy McVeigh's life on the morning of June 11, 2001, at 8:14 in the Terre Haute, Indiana, federal prison. He went to his death displaying the same defiant resolve to the world as he had since the bombing. He made no apology and spoke no final words to the twenty people witnessing his execution at the prison. Instead, he relied on handwritten copies of the nineteenth-century poem "Invictus" to speak for him, famously, with the line, "I am the master of my fate, I am the captain of my soul."

Meanwhile, almost 700 miles away, in an unprecedented bow to the magnitude of his crime, 232 survivors and victims' relatives boarded vans and traveled to Oklahoma City's Federal Transfer Center to watch live video of the execution. It was captured by a camera suspended from the ceiling of the execution chamber, looking down on Timothy McVeigh's face.

One witness told the Associated Press that McVeigh gazed into the camera with a cold, blank stare. "He had a look of defiance and that if he could, he'd do it all over again," a witness said. "I think I did see the face of evil today," Kathy Wilburn, grandmother of murdered toddlers Chase and Colton Smith, told the AP.[42]

In a curious footnote to the execution, the black hearse that police escorted from the prison afterward turned out to be a decoy to prevent "an ambush or something," according to a prison spokesperson. Meanwhile, a prison van transported McVeigh's body to a local funeral home, where cremation took place.

⅄

A few years later, Terry Nichols's Oklahoma state trial put the bombing back in the headlines and gave me an idea. For the second time, Nichols had escaped the death penalty from a deadlocked jury in 2004, though it had convicted him of mass murder. Suspicions about a wider bombing conspiracy had swirled again in media coverage of the trial. I pitched my old friends at *America's Most Wanted* on producing a tenth-anniversary segment about John Doe 2: the terrorist who had eluded one of the world's biggest manhunts to become an enduring legend of the bombing.

While researching that angle, I discovered a committee of citizen investigators in Oklahoma City who were still pursuing the conspiracy theory. Former Oklahoma State Representative Charles Key sent me his committee's nearly 600-page report, published in 2001.[43] The volume showcased evidence, clues, and leads gathered by grassroots activists.

Their survey, beginning within days of the bombing, challenged the official story of Timothy McVeigh, the lone-wolf terrorist. The committee concluded that one ammonium nitrate/fuel oil (ANFO) bomb couldn't have accounted for the damage done to the building and credited evidence of a second bomb. The committee believed that McVeigh had multiple accomplices on the bombing run and, most concerning, that the federal government had prior warning of the coming attack.

Key had been a high-profile figure while serving in the state legislature throughout the bombing investigations. However, the national news media mostly ignored his committee's findings and call for a congressional investigation into "the actions of certain federal agencies." Though Key's executive summary did not name those agencies, they undoubtedly included the FBI and the Bureau of Alcohol, Tobacco, and Firearms.

When the report arrived in the mail, I went straight to the section on surveillance videotapes and learned something incredible. As of 2001, after six years and two bombing trials, the FBI had never released the videotapes it seized at the crime scene. An appendix to the report included a clip from a magazine story with tantalizing details I had never seen in the national media: claims of surveillance video shot from the nearby YMCA and Regency Tower apartments that showed "excellent footage of the Ryder truck and the suspects—McVeigh and John Doe 2—leaving the vehicle."[44]

"These photos have the potential to prove or disprove many eyewitness accounts of events in Oklahoma City on the day of the bombing and the days leading up to it," the report concluded. "They could shed light on the issue of John Doe 2 and others who may have been involved in the bombing. If, as the government claims, there is nothing of this nature on the tapes, then release them and set this issue to rest."[45]

The committee's coverage of the trials, structural damage to the building, the search for John Doe 2, and government improprieties called into question the very foundation of the bombing case. Removed in time from the emotions triggered by the tragedy, the case seemed shaky. Wasn't it a stretch to believe that an unemployed twentysomething with a grudge against the government built and delivered a bomb big enough to blow up the Murrah Building practically by himself?

For the report's cover, the committee chose the graphic image of a call to action that a first responder had scrawled on a damaged wall of the Journal Record Building near the blast site. A decade later, the raw emotion of that plea struck me as more arresting than ever:

> We Search for the Truth
> We seek Justice.
> The Courts Require it.
> The Victims Cry for it.
> And GOD Demands it!

I was hooked on the mystery all over again. However, it wasn't the courts, victims, or God who would make the call on my story. It was the executive producer of *America's Most Wanted,* and he passed on my pitch. It was maddening not to get the green light. If John Doe 2 wasn't a manhunt story for TV, who would investigate?

The surprising answer came a few months later. I was in my studio when the phone rang. Jannie Coverdale, the grandmother of two toddlers killed in the blast and a member of Charles Key's committee, was calling. "We need your help out here," she declared with the force of a process server. Jannie had heard from

Key that I was investigating the bombing case for *America's Most Wanted*. She was expecting results. Before thinking twice about it, I was on a plane to Oklahoma City.

The stout African American woman with a knowing laugh and quick wit who greeted me at the door of her modest apartment was through waiting for the justice that the president of the United States had personally promised her. Jannie had attended all three bombing trials and witnessed McVeigh's execution. But she never got the answers that authorities had promised were coming. After single-handedly pursuing all clues and some surprising contacts, Jannie now believed a wider conspiracy was behind the crime.

She led me past a hallway shrine in her apartment with portraits of Aaron and Elijah, ages five and two, her grandsons killed in the blast. Around Jannie's dining-room table, I joined a writer for the John Birch Society's *The New American*, which had delivered scalding coverage of the government's bombing prosecutions. A local member of the society rounded out our circle. From the apartment's galley kitchen, Jannie refilled cups of coffee and fired off questions and answers about novel pieces of the case that everyone except me seemed to know. I was happy to be a fly on the wall, riveted by the blizzard of inside information.

Jannie had been corresponding with Terry Nichols, serving his prison sentence as McVeigh's convicted coconspirator. She read an excerpt from one of their letters, trying to convince Nichols to do the right thing and reveal all he knew.

The mention of someone named "Poindexter" prompted Jannie to bring up the theory, which somehow came from McVeigh himself, that the unidentified severed leg found in the bombing rubble belonged to the bombmaker, whose name, or code name, was Poindexter. Severed leg? I recalled this detail from McVeigh's trial, but the Poindexter moniker was an entirely new element to me.

If this claim about the leg was valid, Jannie declared, it was an outrage that the bombmaker's remains lay buried in the sacred grounds of the bombing's memorial grove, along with other unmatched body parts belonging to victims. When I broke in to seek clarification, Jannie offered the name Jesse Trentadue, a lawyer who knew the Poindexter story and much more. Jannie said Jesse and I needed to talk.

I suddenly felt I was entering a parallel universe to the bombing case as I thought I knew it. Here at ground zero of the atrocity, I had found someone who had lost the grandchildren she loved, her most precious possessions in the world. She constructed her own version of what had happened to fill a void of information, placing her trust in risky and unknown sources. Yet, who was I to say? If not Jannie Coverdale's version of reality, then whose version was I betting on?

Jannie, the young Native American boy she was fostering, and I went out that evening to meet Charles Key and a couple more committee members. On the way home, Jannie told me the boy sometimes asked her whether Aaron and Elijah were his older or younger brothers. He knew they would be older than he was if they were still alive. But they were younger in Jannie's home pictures, which was confusing. Heartbreaking, unanswerable questions just kept coming.

The next day, sitting in Jannie's living room near the portraits of her "babies," as she still called her grandsons, she recounted the day the bomb killed Aaron and Elijah. She had walked them to the daycare center that morning, as always. Jannie was at work in a downtown office building when the blast triggered an evacuation. At first, Jannie said, she thought the smoke she could see down the street was coming from the Regency Tower, her apartment building. But when someone said it was the federal building, and knowing the boys' daycare center was on the second floor, Jannie and two coworkers took off running—toward the unthinkable.

"There was nothing there, nothing at all," she told me as if still standing there in that bewildering moment. "I remember policemen taking hold of me and telling me I couldn't go in there. But there was nothing to go into anyway."

From that Wednesday morning, Jannie hoped her grandsons were still alive. She searched the city's hospitals and waited for news at a local church. It took four days for recovery workers to find the boys' remains late on Saturday night. Jannie buried her grandsons together in a single small coffin.

Before I left Oklahoma City, I visited the Outdoor Symbolic Memorial at the National Memorial Museum with its haunting courtyard of empty bronze chairs—large ones for the deceased adults and small ones for the children. Nearby, preserved as part of the memorial, was the Team 5 first responder's fierce message scrawled on the wall. I thought of the steely hope Jannie Coverdale had displayed again yesterday. If someone could solve the bombing's mysteries, Jannie might still find closure and justice for Aaron and Elijah.

Jannie said lawyer Jesse Trentadue had a theory about John Doe 2's identity. That was going to have to be enough to go on. I stowed away my doubts. I would make the trip to Salt Lake City to meet the man who might be Jannie Coverdale's last best hope.

⅄

Jesse Trentadue and I sat on chilly bronze benches outside his law office on a winter day in 2006. Out there, Jesse could take some comfort from a cherished Toscanello cigar, which he admitted looked much like "a dried dog turd," while reliving the worst moments of his life.

Behind sturdy black glasses, this compact man in his late fifties, dressed in a tweed jacket and cap, fixed me with a penetrating stare. Then he floated a question that threatened to end our talk before it began.

"Margaret, are you working for the government?" he asked.

"No," I stammered. That seemed to pass muster, and we carried on.

"The FBI killed my brother," Jesse began matter-of-factly. These were startling words coming from a trial lawyer and, before that, a law school professor, a United States Marine, and an all-American track star at the University of Southern California.

The families of murder victims have had my ear ever since *America's Most Wanted*. Still, I never met anyone with Jesse's combination of outrage and lawyerly skill, as the tale about his brother and the Oklahoma City bombing that he was about to tell me would reveal.

Jesse wanted me to know something else: In his family, he told me, justice meant an eye for an eye. "When you kill one of ours, we will come for you," he explained with a calm that added menace to the words. Jesse was referring to his family's West Virginia roots as proud descendants of the notorious Hatfield clan. They clashed murderously with the McCoys in America's most legendary family blood feud. The pledge Jesse quoted was part of the Trentadue family code, along with God and country.

Jesse and Kenney, as he called his younger brother, grew up in "Number 7 Holler," a small coal camp in the Cumberland Mountains of Appalachia, home to snake-handling religion, bootleggers, and crushing poverty. They shared a bed and an outhouse and hunted raccoons and squirrels to help feed their family. In the early 1960s, some Number 7 residents, including Jesse's family, had had enough. They pulled up stakes and moved to Southern California.

Jesse told how two Appalachian women transplanted from their West Virginia mining camp to Hollywood broke the audience applause meter with their hard-luck stories on the television show *Queen for a Day*. Crowned winners took home a case of Chesterfield cigarettes and various household appliances and furnishings. But after the second coronation, the show's producers put a lifetime ban on ladies from Number 7 Holler competing on *Queen for a Day*. In the hard-luck department, they had too big an advantage.

Running through the Cumberland Mountains to keep up with hounds had been excellent training for young athletes. The Trentadue boys starred in track and field in high school after the family settled in Westminster, California. As a thirteen-year-old, Kenney, three years younger than Jesse, set a national age-group record in the two-mile run until an injury sidelined him. He dropped out of high school and enlisted in the Army at age seventeen, following a long family tradition of military service dating back to the Revolutionary War. He came home addicted to heroin and turned to committing armed robberies to pay for his fixes, hitting up pharmacies at first, then on to savings and loans.

With a big brother's grim loyalty, Jesse explained that Kenney took down whole banks, not just the tellers, by himself, purposely using weapons he had emptied or disabled. That was his code. "Robbery is one thing. Murder is something different. Money isn't worth that," Jesse told me, quoting his brother. When the law caught up with Kenney, Jesse explained: "He didn't cry about it. He went in, pled guilty, and served his time," but using the alias Vance Paul Brockway, which would spell disaster years later.

Meanwhile, the older brother's fortunes were soaring. Jesse won a full athletic scholarship at the University of Southern California, excelling in track and field as a three-time all-American middle-distance runner. O. J. Simpson was a teammate. Their name plaques hang side by side in the university's athletic hall in Los Angeles.

After graduation, Jesse served a hitch in the US Marine Corps. He earned a law degree, scored a clerkship for a distinguished federal judge and then a teaching position at the University of North Dakota School of Law. After marrying, Jesse and his wife, Rita, settled in Salt Lake City, where Jesse has conducted courtroom combat for several decades as a trial lawyer for insurance companies and public agencies, one of the most unforgiving branches of the law.

A good life carried Jesse far from Number 7 Holler, his Hatfield ancestors' blood feud, and even his kid brother's crimes and punishment. Jesse was at his law office when the news of Kenneth's death hit like an avalanche on the morning of August 21, 1995. I've read the transcripts of Kenneth's last phone calls with Jesse and other family members in the days before his death, preserved as evidence in the family's wrongful death lawsuit.

Nothing except the dates on those transcripts contains any hint of what was coming.

In calls with Jesse, their "sis," Donna, and Rita, Kenney rallied the family to help him corral parole documents that might straighten out a records mix-up he believed could reduce his penalty for parole violation. Kenney was still determining when his hearing would take place. The transcripts reveal his stress as he processed out loud the vagaries of counselors' schedules and the heavy caseload of a new hearing system, frequently punctuating his musings with the question: "You know what I'm saying?"

Jesse had heard it all before. He listened patiently to his troubled brother, then asked a fundamental question: "Will they give you a lawyer?... You need one." Kenney fretted about mail left behind in California and asked his sister to have his wife, Carmen, send money. He regretted missing a trip to the beach with Jesse's son and asked after their parents. Kenney's last call with Jesse, on the night of August 19, ended with a promise.

Kenney: Okay then, I'll yell back tomorrow then, okay?
Jesse: Okay, take care.
Kenney: Okay then, love to everybody. Bye.[46]

Two days later, Kenney would be gone, timestamping forever this final exchange between brothers and leaving his whole family in grief and disbelief. Two years later, Kenneth's widow, Carmen, recalled his resolve to start over after prison. On a camping trip following his parole in 1987, Kenneth had brought stacks of letters and threw them on the campfire. "We decided this was the past," Carmen told a reporter. "He tried to build something out of his life, be somebody else."[47] She hoped that Kenneth's death would not go unnoticed just because he was a prisoner.

"They're still human beings," she said. "They still have families that love them."[48]

Sitting on that bench, listening to Jesse's story, I could sense the love and loss. I forgot the cold. Jesse led me through his decade-long crusade to solve Kenneth's murder—the awful news from the prison, the horrific secrets hidden in Kenneth's coffin, the anonymous tip, a federal grand jury's pivotal 1997 decision not to bring criminal charges, and finally, the million-dollar judgment that, in Jesse's belief, still failed to call murder by its name.

As he spoke, Jesse occasionally relit his Toscanello. In one of those pauses, I could tell that something profound, imposing an almost tangible sense of menace, had followed Jesse out of the trial. With eerie clarity, the death of prisoner witness Alden Baker personified that threat.

Jesse believed that someone inside the federal government was hiding a terrible secret about who killed Kenneth and why. Why else would the prison bureaucracy go to such elaborate lengths, exposed by the family's civil trial, to protect the killers of one obscure federal inmate—*and* the killers of the inmate witness to that murder? If Kenneth's killers were rogue guards acting independently, Jesse was sure the prison would not bother to protect them. Disturbing as it was to contemplate, simple logic pointed to those who held the keys to both cells and to their superiors up the chain of command in federal law enforcement.

⅄

"It was such a simple homicide—the broken hyoid bone, the blood, the injuries he couldn't have inflicted himself," Michael Hubbard, former top investigator for the US Senate Judiciary Committee, told me, recalling the Kenneth Trentadue case.[49] Hubbard is also a former Washington, DC, police officer. As he told me, "[I] saw more than my share of dead bodies on the street." Hubbard knows murder as well as he knows politics.

Reporting to Senator Orrin Hatch, the powerful chairman of the Judiciary Committee, Hubbard's hefty investigative caseload between 1995 and 1997 included Waco, Ruby Ridge, TWA Flight 800, and the Trentadue case. Hubbard was Jesse's tireless ally on Capitol Hill during the tumultuous spring of 1997. As the Trentadue grand jury investigated in Oklahoma City, the heat of national media coverage of the case rose, and Jesse's attention turned to Washington. As Hubbard knew, the forensics might be simple, but the politics were deep.

Mary A. Fischer's first *GQ* story, "A Case of Homicide?" in September 1996, short-listed for a National Magazine Award, brought high-profile attention to the Trentadue case. However, as her editors noted in their introduction to her follow-up story, "Cover-up in Cell 709A," in the December 1997 issue of *GQ*:

> The second part of the story is, in many ways, more disturbing than the first. What began as a tragedy for those close to Kenneth Trentadue is now, two years after his death, overshadowed by a larger story of bungling or worse within the Department of Justice, which oversees the FBI and the BOP.

Fischer's first story, published two months after the Trentadue federal grand jury began deliberating, had ignited a firestorm of political controversy in Washington, as Jesse had hoped. If the grand jury brought indictments for perjury or obstruction of justice, federal prosecutions might pressure guilty parties to reveal the rest of the truth about Kenneth's murder. However, as Jesse was about to learn, the media exposure also raised the stakes for forces opposing him.

Federal grand juries operate under a cloak of near absolute secrecy, so leaks about the Trentadue grand jury were and are challenging to verify. Still, the rumors were out there: This jury only met once a month for a few hours. Perversely, the prosecutors the Department of Justice had hand-picked to run it were attacking the murder theory instead of presenting it.

For the second year in a row, the DOJ installed federal prosecutors from Washington to manage a high-profile Oklahoma grand jury. In both cases, DOJ stars who would one day rise to become United States attorney general—Merrick Garland on the bombing case and Eric Holder on the Trentadue case—played influential roles in Washington in the outcomes of those grand juries.

However, as revealed by Hoppy Heidelberg's rogue leaks from the bombing grand jury and confidential materials Jesse extracted in his civil lawsuit, troubling ethical questions cast doubts on both grand juries. For Jesse, in the spring of 1997, the weight of Washington's hand on the scale felt like a palpable threat.

By then, TV network news was onto the story of a possible cover-up of a high-profile prison murder. On April 11, 1997, while the grand jury deliberated, NBC's primetime newsmagazine *Dateline* covered the case. Dr. Jordan, Oklahoma's medical examiner, doubled down on his doubts about the story of Kenneth's death. When asked if he had ever seen a suicide like this, Dr. Jordan responded emphatically: "No! Not only have I not seen it in almost twenty years of forensic practice…I presented this informally to colleagues from other states, and I have not encountered one who had ever seen anything like this before in a suicide."

When asked if trauma to Kenneth's body was self-inflicted, Dr. Jordan answered: "No, I think that was done by someone else."

On the same broadcast, Senator Hatch weighed in with equal force, calling the Justice Department's handling of the Trentadue case "colossal incompetence" and saying that the "possibility of cover-up" is "certainly something you can't ignore."

Pledging his commitment to getting answers, the Senate Judiciary Committee chairman declared: "There are a lot of things that just are phony about this, that just don't add up.... There is no excuse for anybody covering this up. This case isn't going to go away. Congress isn't going to go away. We want answers to this. We want to know what happened."

Attorney General Janet Reno dodged Senator Hatch's inquiries about Kenneth's case for several months. However, on May 1, 1997, a few weeks after the *Dateline* broadcast, Senator Hatch ambushed Reno at an oversight hearing, confronting her about graphic photos he had seen of Kenneth's body and reports that the grand jury was intentionally slow-walking the case.

"It is apparent to me that not only are the facts suspicious, it looks like someone in the BOP or someone having relations with the Bureau of Prisons murdered the man," Senator Hatch declared for the record.[50] In reply, Attorney General Reno offered only: "We will do everything we can to see that the matter is vigorously pursued." In the clip I watched, the AG seemed to give this pledge with more irritation than commitment.

No one escaped the extraordinary pressures driving the Trentadue case. Mary A. Fischer reported in *GQ* that while the power play between Senator Hatch and Attorney General Reno was running its course in the spring of 1997, the senator's office received an unusual phone call. A senior Justice Department official posed a highly improper question: "What would it take to make this go away?"

"People in handcuffs," Hatch's indignant aide shot back.

Inside Senator Hatch's office, Michael Hubbard felt the heat personally. He told me that an FBI official warned a lawyer friend of Hubbard's assigned to the Judiciary Committee that he could face indictment for obstruction of justice, apparently for his diligent digging into the case as the committee's top investigator. Hubbard ignored the threat.

Jesse may also have been a target for indictment, as he discovered later when the discovery process in the family's civil lawsuit allowed him to uncover confidential DOJ records. An investigative diary Jesse kept from 1995 to 2003 covers a March 25, 1997, DOJ meeting of attorneys in the department's Civil Rights Division to discuss the possibility of indicting Jesse for obstruction of justice or fraud.[51]

According to confidential notes from that meeting, the DOJ lawyers planned to use as a witness an inmate who would place a "yoke of silence" around Jesse's neck. The inmate would testify that Jesse paid other prisoners to perjure themselves during the *GQ* investigation—a claim Jesse categorically denies. The real reason for such an extreme move against Jesse may have been an accusation floated at the meeting that he was on a "campaign to discredit the federal Government." According to Jesse's diary, the inmate in question did testify before the grand jury, even though he failed a polygraph test.

Political hardball was the standard operating procedure in the Trentadue case, and no one felt more heat than Oklahoma's medical examiner, Dr. Fred Jordan. If he changed his cause-of-death finding of "unknown," which he had steadfastly defended for two years, to "suicide," that would probably ensure a "no bill," meaning no criminal charges, from the grand jury. On the other hand, if Dr. Jordan stood his ground, the outcome was less certain.

The DOJ prosecutors running the grand jury attempted to bypass Dr. Jordan. In a move that must have stung him, they chose another respected expert, Dr. William Gormley of the Armed Forces Institute of Pathology, as their grand jury expert on the cause of death. However, Dr. Gormley reported that he agreed with Dr. Jordan's finding on the cause of death as "unknown." Further, Dr. Gormley stated his opinion that Kenneth Trentadue was a victim of assault, a vital element of the case for murder versus suicide.[52] The DOJ lawyers would need to regroup, and in May 1997, they approached Dr. Gormley with a new request.

According to Jesse's diary for May 29, 1997, they asked: Would Dr. Gormley be willing to testify to the grand jury that "it might be possible these injuries are self-inflicted"? The move backfired. Dr. Gormley refused. Instead, he immediately notified Dr. Jordan's office, recounting the lawyers' gambit and saying he was now even more convinced "that this man was murdered."[53]

The conflict between Dr. Jordan and federal prosecutors had now escalated into a full-blown feud. In July 1997, a month before the grand jury's decision, Dr. Jordan told an assistant US attorney for the Western District of Oklahoma "that the federal grand jury is part of a cover-up" and that he believed "it is very likely this man was killed."[54]

Two days later, Dr. Jordan went on KOKH TV, Oklahoma City's Fox affiliate, and repeated his opinion about Kenneth's cause of death: "I think it's very likely he was murdered."[55]

Dr. Jordan added, however, that because of the destruction of the crime scene: "I am not able to prove it." He slammed the

Justice Department's destruction of the scene, saying: "It was botched. Or worse, it was planned."

With such outrage on display nationally over the seeming cover-up of a shocking miscarriage of justice, it would take more than political hardball to keep the lid on the Trentadue scandal, no matter what the grand jury decided.

Six weeks later, on August 13, 1997, the grand jury returned a no-bill, declining to bring any criminal indictments in the case. Crime scene meddling, preventing Dr. Jordan from ruling Kenneth's death a homicide, undoubtedly was a critical factor. However, secrecy that went beyond even usual strict grand jury confidentiality entirely shrouded the outcome. In a stunning lack of transparency, no one outside the Department of Justice would even learn that the grand jury had reached its decision for two more months.

Only one obstacle remained for those seeking to shut down the Trentadue case from criminal prosecutions. With or without grand jury indictments, Senator Hatch's promised investigation seemed almost inevitable. To prevent that, Deputy Attorney General Eric Holder stepped up to manage a Justice Department influence campaign aimed at Capitol Hill. Operating with the advantage of secrecy, which kept even the Trentadue family in the dark, Deputy AG Holder went to work on what his staff called the "rollout" plan to announce the grand jury's decision while preventing a Senate investigation.

Later, when the discovery process in the civil case disgorged email fragments of the Holder spin campaign, they infuriated Jesse. Team members on the "Trentadue Mission" exchanged a glib message referring to their list of agenda items as "Trentadoes." One email likened their orchestration of Senate notifications of the grand jury's no-bill to World War II's "Normandy Invasion." As the publication of the DOJ's October 9, 1997, press release announcing the decision neared, one staffer summed up the campaign's political goal: "We ain't looking for press on this. Hill takes priority."[56]

"These documents paint a clear picture of a wide-ranging and cynical scheme, run directly by Mr. Holder, to quash my family's efforts to have my brother's murder investigated and to deflect congressional oversight and media attention from the shocking circumstances of his death," Jesse would write in a 2008 letter to Senator Patrick Leahy, chairman of the Judiciary Committee, opposing Holder's nomination as attorney general."[57]

In the short run, diplomacy wasn't enough, even capped off by Deputy AG Holder's visit to Senator Hatch the night the press release went out. Unpersuaded, Senator Hatch went on Fox News the next day, promising the hearings Holder had tried for two months to prevent. "There is a lot wrong with this case, and I hope somebody will get to the bottom of it," Hatch declared. "But apparently, the federal government hasn't been able to do so.... Yep, it has the aroma of a cover-up.... And like I say, it does look bad. Somebody has not told the truth here, and somebody is, in my opinion, covering up."

This declaration from Congress's top watchdog over the Justice Department sounded resolute. Yet, once again, the truth would soon wind up on the back burner. After more pressure from Washington, including two visits by contingents of FBI agents, who traveled to Oklahoma's influential senior Senator Don Nickles's home office, the matter finally faded away on Capitol Hill. On Senator Nickles's recommendation, despite Senator Hatch's fighting words, the promised hearings were never gaveled in. The message from Washington was consistent: Nothing to see here.

At this discouraging moment of the story, as we sat on the benches outside his law office that winter's morning, Jesse applied a match to his cigar, signaling that a twist in the story was coming. Two journalists drawn to Jesse's cause had connected Kenneth's murder to the Oklahoma City bombing and a scandalous cover-up of the crime inside the Department of Justice. Jesse paused before telling me about their breakthrough, gesturing with the Toscanello as if tapping out a coded message.

If cigars could speak, this one would say, "Helluva story."

CHAPTER 4

THE OUTSIDER

FROM THE BEGINNING, the Oklahoma City bombing was a Washington, DC, news story. No matter how many reporters, producers, and camera operators major news organizations dispatched to the nation's Midwest, it would remain a Washington story. In one nearly disastrous early misstep, CBS News flew its celebrity anchor, Connie Chung, to the disaster scene. She insulted the city's fire chief by asking: "Can the Oklahoma City Fire Department handle *this*?" But big-league journalism quickly took control of the story and owned it.

That made the rise of J.D. Cash, reporting for the diminutive *McCurtain Daily Gazette* (circulation 6,000) in Idabel, Oklahoma, even more extraordinary. National news reporters and producers took their cues on the bombing story from the Justice Department in Washington, DC. Top journalists often quoted unnamed federal law enforcement sources in Washington for their exclusives. Back in Oklahoma, J.D. Cash was practicing old-school journalism, hitting the streets or open roads to interview witnesses and sources, often face-to-face.

When the bomb exploded, John David Cash, ("J.D." to friends), wasn't even a journalist. After working as a mortgage broker and divorcing, he retired in his forties, relocating to a rustic cabin he inherited from his father in rural eastern Oklahoma, near the Arkansas border. There the passionate outdoorsman planned to drive the backroads, fish, and write a novel about lost Nazi gold. All that changed when a friend from law school died in the Oklahoma City blast.

Following the news coverage, J.D. was frustrated that reporters weren't digging hard enough into unanswered questions. He tapped some real estate sources, drafted his first newspaper story, and personally handed it to Bruce Willingham, the *Gazette*'s editor and publisher. Willingham took a few days to check the facts and have the story rewritten, then published it under a joint byline with a *Gazette* staff writer. The story ran on May 4, 1995, under the headline: "Secondary Explosion Revealed in Murrah Blast: Were High Explosives Removed from Floor Above Day Care Center?" The story won a state journalism prize for best investigative reporting that year, though federal authorities and the media disregarded its expert's findings.[58]

J.D's exclusive report quoted University of Oklahoma geophysicist Dr. Raymond Brown, concluding, based on seismographic evidence, that not one but two explosions, eleven seconds apart, destroyed the Murrah Building. It was big news, but the Associated Press did not even pick up the story. As the *Gazette* reported on June 18, 1995, the US Geological Survey quickly moved to discredit Dr. Brown's theory. Soon after, the AP reported on the USGS conclusions without quoting Brown.[59] The shunning of J.D. Cash by the nation's journalistic establishment had begun on his very first story in print.

Still, this natural-born star reporter was off and running. J.D. Cash had found his true calling in middle age. Now he needed solid sources in Oklahoma City to compete on this high-profile story. He found them in Glenn and Kathy Wilburn, grandparents of murdered toddlers Chase and Colton, ages three and two, who had lived with the Wilburns, along with their mother, Kathy's daughter, Edye Smith. Soon after meeting Glenn and Kathy, J.D. began camping out in their home for days, sleeping in a spare room down the hall from the boys' bedroom. J.D. was now the third principal player in a grassroots journalistic juggernaut.

The Wilburns weren't professional journalists, but they had skills and learned fast. Glenn was a natural investigator. He was organized, whip-smart, and detail and document-oriented as an accountant. Kathy was a natural street reporter, an extrovert by nature. She was also a disarmingly attractive redhead who would knock on doors and win hearts. "I lost my two grandsons in the bombing," she would tell strangers, "and I need you to help me find out the truth about what happened." Not many people could say no to "Big Red," as Glenn called Kathy. They had exclusive access to sources and witnesses, including friends, neighbors, and fellow survivors. The horror they had all experienced shocked them into raw candor.

By midsummer of 1995, the national news media had focused the bombing story on the frightening psychological riddle of a criminal monster, still in his twenties, who was also a paragon of politeness and a recipient of the Army's Bronze Star while serving his country in Iraq. They were documenting Timothy McVeigh's path to trial as the bombing's lone-wolf terrorist mastermind. Meanwhile, on the ground in Oklahoma City, J.D. Cash and the Wilburns uncovered troubling, contradictory revelations. It was almost as if they covered the story in a parallel universe.

Glenn Wilburn learned from the Oklahoma City Fire Department's dispatch chief about a phone call from the FBI on the Friday before the bombing, warning of a possible terrorist threat. Did the federal government have prior knowledge that the bombing was coming yet fail to warn the victims? From families in the Wilburns' circle came other inklings of prior knowledge: sightings of a sheriff's department bomb squad in the early morning hours before the blast and sightings of unknown uniformed agents prowling different areas of the city with hoop-like devices. Were they trying to pick up transmitter signals from a vehicle they were tracking, one that had gone missing?[60]

Minutes after the blast, a frantic husband searching for his wife, who worked in the Murrah Building, encountered an ATF agent at the blast site, who told him ATF agents had been tipped off on their pagers not to come in to work that day.[61] J.D. featured the circle of victim and survivor families in his *Gazette* coverage.

Hoppy Heidelberg, the grand juror dismissed for going public with his concerns about prosecutorial misconduct, had earned local legend status with some families for continuing to speak his mind. Heidelberg allowed J.D. to quote him in the newspaper after the judge threatened to send him to jail if he violated the grand jury's rules. In J.D.'s January 21, 1996, story about doubts haunting the survivors, Heidelberg elaborated on his suspicion that John Doe 2 was a government informant or operative.

"Was this a sting operation by the government that went bad?" the ex-grand juror wondered. "If it was, so be it. They should take responsibility for their mistakes—just like the rest of us have to. None of us is above the law!"

A few days later, on January 24, 1996, J.D. broke a two-part *Gazette* exclusive. The timing made the story, sourced in eyewitness accounts of John Doe 2, even more explosive. Within weeks of the launch of the global John Doe 2 manhunt, the FBI had curiously begun backing away from it. On May 8, 1995, the bureau pulled the plug on the John Doe 2 tipline. In mid-June, it unveiled the shaky Private Bunting theory, suggesting that innocent soldier Todd Bunting may have been mistakenly identified as John Doe 2.[62]

Soon, just a few days after the publication of J.D.'s eyewitness story, the DOJ would seek to set that theory in stone by filing court papers in the McVeigh case asserting that mechanic Tom Kessinger's description of John Doe 2 at Elliott's Body Shop had indeed been a mistake.[63] The message was loud and clear: The witnesses who swore they saw John Doe 2 got it wrong.

But did they?

Based on sightings by nine eyewitnesses at or near the Murrah Building the morning of the bombing, J.D.'s story counted down the final hour leading up to the blast. His witnesses were ordinary men and women starting an ordinary workday in an ordinary American city, only to become part of a real-life horror story. Lone-wolf terror? In vivid details possessing the ring of truth, J.D.'s eyewitnesses recounted seeing a strike force of at least four terrorists—McVeigh, John Doe 2, and two unknown others driving at least three different vehicles as they mobilized with military precision to detonate a weapon of mass destruction.

At 8:00 a.m., motorist Leonard Long nearly collided with a brown pickup truck racing out of the Murrah Building's parking lot. Inside the vehicle, he saw a man resembling Timothy McVeigh and another man matching the description of John Doe 2.

At 8:35 a.m., businessman Kyle Hunt saw three white men in a pale sedan following a yellow Ryder truck near the intersection of Main and Robinson in downtown Oklahoma City.

Also around 8:35 a.m., a few blocks from the Hunt sighting, warehouse foreman David Snider saw a Ryder truck coasting slowly through the Bricktown warehouse district.

At 8:40 a.m., mechanic Mike Moroz shook hands with McVeigh after giving him directions to the nearby Murrah Building. Moroz noticed a man resembling John Doe 2 sitting in the passenger seat of the Ryder truck.

At 8:50 a.m., an anonymous witness, later identified as Leroy Brooks, was visiting the post office a half block from the Murrah Building. He noticed McVeigh and two other men standing behind a Ryder truck while another man in a ball cap sat in the truck's passenger seat.

At 8:56 a.m., while running an errand to retrieve uniforms from his pickup truck, pressman Gary Lewis passed a man behind the wheel of a dirty yellow sedan with its engine idling in an alley near the Murrah Building.

At 8:57 a.m., motorist Lea Mohr was annoyed to discover the Ryder truck parked in her usual handicapped parking space at the Murrah Building. She snapped photos of the offending vehicle, which the FBI confiscated and never returned.

At 8:58 a.m., the witness, Brooks, at the post office again saw the Ryder truck, now parked down the street in front of the Murrah Building. The same tall, thin man Brooks had seen before, whom he later would identify as McVeigh, was hurrying away from the vehicle. A customized Chevy pickup truck parked a few spaces ahead of the Ryder truck also caught this witness's attention.

At 8:59 a.m., Lewis, the pressman, was rushing back across the parking lot carrying his uniforms when he leaped aside to avoid being struck by a dirty yellow sedan as it hopped a car guard. He believed Timothy McVeigh was the car's driver, and the passenger resembled John Doe 2.

At 9:00 a.m., young mother Daina Bradley was people-watching from inside the Murrah Building while visiting the Social Security office on the first floor. Just before the blast, through the building's tall glass windows, she saw John Doe 2 exit the passenger side of the Ryder truck and walk away.

At 9:02 a.m., five blocks south of the Murrah Building, glass rained down on the pavement when the explosion shattered windows above. An anonymous pedestrian about to cross the street stepped back onto the curb to avoid being hit by a brown pickup truck racing away from the Murrah Building.

The *Gazette*'s editor, Bruce Willingham, bannered the story's significance this way: "The findings of *Gazette* investigative reporter J.D. Cash defy all previous government assertions that there were no additional co-conspirators involved." The editor was right. There was simply no way to reconcile what the eyewitnesses saw with the government's theory that McVeigh drove the bomb from Kansas to Oklahoma City alone and detonated it by himself at the Murrah Building.

Most of the witnesses allowed J.D. to use their names, and most had reported their sightings to the FBI, which enhanced their credibility. Yet strangely, prosecutors did not call any of them before the grand jury or to testify at McVeigh's trial. Over the years since the story's publication, additional eyewitnesses to John Doe 2 have come to light. All told, official records and credible media reports have identified twenty-six such eyewitnesses, some with multiple sightings, who observed McVeigh with others unknown in Oklahoma City in the three hours before the bombing, including sixteen witnesses—almost twice Cash's total—who saw a man resembling John Doe 2 with McVeigh.[64]

How many terrorists does it take to blow up a nine-story building? Is the number one? Or more like four, as J.D.'s eyewitnesses reported? Still, prosecutors ignored the witnesses and settled on McVeigh committing the crime solo.

In the following months, J.D.'s reporting took a pivotal turn, leading him into the secluded white separatist community of Elohim City, to its shadowy paramilitary trainer, the German national Andreas Strassmeir, and to the Aryan Republican Army gang that sometimes hid out there in 1994–95. The 400-acre Elohim City compound on the Oklahoma-Arkansas border was either a harmless rural outpost where a few dozen families lived and worshipped in seclusion or a toxic white supremacist cult indoctrinating residents into radical anti-government violence. Someone badly needed to separate appearance from reality here.

As an Oklahoman, J.D. knew something about the bombing story that the visiting national news media, mostly from the East Coast, didn't, giving him a tremendous edge. For them, the bombing came as a bolt from the blue. Why would terrorists bother targeting a building in remote Oklahoma to make their statement? Why not New York City or Washington, DC? But J.D. knew that anti-government sentiment was surging in the nation's Midwest.

A recent wave of federal gun raids had escalated a fearsome rebellion in the making, spilling the blood of innocent women and children at Ruby Ridge, Idaho, in 1992 and then at Waco, Texas, in 1993, two years to the day before the Oklahoma City bombing. As desperate people searched for answers, some extreme ones emerged in strange quarters. Preachers of an obscure and racist religious doctrine calling itself Christian Identity taught followers that white DNA made them genetically superior to "mud people," as its movement labeled Blacks and Jews. At Elohim City, the community's patriarch, the Reverend Robert Millar, preached white supremacy and delivered a stark political message too. The federal government is coming for your guns. Arm yourselves. Prepare to stand and fight. The message was extreme, but after Waco, it was gaining followers.

Understanding the white power movement's role in the Oklahoma City bombing—as an inspiring force or even, as J.D. came to believe, as an active player in the bomb plot, overshadowing Timothy McVeigh's role—would distinguish J.D.'s reporting. He had a firm grasp on the history of America's radical white power movement, dating back to 1983, and a toxic struggle against poverty and powerlessness in predominantly white rural America. What he didn't know, he was about to learn.

After twenty years of brutally hard times, many Midwesterners and Westerners had come to view the federal government as their enemy. Sky-high interest rates claimed family farms. The Vietnam War claimed sons, brothers, and husbands. In a time of need, farmers saw their government turning a blind eye to those who provided food for America's tables. Record numbers of farmers put guns to their heads and ended their misery in suicide. Far from white supremacists defined by privilege, they were struggling to survive.

Caught in a regional economic doom spiral, some on the anti-government fringe turned to violence. J.D. knew this grim history too. The rage driving these radicals manifested itself in fiery criminal assaults on federal institutions and personnel. Federal law enforcement fired back. In 1983, war broke out in America's Heartland when a group of extremists convened in Hayden Lake, Idaho, to formulate a response to a criminal manhunt by federal law enforcement that had killed one of their own.

Anti-tax activist Gordon Kahl had killed two deputy US marshals attempting to serve a subpoena on him. A federal posse tracked Kahl down in Arkansas, and he burned alive after they dropped a flare down the chimney of his safe house. Kahl's death transformed him into a martyr in the eyes of the movement. The first shots had landed in a blood feud with federal law enforcement that would spiral into unimagined atrocities for another dozen years.

Movement leader Kerry Noble drafted a four-page declaration of war against the US government. The document stated that "it is inevitable that war is coming to the United States of America" and called for meeting force with force: "Terror will succeed only until it is met with equal terror!"[65]

With the battle cry "War in 84," the white power movement envisioned 1984 as the year of the second American revolution. Its goal was to incite a race war that would bring down the government and pave the way for the establishment of an all-white homeland. The battleground would be the rural, wide-open spaces of the Midwest and West. That's where the insurgents mostly lived and where Oklahoma City and Tulsa were high-value targets in practical striking distance. In a 1998 memoir, Noble said the movement's ultimate goal was to bomb Oklahoma City's federal building.[66]

A kinder, gentler movement leader, Kerry Noble, appeared in HBO's 2024 documentary *An American Bombing: The Road to April 19th*. The reformed white supremacist and domestic terrorist recounts participating in targeting a gay church for attack as a member of the 1980s white power group calling itself "the Covenant, the Sword, and the Arm of the Lord" (CSA). However, in a moment Noble describes as a turning point, ending his radicalization, he discovered that the gay targets of terror were just churchgoers, like any others.

Before his awakening, though, Noble helped CSA founder and Christian Identity preacher James Ellison helm the Arkansas-based group's violent mission. The CSA plotted to poison the water supplies of New York City and Washington, DC, with sodium sulfate. In 1983, Richard Snell, a self-proclaimed "messenger" between the CSA and Elohim City, was a crucial player in a CSA plot to destroy the Murrah Building with rocket launchers. The plot failed when a rocket blew up in the hands of its expert in munitions. The conspirators took the violent mishap as a sign from God and stood down.

Twelve years later, in a coincidence that spoke volumes to J.D., on the same day as the Oklahoma City bombing, Richard Snell was executed in Arkansas for the murder of a pawnbroker he mistakenly believed was Jewish. Elohim City's Reverend Millar served as Snell's pastor, took his body back to Elohim City, and presided over his burial there.

A year after the collapse of the 1983 Murrah Building plot, the spectacular rise and fall of the white power movement's most notorious outlaw gang, known as The Order, engulfed the CSA and extinguished all its destructive plans. Inspired by Kahl's martyrdom and the momentum of the "War in 84" movement, Robert

Mathews stepped forward to create a domestic terror group to lead the insurgency. He called it the Silent Brotherhood. However, members soon renamed it The Order after William Pierce's fictional strike force in *The Turner Diaries*, Pierce's apocalyptic 1978 novel glorifying a white supremacist insurrection. It was Timothy McVeigh's favorite book and, according to federal prosecutors, the blueprint for the Oklahoma City bombing.

In June 1984, the gang murdered Denver talk show host Alan Berg—for being Jewish and for using his radio broadcast to oppose right-wing extremist organizations, notably Tom Metzger's California-based hate group WAR, short for White Aryan Resistance. The following month, The Order robbed an armored car in California of $3.8 million, distributing a portion of the stolen money to various militant white supremacist groups. The crime spree triggered the white power movement's second fiery martyrdom.

In December 1984, FBI agents tracked The Order to an island in Washington State's Puget Sound. After a thirty-hour gun battle and Mathews's refusal to surrender, the FBI's Hostage Rescue Team fired flares into the cabin where he was barricaded, exploding stored ammunition into a firestorm and burning Mathews alive. Near the end of the siege, he wrote: "I have been a good soldier, a fearless warrior. I will die with honor and join my brothers in Valhalla."

Months later, in a ripple effect reaching the CSA in Arkansas, the FBI tracked the last of The Order's fugitive gang members to James Ellison's CSA compound. The 200-acre property featured a paramilitary training camp equipped with pop-up targets of Blacks, Jews, and police officers wearing Star of David badges.

The FBI had learned that the CSA manufactured some of the guns used in The Order's crimes.[67]

FBI Hostage Rescue Team leader Danny Coulson moved in with 200 agents and called on Noble as a negotiator. According to Noble, Coulson told him that if anyone fired a shot at the FBI he would send up a helicopter with a 50-caliber machine gun, and in thirty seconds all the men, women and children in the compound would be dead. The strategy worked. The FBI shut down the compound and arrested Ellison without violence.

The CSA siege began on April 19, 1985, Patriots' Day, observed by the white power movement as a banner day of defiance in its ongoing struggle against the federal government. That year, however, federal law enforcement owned the day with an overpowering show of force. The CSA's grand plan to bomb Oklahoma City's federal building was left smoldering in the ashes of history, along with the larger-than-life outlaw legend of The Order, at least for the time being.

While investigating Mathews's gang, the FBI had developed information that prominent white supremacist organizations had orchestrated The Order's terror spree. In a high-profile prosecution aimed at crushing the white power movement in federal court, the Justice Department charged fourteen prominent movement figures—including neo-Nazi leader Louis Beam and CSA member Richard Snell—with sedition.[68] The CSA's Ellison made a plea deal and became a star witness for the government in the 1988 sedition trial in Fort Smith, Arkansas. However, that trial ended in disaster for the government when the jury acquitted all the defendants on all charges. The white power movement would live to fight another day.

For J.D. Cash, the question was: Was that day April 19, 1995?

The movement's recent history and McVeigh's possible role were opaque, a cunningly deceptive puzzle for J.D. to solve. A pivotal development came in 1992 when Louis Beam unveiled his influential "leaderless resistance" strategy in a widely circulated essay. The innovative concept Beam set forth featured small independent terror cells made up of two to five "silent warriors," operating independently of each other, to commit robberies to finance the movement's war and to carry out bombings to damage the enemy federal government.

For Timothy McVeigh, the timing of Beam's call to action could not have been more potent. That same year, 1992, the young Desert Storm veteran McVeigh pulled up stakes in Buffalo and headed west to Michigan and Arizona into the hotbed of white power activism. Constantly on the move, McVeigh racked up thousands of miles driving through the Midwest and West, selling copies of his cult bible, *The Turner Diaries*, and dispensing his brand of anti-government fundamentalism from rented tables on America's busy gun show circuit. One show, one city at a time, McVeigh might have cut the figure of a youthful, self-styled itinerant preacher in training, following in the footsteps of the Reverends Ellison, Millar, and their like.

Timothy McVeigh's war veteran profile would have held strong appeal for white power sympathizers frequenting those gun shows. The activists now called themselves "patriots," bonding under the banner of a second American revolution. But did Timothy McVeigh have other business on the gun show circuit beyond sermonizing? Did he make contacts in the white power underground, a fluid, almost invisible mosaic of violent groups dedicated to continuing The Order's mission of robbery and revolution in the 1990s and beyond? Was Timothy McVeigh a silent warrior under the banner of Louis Beam's leaderless resistance?

⅄

Patriots' Day. *The Turner Diaries*. The Order. Elohim City. The Murrah Building. Timothy McVeigh. The story was there for the taking, and J.D. Cash scooped the nation's premier news organizations multiple times in 1996.

On February 4, 1996, the *Gazette* published an exclusive story based on J.D.'s reporting, headlined "Mystery Surrounds German's Link to Bombing." Tapping into Timothy McVeigh's phone records through his defense team contacts, J.D. was the first journalist to report that Timothy McVeigh phoned Elohim City asking for Andreas Strassmeir on April 17, 1995, the day the bomb truck was rented in Kansas. Earlier reports had disclosed that McVeigh called Elohim City on April 5, asking for Strassmeir, at a time when the FBI believed McVeigh was trying to recruit an accomplice.

When J.D.'s story broke, the national news media rained down on Elohim City with questions but without persistence. Reverend Millar assured reporters that no one there knew anything about phone calls from Timothy McVeigh. The media took the patriarch's word that there was nothing to see here. But Reverend Millar was playing possum.

Later, when J.D. interviewed him for a *Gazette* story on July 14, 1996, the reverend flip-flopped, admitting that McVeigh had called Elohim City at least once on April 5, 1995, and maybe more than once. Reverend Millar also revealed to J.D. that McVeigh had been trying to reach Andreas Strassmeir when he called, referring to Strassmeir as the community's "security chief," a claim Strassmeir's lawyer would dispute.

From that early story, Andreas Strassmeir became a permanent target of J.D.'s reporting, but direct answers from Strassmeir would take a lot of work. Under pressure from the discovery of McVeigh's phone calls, Strassmeir had fled the US across the Mexican border and on to Germany. He traveled with David Holloway, deputy director of CAUSE, a legal foundation with close ties to the white power movement, whose director Kirk Lyons was Strassmeir's lawyer.

In a statement drafted by Lyons, Strassmeir stated that he only met McVeigh once, if at all, at a Tulsa gun show in 1993.[69] Strassmeir also said he traded a knife for McVeigh's military fatigue jacket and gave him a card with Elohim City's phone number. Despite Strassmeir's admitted ties to McVeigh, and his immigration status as a German national on an expired visa, the FBI left Strassmeir out of some 25,000 interviews it conducted on the bombing case.

On March 24, 1996, J.D. delivered another exclusive story connecting Timothy McVeigh to a 1990s resurgence of The Order, calling the terror group "one of the most radical and subversive underground political movements in America." J.D.'s unnamed source had access to FBI interviews of former McVeigh Army buddy Michael Fortier, which led to his plea deal in the bombing case in exchange for testifying against McVeigh. According to J.D.'s source, McVeigh told Fortier a few weeks before the bombing that he was going to Colorado to join The Order.

It sounded stranger than fiction. Was it possible that from the ashes of Robert Jay Mathews's notorious terror organization, the white power underground of the 1990s had created a new Order?

If so, no wonder McVeigh was obsessed with *The Turner Diaries*. If J.D.'s source was right, here was the bombing's direct connection to organized white supremacy. And if this information did come from Fortier's FBI interviews, then the bureau and McVeigh's prosecutors knew it also, even while they were constructing a disastrously misleading case of lone-wolf terror.

According to J.D.'s source, Fortier said that McVeigh spoke often about the coming execution of Richard Snell, a member of the original Murrah Building plot, on the same day of the bombing. This detail matched reports from death row guards that Snell seemed to know in advance that the bombing was coming. On the day of his execution, Snell reportedly smiled and laughed while watching television coverage of rescue workers bringing bodies out of the Murrah Building. Then, on the gurney in the death chamber, while awaiting lethal injection, Snell declared, "Hail his victory."[70]

Next came Richard Snell's burial at Elohim City, with Reverend Millar presiding. To J.D., the connections were too rich and too many to explain away as coincidence. All roads in his reporting led to Elohim City.

Others in Snell's inner circle also seemingly knew the bombing was coming. According to Cheri Seymour, then secretary to the Aryan Nations, Snell's close friend Louis Beam visited Snell's wife, Mary, three weeks before the bombing and gave her a message to pass along to her condemned husband that "Armageddon was coming on the day of his death."[71] Asked by journalist Andrew Gumbel if he believed Beam was in on the bomb plot, Bill Buford, the ATF's top agent in Arkansas at the time of the bombing, said: "I have no solid information, but the pieces fit together too neatly for him not to have known."

J.D.'s March 24 story uncovered another clue to the breadth of McVeigh's white power network. J.D. reported on multiple pre-bombing calls McVeigh placed to a message center operated by the National Alliance in Arizona, founded by *The Turner Diaries* author William Pierce, and a forty-minute call to the CAUSE Foundation's Holloway the day before the bombing.

According to Holloway, he only discovered McVeigh's identity later, when an investigator tracked the lengthy pre-bombing call to him. He remembered the young man on the phone launching a rant about a Waco lawsuit the foundation had filed, charging that it did not go far enough. "It was time to send the government a clear message," the caller had ominously said.[72]

Separately from J.D., in 1996, Morris Dees of the Southern Poverty Law Center drew an even closer connection between McVeigh and *The Turner Diaries*' Pierce. In his memoir *The Gathering Storm,* Dees cited reports to CNN by two separate law enforcement sources that McVeigh placed a lengthy call to Pierce's unlisted number in West Virginia in the weeks before the bombing. Pierce denied receiving the call or knowing McVeigh.[73]

In search of more on McVeigh's white power connections for the March story, J.D. tracked down former CSA leader James Ellison at Elohim City, where he had settled two days after the bombing following his release from prison. Asked point-blank by J.D. if The Order still existed, the former CSA leader Ellison replied, "The Order is certainly still a functioning group in this country. The only man who knows who *all* the members are is William Pierce of the National Alliance."

On June 9, 1996, J.D. broke another exclusive story headlined, "More Arrests Pending in Oklahoma City Bombing Case?" He based the story on field reporting in Kansas and Wyoming, where he had picked up Timothy McVeigh's trail in Junction City, Kansas, in the summer of 1992, keeping surprising company. J.D.'s source for the story, a young woman named Catina Lawson, told him that as a high school girl, she socialized at "pasture parties" with McVeigh and his circle of friends, including Andreas Strassmeir, Michael Brescia, and Michael Fortier.

If Lawson's account, echoed by her mother, was accurate, McVeigh, Fortier, Strassmeir, and Brescia seemingly had some hidden association back in 1992 in Junction City, which would become the staging ground for the bombing three years later.

Days after the blast, as soon as Lawson saw the John Doe 2 wanted poster, she called the FBI because of Brescia's strong resemblance to the poster. From all appearances, however, the information she and her mother gave the FBI produced no follow-up with Strassmeir, Brescia, or Fortier, whom Lawson described as a close friend.

⅄

Back in Oklahoma after the Kansas field trip, J.D. gathered two fresh mysteries into his sprawling probe in a *Gazette* story on July 16, 1996, headlined, "Agents Probe OKC Bombing Links to Bank Robberies." Strictly speaking, J.D.'s coverage of the Mueller family murders and terror leader Richard Guthrie's mysterious death didn't qualify as exclusives, but they would propel his investigation forward, focusing it intently onto the Aryan Republican Army.

What stood out for J.D. was the same common denominator he had found on the Kansas road trip: Elohim City. Strassmeir and Brescia, the Elohim City roommates feared as a threat by the gun dealer Mueller, were in Guthrie's orbit through fellow ARA gang member Brescia. Was there some still unseen connection between Mueller and Guthrie? J.D. didn't have that answer, only a searching interest in the bombing and the current angle he was pursuing most aggressively, the white power movement's possible role.

J.D.'s story reported that investigators were looking into curious parallels between a $50,000 robbery of silver, gun parts, and ammunition from the Mueller home in early 1995 and, coincidentally, a $60,000 robbery a few months earlier of another Arkansas gun dealer, Roger Moore, which had been tied to the Oklahoma City bombing. Was the Mueller robbery somehow also connected to the bombing? J.D. didn't pose that question outright, but it floated between the lines of his story.

Delving deeper into Guthrie's mysterious hanging death, J.D. reported that the terror leader's plea deal with prosecutors had confirmed the ARA gang's mission of financing the white power movement. Could robbery and revolution be the thread that tied the bombing to the movement, maybe even by way of crimes against gun dealers William Mueller and Roger Moore?

Those possibilities went beyond the limits of what J.D. Cash knew as fact. Still, for a journalist with his head wrapped around the violent legacy of Robert Mathews and The Order, the discovery of Guthrie and his bank robbery gang, twelve years after Mathews's fiery demise, must have struck the journalist like an encounter with a ghost. Robbery and revolution were The Order's creed. Was the Aryan Republican Army, in reality, The Order 2.0, functioning as the financial arm of the Oklahoma City bomb plot in a renewal of the movement's failed original strike on the Murrah Federal Building?

When J.D. circled back once more to Elohim City in the summer of 1996, his sources there brought that specter into chilling focus. J.D.'s most revealing interviews yet suggested that The Order rebooted might have been hiding in plain sight in 1995 in an underground way station in America's Midwestern Heartland, where the ARA gang hid out between bank robberies and the shadowy figure of Andreas Strassmeir trained up white power warrior youths.

In a *Gazette* story on July 16, 1996, J.D. quoted a confidential state law enforcement source confirming that Strassmeir might have operated a terrorist training camp in Elohim City. "Every few months, 15 to 30 individuals from around the US would show up for a few weeks of military-style training," J.D.'s source said.

"The recruits were primarily members of the Aryan Nation," the source continued, adding that one of the participants was Timothy McVeigh.

For the record, Elohim City's leadership steadfastly insisted that it was a peaceful religious community and rejected the suspicion of any terrorist training activities operating there. Also for the record, Strassmeir's lawyer denied that he ever served as Elohim City's security chief.

J.D.'s reporting suggested otherwise. Previously tight-lipped residents opened up. Zara Patterson, Elohim City's former security chief, told J.D.: "As soon as Andy arrived here, he told me he wanted to take over the security job. I didn't care…It was one less headache for me." However, Patterson reported: "Strassmeir went out and replaced all our deer rifles with assault weapons. Next, he wanted us to start doing illegal stuff."

Reverend Millar emphatically spelled out those activities for J.D. as "the illegal gun business!" Every Elohim City resident J.D. interviewed said that the elders eventually stripped both

Strassmeir and Michael Brescia of their security roles in the community because of training exercises deemed "too violent."

⅄

In 1996, J.D. Cash's year of reporting dangerously, he had amassed astonishing credible evidence of a bomb plot that went far beyond Timothy McVeigh, possibly originating in the dark heart of America's underground neo-Nazi movement. Taken together, McVeigh's phone calls and reputed visits to Elohim City before the bombing; his contacts with nationally known white supremacy influencers in the run-up to the bombing; and his 1992 summertime association with Strassmeir, Brescia, and Fortier in Junction City, the bombing's staging area to be, revealed the troubling extent to which the lone-wolf bomber had not been alone at all.

Meanwhile, federal prosecutors were building their lone-wolf terror case against McVeigh as if J.D.'s reporting never happened. The Oklahoma City bureau of the Associated Press assisted the blackout by making it a policy not to pick up J.D.'s stories for national distribution, claiming that he wrote in a magazine style. Moreover, the wire service couldn't devote its staff's time to rewrite his stories. Bruce Willingham was skeptical. "You had to wonder what was going on," he said in 2018, looking back.[74]

J.D. Cash's coverage of the bombing story was the proverbial tree that fell in journalism's forest with no one to witness it. Did it even happen? Yes, it did. By the summer of 1996, a reckoning between two journalistic narratives was coming. In the dominant national news story, Timothy McVeigh, the lone-wolf bomber, was facing justice for mass murder in the Heartland. In J.D. Cash's upstart reporting, the federal government was turning a blind eye to justice for the 168 victims of a neo-Nazi terror attack.

An ABC News team was about to land on J.D.'s turf and begin working their story with his core sources, the Wilburns and their circle of surviving families. The network news team was coming armed with confidential FBI files leaked from the office of McVeigh's defense attorney. What would these network journalists tell millions of viewers from their influential national platform just three months before the opening of Timothy McVeigh's trial for the bombing.

J.D. Cash was going to have something to say about that.

CHAPTER 5

MARINE LANDING

MYSTERY DEATHS are a part of Washington's landscape, along with presidential motorcades, twenty-one-gun salutes, and Fourth of July fireworks. To some, these tragic exits from the scene offer fleeting glimpses of diabolical political intrigue lurking beneath the Capital's surface. To others, they signal paranoia in those who overthink them. By 1996, when ABC News launched its high-profile Oklahoma City bombing story, the Clinton presidency had already seen three such high-profile deaths.

In 1993, White House counsel Vincent Foster, embattled by the Whitewater scandal and Travelgate, was found dead in broad daylight in suburban Fort Marcy Park with a gun in his hand but no fingerprints on it. His death was declared a suicide. In May 1996, the body of former CIA director William Colby turned up on a sandbar of the Wicomico River in southern Maryland. Just a month before, a former colleague had predicted the agency's old guard would assassinate Colby for snitching to Congress back in 1975 about the CIA's hidden history of spying on US citizens and plotting to assassinate foreign leaders. Colby's death was declared a nighttime drowning accident, though there was no paddle near his sand-filled canoe, his custom life jacket was missing, and he left his dinner half-finished back at home, his radio and computer still turned on.

That same month, Admiral Jeremy M. Boorda, the Navy's chief of operations and its highest-ranking officer, went home for lunch at his private quarters in the Washington Navy Yard, where he died from a gunshot wound to his chest, declared a suicide. An unlikely ripple effect from Admiral Boorda's death would lead journalist Roger Charles into a plum assignment as ABC News producer Don Thrasher's number two on a high-profile bombing story for the network's primetime newsmagazine *20/20*.

Following a tour of duty in Vietnam and a twenty-year Marine Corps career at the Pentagon, Roger had retired as a lieutenant colonel and transitioned into journalism. His first byline was on "Sea of Lies," a 1992 cover story for *Newsweek* exposing the shoot-down of an Iranian commercial airliner by a US Navy Aegis cruiser and the Pentagon cover-up that followed. Four years later, he was on staff at a military affairs wire service in Washington.

Roger worked on the Admiral Boorda story for *Newsweek* as lead researcher for the magazine's military affairs analyst, Colonel David Hackworth, Roger's journalism mentor and good friend. Their reporting was about to uncover that Admiral Boorda had worn unauthorized valor medals for service in Vietnam. With the *Newsweek* interview impending, the admiral drove himself home to his quarters on the afternoon of May 16, 1996, and died in the garden.

Questions swirled as to why the admiral did not sign either of two suicide notes he left behind, why the Navy did not release the notes to the public, why it kept his autopsy secret, and why, if this was a suicide, would a career military man shoot himself in the chest?

When Roger told me the story years later, what still haunted his memory was President Clinton's reaction, which was captured on live television as an aide passed him a note during a meeting. The president's shoulders slumped, and his face froze into a rictus of horror. Did this moment of television truth signify something more to a tragic story? If a Washington secret lurked behind the president's reaction, would the public ever find out? That troubling gap between appearance and reality would preoccupy Roger's thoughts about Washington-related secrets in the Oklahoma City bombing story for years to come.

Still, Roger was a paragon of discretion, thoroughly trained in need-to-know protocols from his midshipman days at the US Naval Academy and his extended tour of duty at the Pentagon. Villainy did not surprise Roger, deter him from his duty, or disturb his implacable, well-mannered calm, almost ever. In the 2015 film *Truth*, portraying CBS producer Mary Mapes's ill-fated investigation of President George W. Bush's military background, Hollywood A-lister Dennis Quaid played Roger, who was on Mapes's team. The actor perfectly captured Roger's gentlemanly affability under fire.

By year's end in 1996, a story in *Washingtonian* magazine laid the Admiral Boorda mystery to rest, settling his death as a tragic suicide with the publication of the suicide notes the Navy had kept secret. "What I'm about to do is not very smart, but it is right for me," he told the sailors he had commanded. "You see, I have asked you to do the right thing, to care for and take care of each other, and to stand up for what is good and correct."

Shockwaves over the admiral's death rocked Roger's news agency. In the fiercely loyal military, someone had to pay the price for the public stain on the admiral's and the Navy's honor. Roger was the one to go, which was how he came to leave the news agency and become available to move into the big leagues of broadcast journalism at ABC that summer.

Over at the network's Washington bureau, producer Don Thrasher had dug into the Oklahoma City bombing case. Thrasher could be brash. He scoffed that some news executives didn't have a curious bone in their bodies. "They get their ideas from *USA Today*," Roger remembered him saying. Thrasher could get away with attitude because he consistently delivered stories that made on-camera correspondent Tom Jarriel look great. "Jarriel loved Thrasher," Roger told me. During Roger's tenure at the news agency, they had partnered on several high-profile Pentagon stories for ABC News.

In the summer of 1996, Thrasher tapped Roger as associate producer on his Oklahoma City bombing story for ABC's *20/20*. None of the risks and all the high-flying thrill of working in Washington were on the menu for the journalists that July as they shared pitchers of beer at the Sign of the Whale, their favorite bar and grill. Thrasher's pitch memo had promised that this story was not going to be more mythologizing of accused bomber Timothy McVeigh. It would have an edge unseen in national media coverage to date. Here's an abridged version of the pitch memo Roger shared with me:[75]

> The thought that McVeigh is the mastermind behind [the bombing] borders on the absurd—at least for someone believed to be as smart as he is and who allegedly spent

> months and months planning this. Some of the things are beyond amateur....
>
> The government says that witnesses have picked McVeigh out of a lineup. Well, a couple did—in mid-June—six and seven weeks after his arrest...and his picture had been in the paper a few thousand times. Even then, some witnesses could not ID McVeigh....
>
> In fact, John Doe #2 is actually more positively ID'd than McVeigh—and the government now says, at least publicly, he doesn't even exist and he's not important....
>
> There is no question the FBI now believes there were at least four or 5 others involved. We have their names. It is the defense's contention that McVeigh was either a patsy or the fall guy, and the real terrorists are still out there—and the FBI knows it....

The pitch was classic Thrasher: exclusive information pointing to a sensational scoop—the identification of multiple terrorists the FBI knew had played roles in the bombing. But somehow, the terrorists had walked free after helping commit the crime of the century. Thrasher's source for the story, adding firepower to the pitch, was in the best position to rock the Oklahoma City bombing prosecution: McVeigh's defense attorney Stephen Jones.

ABC's greenlighting of Thrasher's story was a bold move. His interest in John Doe 2 and McVeigh's other unknown accomplices was strikingly out of step with the mainstream news media's evolving narrative. Except in outlier reporting by the Oklahoman J.D. Cash, John Doe 2 was by 1996 a nearly forgotten footnote to a crime the FBI had otherwise apparently pieced together flawlessly. However, when attorney Stephen Jones reached out to Thrasher at ABC early that year, the John Doe 2 mystery was precisely what the lawyer wanted to discuss.

As Roger recounted to me years later, what hooked Thrasher on the story was a leak of confidential FBI files turned over to the defense in the discovery process for the McVeigh trial. On a visit by Thrasher to Jones's law office in Enid, Oklahoma, the lawyer stepped away from his conference room, leaving Thrasher alone with a trove of files. The producer knew what to do. Using his pocket tape recorder, he made a record of FBI interviews of the staff who had witnessed the rental of the bomb truck at Elliott's Body Shop in Junction City, Kansas. Brainstorming over transcripts of those interviews, the producers agreed that they turned the case upside down.

As Jeffrey Toobin reported in his 2023 book *Homegrown: Timothy McVeigh and the Rise of Right-Wing Extremism*, the eyewitnesses at the rental agency were crucial to the government's case against McVeigh. In essence, its laser focus boiled down to one double-barreled claim: McVeigh rented the truck and bombed the Murrah Building. "That was the case that [Principal Associate Deputy Attorney General Merrick] Garland wanted presented to a jury, and lead prosecutor Joseph Hartzler entirely agreed," Toobin wrote, adding this detail: "In the prosecutors' makeshift offices in the former Southwestern Bell office space, Hartzler scrawled out a sign that summed up his philosophy (and Garland's) and taped it to his door: DO NOT BURY THE CRIME IN CLUTTER."[76]

Spelling out the government's storyline at trial, prosecutors would argue that McVeigh rented the bomb truck and built the bomb in Kansas, then delivered and detonated it 275 miles to the south, in Oklahoma City. No physical evidence at the Murrah Building positively tied McVeigh to the crime scene, however. For that, prosecutors would seek eyewitnesses who saw the Ryder truck on its way to the Murrah Building through downtown Oklahoma City. But there was a problem. Almost all the witnesses the FBI eventually located there either couldn't positively identify McVeigh or said they saw one or more other men with him.

This potentially fatal flaw put pressure on prosecutors to prove that McVeigh acted alone in Kansas, renting the bomb truck. Yet, in Junction City, as in Oklahoma City, no forensic evidence tied McVeigh to Elliott's Body Shop. His fingerprints weren't on the paperwork, or the counter where he signed the rental contract, and the handwritten signature wasn't a positive match to McVeigh's. An identification would come down to the eyewitnesses in the room at Elliott's Body Shop.

Roger told me he never thought the FBI sketch of John Doe 1 looked much like Timothy McVeigh. The face in the sketch was a V shape: wider at the top, tapering to a rounded chin. McVeigh's face was a pronounced oval, with no distinctive crease above the chin. And McVeigh's head was not flat like the suspect in the John Doe 1 sketch. When the producers drilled down into the leaked FBI interviews of the witnesses at Elliott's Body Shop, they revealed something shocking. It wasn't just that the sketch of John Doe 1 may have missed the mark. The man who rented the bomb truck wasn't Timothy McVeigh.

It was someone else.

As Roger and Thrasher pored over what the three body shop eyewitnesses saw and heard, the producers knew they were onto a significant story. It was all right there in the FBI interview reports. The government was spinning the facts.

The Ryder truck rental had taken place in Junction City, Kansas, at 4:19 p.m. on Monday, April 17, 1995, two days before the bombing. The time is critical because a surveillance camera at a McDonald's restaurant captured McVeigh on videotape at 3:57 p.m., less than half an hour earlier and about a mile away. Owner Eldon Elliott and his two staffers were in the office when the man calling himself Robert Kling walked in. Bookkeeper Vicki Beemer handled the paperwork for the rental transaction. Elliott was busy with other tasks, in and out of the room. Mechanic Tom Kessinger was in the office on a break, eating a snack on a sofa.

All three eyewitnesses told the FBI that Robert Kling, who rented the truck, was five foot ten or shorter.[77] Elliott and Beemer used reliable mental yardsticks. Elliott, who was five-ten, said Kling was about his height. Beemer said Kling was no taller than her husband, also five-ten. There was no way this was Timothy McVeigh, a towering string bean of a man standing six foot two.

There were other striking physical discrepancies. Kessinger and Elliott said Kling weighed about 180 pounds, had a medium build, and a pockmarked complexion. Timothy McVeigh stood five inches taller and weighed fifteen pounds less. McVeigh had a slender build and a smooth complexion with no pockmarks. It was an impossible match.[78]

Using Kessinger as his primary source, backed up by Elliott and Beemer, the FBI's visual information specialist Raymond Rozycki created the FBI's composite sketch of the man who rented the Ryder truck. The FBI wanted poster for John Doe 1, as Kling was known, depicted a man with a distinctive military-style crew cut between five foot eight and five foot nine, weighing 180–185 pounds.[79]

The impossibility that this man was Timothy McVeigh would have become crystal clear a few days later when the FBI held a physical lineup featuring McVeigh. However, the FBI did not ask any of the Elliott's Body Shop witnesses to attend. Instead, Tom Kessinger was shown a photo lineup eleven days after the bombing, on April 30, 1995.[80] This presentation effectively concealed the height discrepancy between McVeigh and John Doe 1 because the McVeigh photo was a torso shot. Based on the photo lineup, and despite the seemingly disqualifying physical description Kessinger had given originally, the mechanic now picked out McVeigh and verified him as John Doe 1 by signing the back of McVeigh's photo.[81]

Eldon Elliott's photo lineup occurred on June 8, six weeks after his original FBI interview.[82] Again, based on a torso shot, Elliott identified McVeigh as John Doe 1 by signing the back of the McVeigh photo, even though Elliott's original physical description of Kling had disqualified McVeigh as too tall and skinny.

Vicki Beemer, the staffer who had been face-to-face with Kling as he did his paperwork, didn't attend the physical lineup, wasn't shown a photo lineup, and never identified McVeigh as John Doe 1.

After six weeks of steering by the FBI, prosecutors got what they needed from Elliott's Body Shop for the McVeigh trial. By June 1995, two of the three witnesses who originally described a suspect almost a half-foot shorter than McVeigh, with other assorted striking physical traits he did not possess, now were prepared to swear that Timothy McVeigh had rented the bomb truck.

More evidence refuting the claim that McVeigh was John Doe 1 soon surfaced. A week after the FBI interviews at Elliott's, the bureau called in private forensic sketch artist Jeanne Boylan for a second opinion. Boylan, a consultant on high-profile FBI cases, interviewed mechanic Tom Kessinger about John Doe 1. This interview produced a striking clue. Here is Kessinger in April

1995, describing John Doe 1 to Boylan, as reported in her book *Portraits of Guilt*:

> He was standing there, and he had these two wads of chew under his lip, you know? Now when a guy chews, he tucks the chaw over to one side or the other so he can talk, know what I mean? But he doesn't divide it in two. This guy standing at the counter had a long, thin face, blue eyes, this short flattop hair like an army guy, and two puffs, like two plugs of chew, one tucked over on each side of his bottom lip. Funniest damn thing I ever seen. I just got fixated on looking at his face, I tell you. I couldn't take my eyes off him, trying to figure it out.[83]

McVeigh, chewing tobacco? This detail was incredible because McVeigh did not use tobacco in any form. But the real John Doe 1 did. His unusual habit of splitting his chewing wad into halves that puffed out his face caused the eyewitness Kessinger to stare. Here was a telltale clue the FBI could have used to track down the fugitive. But by the time Boylan interviewed Kessinger, the FBI already had its man, Timothy McVeigh, and this information was of no help. Boylan's interview of Kessinger never made it into the McVeigh trial. Even when she published her book in 2000, while McVeigh was on death row awaiting execution, nobody corrected the record on this point.

Years later, Roger discovered an FBI interview of yet another staffer at Elliott's Body Shop. For reasons unknown, Fernando Ramos's interview took place separately from the others. But like them, parking lot attendant Ramos told the FBI that John Doe 1 stood about five foot nine and weighed 200 pounds, thus adding another physical description—roughly consistent with Elliott's,

Beemer's, and Kessinger's—that conflicted hopelessly with the actual physique of the towering, skinny McVeigh.[84]

Ramos told the FBI that John Doe 1 arrived at Elliott's not on foot but as a passenger in a blue Jeep Cherokee driven by someone Ramos never saw.[85] This information conflicted with the eventual prosecution claim that McVeigh walked a mile to Elliott's from the McDonald's restaurant in the rain.

A surveillance video camera caught McVeigh on tape just twenty-two minutes before he supposedly signed the rental contract. In the video, he is wearing a sports shirt with rolled-up sleeves and a white T-shirt underneath, not a dark-green T-shirt, as described by the witnesses at Elliott's. Also, in the videotape, McVeigh is wearing tapered slacks, not military fatigues, as the witnesses at Elliott's described.[86] It was a tight timeline for McVeigh to make the trip on foot, even in good weather. But how and where did he change clothes along the way—and in the rain too?

The FBI had initially stated, under oath, at McVeigh's preliminary hearing, that he was "brought" to Elliott's Body Shop, which made more sense.[87] But the official story changed, perhaps in the interest of decluttering. Tight timeline or not, prosecutors would settle on McVeigh coming alone to Elliott's. So he must have walked, even though the witness Ramos said he saw John Doe 1 arrive by Jeep.

Was it more likely, as prosecutors would tell the jury, that McVeigh walked a mile in the rain and somehow arrived at Elliott's in dry clothes—and different ones, too, from those he was wearing in the McDonald's videotape, just in the nick of time to record the rental transaction at 4:19 p.m.? Or was it more likely that McVeigh never went to Elliott's, that John Doe 1 was someone else entirely—the shorter, heavier man Ramos told the FBI he saw arrive in the Jeep? It was a question jurors would never get to weigh. No one would pay much attention to what Ramos said because the FBI classified his interview report as an "insert," supposedly of little testimonial value, ensuring virtual invisibility to curious eyes in the bureau's vast computer filing system.

Disclosures about John Doe 1 weren't the only ticking time bomb of believability embedded in the interviews at Elliott's Body Shop. In time, what the eyewitnesses to the truck rental recalled about Robert Kling's unidentified companion, John Doe 2, would evolve into a discrepancy equally damaging to the official story.

Recall that during the investigation, the man known as John Doe 2 quickly morphed from the world's most wanted criminal, the subject of a global FBI manhunt, into a mass hallucination in the minds of eyewitnesses. But the original FBI interviews of Elliott, Beemer, Kessinger, and Ramos—immediate, spontaneous, and virtually uninfluenced by the media blizzard that followed—set the presence of the second man in stone.

Mechanic Tom Kessinger provided the visual information for the first wanted poster of John Doe 2 that launched the worldwide manhunt. Kessinger described the escaped terrorist as a Caucasian man with dark hair, twenty-six or twenty-seven years old, about five feet ten inches tall, weighing 175–185 pounds, with a muscular build, large arms, and large chest. Facially, Kessinger said John Doe 2 had a large nose, thick eyebrows, and a broad chin, with dark hair trimmed square across the back of his thick neck.[88]

In a telltale clue that would become significant later in Jesse's investigation of his brother's murder, Kessinger said he could see the edge of a tattoo on John Doe 2's upper left arm, peeking out of his shirt sleeve.[89] Eight days after his interview, on April 27, the FBI followed up on this point, showing Kessinger a tattoo replica from an unknown source and asking him if it matched John Doe 2's tattoo. According to the FBI report—and this is all we know about the tattoo investigation, "Kessinger further advised that it was possible that there was something underneath the curved part of the tattoo where the writing is."[90]

After deep-diving into the leaked FBI interview reports in July of 1996, Roger and Thrasher drew the same conclusion. They knew, of course, that McVeigh's attorney, Stephen Jones, had an agenda for highlighting these files. They didn't take everything the defense team told them on faith. But Jones was dead right about the shaky identifications from Elliott's Body Shop that were foundational to the prosecution. The information contained in the leaked FBI interviews was explosive:

- McVeigh wasn't at Elliott's Body Shop.
- McVeigh didn't rent the Ryder truck.
- McVeigh wasn't John Doe 1.
- John Doe 2 was at Elliott's.
- John Doe 1 and John Doe 2 were both still at large.

Unedited and unspun, the interviews from Elliott's demolished half the case against McVeigh—that he rented the bomb truck—as the prosecution's manager, Merrick Garland, had boiled the case down himself. The leak was a bombshell.

⅄

In Oklahoma City, where Roger and Thrasher traveled to investigate their story in August 1996, they found a surprising situation considering the high-priority status of the bombing case.

A year and a half after America's worst domestic terror attack, grieving grandparents-turned-citizen investigators Glenn and Kathy Wilburn were running rings around the FBI. Meanwhile, retiree-turned-reporter J.D. Cash was scooping the nation's major news organizations with his bombing coverage in the *Gazette*.

With their new sources, the producers picked up the trail of John Doe 2, the world's most wanted fugitive, and maybe John Does 3 and 4. The Wilburns had also uncovered evidence of unheeded bombing warnings with devastating political implications. It hadn't been smooth sailing for the rookie citizen investigators either. As they pressed for answers, a bitter disconnect had opened up between the family and federal law enforcement.

On May 23, 1995, a month after the bombing, authorities leveled the Murrah Building in a controlled implosion. Kathy's daughter, Edye Smith, mother of Chase and Colton, gave vent to her anguish in a live interview on CNN.

> [W]e're being told to keep our mouths shut; not talk about it; don't ask those questions.... [Y]ou know, where was the ATF? All fifteen or seventeen of their employees survived, and they live—they're on the ninth floor. They were the target of this explosion, and where were they? Did they have a warning sign? I mean, did they think it might be a bad day to go into the office? They had an option to not go to work that day, and my kids didn't get that option; nobody else in the building got that option.

It was brutally candid live TV, prompting CNN's reporter to end the interview with an abrupt thank-you. But Edye had given voice to one of the Wilburns' most vexing questions: Why were so many ATF officials absent from their office on the morning of the bombing? And where were they?

"By the time Don [Thrasher] and I got there, the Wilburns and John Cash absolutely were convinced it was a sting gone bad—that the government had some role in the bombing conspiracy, and they were hiding that role," Roger told me. "And to not answer the question—'Well, why did the bomb go off if you knew in advance there was this threat?'—that was the whole game."

But who would trust a pair of bereaved grandparents and a rookie reporter with beginner's luck to tell America a scandalous story that could bring down the US Department of Justice or even the president? That was the high-stakes gamble facing Thrasher and Roger when they sat down with the Wilburns in August 1996 to vet the findings of their investigation.

The briefing occurred over two summer evenings at the Wilburns' kitchen table. The room was cozy, lighthearted, and retro, with a life-size cutout of Elvis Presley and vintage Coca-Cola logos hanging on the wall: bittersweet reminders of happier times. But on those nights, the kitchen was strictly business. Two visitors from a television network and two citizen investigators pored over files, audiotapes, videotapes, and news clippings documenting a colossal untold story.

Recalling that briefing, Roger told me: "They knew about Elohim City or knew enough. They knew about the ARA. They knew John Doe 2 was real." What still amazed Roger was that the Wilburns had developed the skeleton of all the significant research that would take place on the bombing case for decades to come.

After Glenn and Kathy had recounted the highlights of their sixteen-month investigation, Roger and Thrasher knew they had their angle. They would call the *20/20* segment "The Families

Want to Know." It would focus on the suspicion that most haunted Glenn: that the federal government somehow had forewarning of the bombing and now was hiding the truth from survivors. The producers would shoot part of the story in the Elvis Presley kitchenette, with some of the survivors and witnesses the Wilburns had found.

The *20/20* segment would retrace Glenn Wilburn's steps as he investigated the FBI's warning call to the fire department and the mystery of the falling elevator: a fraught and telling chapter in the family's ongoing dispute with the government over whether ATF agents were present in the Murrah Building when the bomb went off. Lester Martz, head of the ATF's Dallas office, issued a press release to support the agency's Oklahoma City team. Fifteen ATF employees worked in the Murrah Building—the agent in charge, eleven field agents, and three clerical workers. The ATF claimed that all had been carrying out their assigned duties the day of the bombing. "We were there and we were heroes,"[91] declared Martz.

Still, except for the clerical workers, only Alex McCauley, the agent in charge, and field agent Luke Franey were in the Murrah Building on April 19, according to the ATF. Explanations of court appearances, out-of-town duty, and a golf tournament clouded the matter. Unpersuaded, the Wilburns drilled down and discovered a story made for *20/20*.

According to the ATF, Agent McCauley was in an elevator on the eighth floor at the time of the blast. In a free fall, the elevator had supposedly plunged five floors. After that, in one telling of this story, Agent McCauley squeezed his way out and helped fashion a bedsheet rope for a group of survivors to drop down to a chain of rescuers below.

However, as Glenn Wilburn discovered, and the *20/20* segment, broadcast on January 17, 1997, would document in interviews, the story was incorrect. Roger and Thrasher tracked down the elevator maintenance men who arrived twenty minutes after the blast. "Several of us entered and did a floor-by-floor search to see where the elevators were," said maintenance tech Duane James in an on-camera interview. "And we inspected each elevator and ensured nobody was in [them]," James added.

The Midwestern Elevator Company technicians documented their inspection with extensive photographs, which the producers broadcast to confirm that all the safety cables in the elevators were intact.

J.D. Cash monitored the public relations disaster of the falling elevator story in the *Gazette*. He made sure to poke Lester Martz, the agent in charge in Dallas, about it, prompting this concession by Martz in a *Gazette* story on May 14, 1996: "Well, I have discussed this with the agent, and let's say this, Mr. Cash.... Maybe Agent McCauley just imagined he free-fell."

The story was showcase material for the *20/20* piece. But the crown jewel of the broadcast was a grainy surveillance photograph. It was America's first glimpse of the bomb itself, as the Ryder truck passed by the Regency Tower apartments, a half-block from the Murrah Building.

On its face, the image was nothing special: glass exit doors leading from an anonymous dark-gray lobby to the gray sidewalk outside and a street bathed in glaring white light. But two details catapulted this image to fame. At the top left, the Ryder truck is visible, stopped across the street or heading toward the Murrah Building. Across the image, a time stamp reads 04-19-95 WED 08:57:05:24—four minutes before the bomb exploded.

As of late 1996, that image represented the only known photographic evidence of the bomb delivery. With Timothy McVeigh's trial just a few months away, all mention of the surveillance videotapes of the truck and the escaped terrorist accomplice John Doe 2 had disappeared from public view. It was as if this blurry time-stamped photograph was the only image of the crime the government had in its possession, even though it had more.

The surveillance photo was a massive get for ABC, allowing the network to tout the photo as a coming attraction of the *20/20* segment: sensational incriminating evidence against Timothy McVeigh in his forthcoming trial. At the network's 1996 Christmas party in New York City, *20/20*'s coanchor Barbara Walters gushed praise on Thrasher, admitting that she had doubted he could land this prize for next month's broadcast.

Walters had no clue that her producers would soon be chasing an even bigger quarry. Far from New York, far from the glamour of network television, the free fall of the official story of the bombing was about to accelerate, courtesy of J.D. Cash. Roger had driven down to Idabel, Oklahoma, a few months earlier to meet J.D. over beers at a local sports bar. There, the reporter had offered a double-edged compliment, telling Roger he was "impressed" that the ABC team had gotten this challenge to the official narrative of lone-wolf terror scheduled to air.

J.D. soon went further with a fresh story lead. Knowing the television network could give a story a ride he could only dream about, on Christmas Day 1996, J.D. called Roger at home in Alexandria, Virginia, where he was spending the holiday with his family. J.D. confided that he had found a mystery witness who would turn the bombing case upside down.

His witness, a neo-Nazi trainee turned paid government informant, had told J.D. that she worked as a government spy inside Elohim City for eight months in the run-up to the bombing. While undercover, she said she warned her federal government handlers that an attack was coming on a shortlist of targets that included the Oklahoma City federal building. She said she named names, lots of them, before leaving Elohim City a month before the bombing. But the government did nothing to shut down the bomb plot.

J.D. kept his source's name secret, but Roger told me J.D. played a clip of an audiotaped interview with her, which Roger recorded in his reporter's notebook. "All he wanted to do was go blow up federal buildings," J.D.'s soft-spoken witness said on tape. The twist was that she wasn't talking about Timothy McVeigh. She was talking about Andreas Strassmeir. It was another bombshell.

In J.D.'s opinion, his witness was credible, and she was talking to him exclusively. Her story would be sensational and dangerous if she lived to tell it. Did Roger and Thrasher want to produce it for ABC?

CHAPTER 6

MY BLONDE NAZI

J.D. Cash's witness was twenty-six-year-old Carol Howe, daughter of a prominent Tulsa oil executive, former debutante, competitive equestrian rider, and Miss Teenage America contestant. Over the past few years, however, the petite, beautiful, community college student had undergone a radical transformation into a self-proclaimed neo-Nazi, complete with tattoos, paramilitary training, and a spectacular story to tell.

"It's going to surprise people that Mike Brescia was John Doe 2," J.D. quoted his witness as saying in a phone call to Roger Charles on January 28, 1997. Carol Howe was referring to the dark, handsome Aryan Republican Army gang member Brescia who was Andreas Strassmeir's Elohim City roommate. In an exclusive interview with J.D. Cash, Howe was claiming to unmask a terrorist who had escaped the FBI's dragnet after the Oklahoma City bombing. Roger memorialized this phone call and many more from J.D. in the coming weeks, summarizing Howe's disclosures in his ever-ready reporter's notebook.[92] Her identification of Michael Brescia as John Doe 2 was just the tip of the iceberg.

Carol Howe's story had begun to trickle out into the public on December 14, 1996, when the *Tulsa World* reported that the

FBI had raided the Tulsa home she shared with her radical neo-Nazi boyfriend, James Viefhaus Jr., who was busy promoting an attack against the federal government using the couple's answering machine. His dial-up message: "As in the case of the bombing of the Murrah Federal Building, the revolutionary understands and accepts that no matter how painful, that innocent people must be considered expendable if necessary in order to successfully complete any action."[93] Hotline callers were told to take up arms against the federal government on December 15 or bombs would explode in fifteen US cities.

That was enough for the FBI. Tipped off by a journalist who heard the alarming message, agents moved in and arrested Viefhaus two days before "D-Day." Agents questioned but did not arrest Howe.

After someone in J.D.'s journalistic circle tipped him to track Howe down, she began spilling the untold saga of her undercover spy mission to Elohim City as a paid ATF informant for eight months in the run-up to the Oklahoma City bombing.

Howe's unlikely path to becoming a spy began with an incident in which she severely injured both feet in 1994. Howe claimed she jumped from the second story of a building in a Tulsa public park during a concert to escape a group of black youths who were chasing her. Her ex-husband disputed the pursuit scenario but not what happened next, in journalist Jon Ronson's 2023 podcast, *The Debutante*. During Howe's recovery, she called a "Dial-a-Racist" hotline run by Dennis Mahon, a bombastic Tulsa-based propagandist, former KKK imperial dragon, and, at the time Howe reached out to him, a high-ranking official in neo-Nazi leader Tom Metzger's violent White Aryan Resistance

(WAR). Still on crutches, Howe met Mahon, and they started spending time together.

He took her to Elohim City, where he kept an Airstream travel trailer for overnighting, and introduced her to the community's white separatist ideology and paramilitary training program. Howe and Mahon appeared together in a photo in which she brandished a semiautomatic assault weapon and dressed in neo-Nazi paramilitary gear, including a swastika armband. By that summer, however, they had fallen out. He said they had been lovers. She said he sexually assaulted her.

The same day in August 1994 that Howe applied for a restraining order against Mahon, the ATF moved in, offering her $120 per week, plus expenses, to go undercover to Elohim City and spy on Mahon. Howe agreed. A federal undercover surveillance operation targeting WAR's Dennis Mahon for suspected terror activities related to illegal firearms and explosives was now underway at Elohim City, with information to be developed by CI-183, as Carol Howe would now be known.

J.D. barely spoke his source's name for a month after his Christmas Day phone call to Roger Charles. She was "The Girl," "My Blonde Nazi," and "Sweet Thing" in phone calls to Roger, reporting on exclusive interviews with Howe. She told J.D. she had operated as a government spy at Elohim City from August 1994 until March 1995, a month before the bombing. During that time, she claimed to have filed fifty to one hundred written reports with her ATF handler, Agent Angela Finley. "Angela showed up every week...paid [Howe] in cash...signed receipts, and Angela took all the papers and kept them," J.D. told Roger in a phone call.

The bomb plot Howe said she had witnessed as it unfolded bore almost no resemblance to the one America would hear prosecutors describe a few months later at Timothy McVeigh's trial. Howe said the conspiracy had three leaders at Elohim City—"the Big Three," as she called them, according to J.D. in a January 26, 1997, phone call to Roger. First, Dennis Mahon, the primary target of her spy mission; second, Andreas Strassmeir; and third, the Aryan Republican Army's Michael Brescia, who was engaged to marry a granddaughter of Elohim City patriarch, the Reverend Robert Millar.

Howe told J.D. of her attempts in late 1994 to get close to her targets. "She tried to date Strassmeir...[and] tried to date Brescia, but his girlfriend stopped that," J.D. told Roger in a phone call. Howe recalled hosting a Halloween-themed dinner party at her Tulsa apartment after the ATF installed surveillance cameras. The hidden cameras recorded the scene as Strassmeir and others from Elohim City painted empty grenade hulls to look like jack-o-lanterns. They had no idea this was part of a scheme to catch Dennis Mahon illegally converting hulls into live grenades.

At the Wilburns' home in late January 1997, J.D. played part of an interview with Howe for Roger and Thrasher covering the time frame of late 1994. Roger took notes on J.D.'s tape-recording as it played:

> CH: There's something wrong with Andy. Didn't want to settle down, wanted to go blow up federal buildings.... Put his hand under my blouse—feeling for a wire.
>
> J.D.: When did he first start talking about blowing up federal buildings?
>
> CH: About September or October.

Howe had only been undercover for a couple of months when this exchange with Strassmeir allegedly occurred. But the bomb plot was already entering its decisive phase. According to Howe, the terrorists had developed a list of three potential bombing targets including Oklahoma City's Murrah Building. Howe said the conspirators made three separate scouting missions there in 1994 and 1995 including one accompanied by Mahon and Strassmeir in December 1994.

As for Timothy McVeigh and his role in the conspiracy, Howe told J.D. that McVeigh operated a satellite cell outside Elohim City, independent of three other conspiracy cells. "There were fifteen or twenty-one guys in the group...McVeigh's cell...Elohim City... Langan's cell," J.D. told Roger—referring to Peter Langan, coleader of the ARA gang. "I'm lacking one other cell, and she's going to help, but she's really scared," J.D. added.

In their exclusive interviews, Howe told J.D. that she knew McVeigh by his Tim Tuttle alias. She heard others at Elohim City talking about McVeigh, but Howe only placed him there physically once, in late 1994. "Sometime before Christmas, a lot of guys showed up at [Elohim City]," Howe said. "One that I recall was Tim.... I never spoke to him. He was considered a 'good soldier' by the members of the ARA, not a leader. He was just someone you sent out on jobs because he was reliable."

J.D. wanted to know more. "I asked who directed him, and she said Strassmeir," J.D. told Roger in a phone call.

J.D. had other sources who claimed that McVeigh visited Elohim City more than once. In October 1993, he got a traffic ticket for speeding fifteen minutes from Elohim City. Almost a year later, on September 13, 1994, motel records showed that McVeigh was in Vian, Oklahoma, again just a few miles from

Elohim City. That was the day prosecutors denoted as the beginning of the bombing conspiracy without ever explaining why. McVeigh's presence in remote Vian on that day was a logic-defying coincidence if it was unrelated to the bomb plot.

In a *Gazette* story on June 30, 1996, J.D. reported that Morris Dees of the Southern Poverty Law Center had told journalists at a recent news conference that McVeigh visited Elohim City "more than a dozen times prior to the bombing." One of J.D.'s state law enforcement sources put the number higher, at twenty trips by McVeigh to Elohim City.[94]

At the federal trial of McVeigh's accomplice Terry Nichols, Carol Howe testified that in the summer of 1994 she saw McVeigh at an Elohim City Ku Klux Klan rally in the company of two other men. Why it took Howe two years to report this sighting is unknown. As J.D. kept saying, she was scared. Her testimony:[95]

> Q: Did you ever see Timothy McVeigh at the Elohim City compound?
>
> A: I believe I did.
>
> Q: All right. When did you see him?
>
> A: It was in July of 1994....
>
> Q: And was he accompanied by any other individuals who you know?
>
> A: Yes, he was.
>
> Q: And who were they?
>
> A: A man named Peter Ward and a man named Andreas Strassmeir.

The revelations streaming in from Carol Howe through J.D. to Roger were astonishing. Some twenty domestic terrorists in a bomb plot the government claimed McVeigh planned and carried out virtually by himself. Mahon, Strassmeir, and Brescia in leading roles in the plot. McVeigh, not as the mastermind, but a satellite figure who followed orders as a good soldier. Brescia revealed as the mystery man of the bombing case, John Doe 2.

Howe's naming of Michael Fortier, or "Mike Fontaine" as she said she knew him, was another explosive allegation: Fortier was the only person Howe placed in McVeigh's bomb plot cell. She didn't name Nichols.

By Fortier's account, in support of his plea agreement, he had no direct role in the crime. McVeigh's prosecutors portrayed Fortier practically as a bystander to the terror attack. The only charges against him were for helping McVeigh transport stolen weapons and neglecting to inform authorities about the bomb plot. In contrast, Carol Howe's narrative cast Michael Fortier as an active participant in the conspiracy.

J.D. told Roger: "No question Fortier was in downtown OKC with McVeigh."

This claim did not surprise J.D. For someone who was supposed to have almost nothing to do with the bombing, Fortier seemed to pop up everywhere in J.D.'s field reporting—from Catina Lawson's account of Fortier as being part of McVeigh's social circle in Junction City, Kansas, during the summer of 1992 to the FBI interview report placing Fortier with McVeigh at Lady Godiva's night club in Tulsa eleven days before the bombing.

By January 1997, as J.D. spilled more details to Roger of what Howe was telling him, the tragedy of the Lady Godiva trip still weighed on him. Only by hours had he missed the chance to interview Shawn-Tea Farrens, the young dancer heard on videotape agreeing to party "later" with McVeigh and company. Now, four months later, he found himself face to face with another vulnerable young woman telling her version of the same dangerous and unauthorized story.

Carol Howe was naming the same names that had flowed from Lady Godiva's—McVeigh, Strassmeir, Brescia, and Fortier—and pointing to potential McVeigh accomplices in the Oklahoma City bomb plot who had escaped justice. Her story was so explosive that J.D. wondered aloud if someone would kill her before she could tell it. He knew that Roger had contacts on Capitol Hill and asked him to explore getting Howe into a safe house under congressional protection. Roger made inquiries, but they failed to produce results.

With Carol Howe's revelations, my story crosses into uncharted territory along with hers. Howe's ATF handlers, federal prosecutors, Dennis Mahon, and her ex-husband have all attempted to discredit her as mentally unstable or deceitful. Following the sensational events triggered by the FBI raid of her Tulsa home, Carol Howe went underground in 1997 and became a "ghost" who can't be asked whether she stands by her story today. Yet dismissing her account, as she told it to J.D. Cash, risks jettisoning precious buried truth about the bombing.

Investigators and prosecutors in the case had every reason to push back against Howe when she went public in 1997, and they did so with no holds barred. She divulged secrets that could upend the highest-stakes federal criminal prosecution in decades. But were the secrets true? Or was she crazy? Or a terrorist? Or a vengeful ex gone way over the top? As a practical matter, with their story on the line, this was the challenge confronting Roger Charles and Don Thrasher as they probed the details of what Carol Howe was telling J.D. Cash.

Where were the written reports Howe claimed she submitted to her government handlers? J.D. had yet to see a single scrap of that paperwork. Roger knew that wasn't going to fly at ABC. Was Carol Howe for real? Or had she somehow fed J.D. a made-up story that supported his reporting—and no one else's?

⅄

The producers would soon head west again in January 1997 to vet their new story with McVeigh's lawyer, Stephen Jones. Before departing, though, they received a series of unusual phone calls that might have almost seemed like an omen of trouble that was coming their way. The caller was Joseph Hartzler, lead prosecutor on the bombing case, telling them on January 14, 1997, that he was worried about where their investigation was heading.[96]

Hartzler often projected an image about as close to a choirboy as the Justice Department could have hoped when it chose him to prosecute Timothy McVeigh. He was usually soft-spoken with a gentle demeanor. Multiple sclerosis confined him to a wheelchair, enhancing the impression of a lawyer the bombing victims could trust to keep them at the forefront of the coming trial.

But Hartzler had an edgier side, as when he announced his desire to send Timothy McVeigh "to hell."[97] Or when he tracked down Thrasher and Roger by phone at the ABC bureau three days before the broadcast of their *20/20* story, "The Families Want to Know." The call's urgency was apparent. It was Hartzler himself, not a staffer he could easily have assigned to the task. Also on the line was Leesa Brown, the Justice Department's public affairs representative. Hartzler had a witness, and Thrasher did too.

The Justice Department had declined the producers' request to interview Hartzler on camera, citing the court's gag order in the McVeigh case. But with Hartzler on the phone, Thrasher pounced as Roger took notes:

> DT: Was there any prior warning...a phone call [from] the FBI?... A memo by the ATF to field offices...?
>
> JH: I've answered this in court.... This is a no-brainer.... Where are you going?... I can't believe you believe the government had prior warning.

Thrasher didn't let the prosecutor deflect. He asked again:

> DT: Was there any type of specific warning to the Murrah Federal Building? Or any type of general warning of possible terrorist activity?
>
> JH: No.

There it was, on the record. The lead prosecutor in the McVeigh case had put the government at odds with the citizen investigators, who had amassed a solid body of evidence that there had indeed been advance warning.

Hartzler's ambush had missed the mark. The producers had zero doubt that his Washington bosses had ordered him to place this unusual call. They didn't have much time for guesswork, however. Ten minutes later, Hartzler called back. By now, word had spread through the ABC bureau, and Tom Jarriel, one of the network's most senior correspondents, who would present the *20/20* segment on air, was in the room.

Jarriel pointed out to Hartzler, as the story's script would also do, that ABC had found facts to support the families' suspicions of prior warning. These included sightings of the bomb squad truck before the blast, which Hartzler had tried to explain away as an exercise, and the ridiculous falling elevator story, highlighting the controversy over ATF absenteeism from the Murrah Building on the day of the bombing.

Now Hartzler became indignant. Roger's notes reflected that he dismissed the idea that the ATF had issued a nationwide warning. "Put yourself in my shoes," Hartzler said. "You come up with information that there's a threat, and then what would you do after you found out?"

His answer to his own rhetorical question was fierce. "Heads would roll," he declared. "More than people losing their jobs.... What incentive would I have not to go after the people responsible so that it could never happen again...[to] bring the entire weight of the federal government down on them?"

A third call from Hartzler followed the next day. Was the prosecutor stalking the producers? His call reached Thrasher at home, though Thrasher had never given the Justice Department that number. "I took it as a threat," he told Roger. On the call, Thrasher said he pointedly reminded Hartzler of his pledge to go after anyone in the government if he found out they had prior warning of the bombing. Now, though, Thrasher said, the prosecutor warned him: "He'd go after me with the same passion if I jeopardized the case," Thrasher told Roger.

The producers had a problem. Armed with J.D.'s informant story, jeopardizing the McVeigh case was exactly what they were about to do.

Nonetheless, January 17, 1997, brought a brief reprieve from concerns about Joseph Hartzler, the Justice Department, and even doubts the producers might have had about the credibility of J.D.'s witness. "Around the world and into your home, the stories that touch your life," was *20/20*'s catchphrase. On this edition, the newsmagazine would broadcast the results of its investigation into the disturbing question: What did authorities know in advance that federal workers and children in the daycare center weren't told?

"For seven months, *20/20* has looked into just that question," Tom Jarriel told viewers across America. "And we have found solid facts which tend to support their suspicion." Jarriel's reliably earnest delivery of the bold script for "The Families Want to Know" left no doubt whose side of the story the network was backing. Leaning into the evidence gathered by Thrasher, Roger and their primary sources, citizen investigators Glenn and Kathy Wilburn, Tom Jarriel cited government documents, eyewitnesses, recorded interviews, and pictures to underscore credibility.

The segment unfolded as an arresting tour of evidence supporting the government's suspected "prior knowledge" of the bombing, from sightings of a bomb squad truck, to personnel and sniffer dogs downtown before the blast, a witness told by an officer in an ATF jacket that the agency's staff had been tipped by their pagers not to come to work that day, and Glenn Wilburn buttonholing a fire department dispatcher to confirm that an FBI warning had been received five days before the blast.

"Prior knowledge" was an oddly mild and almost academic way to sum up the magnitude of the questions the story raised about what the government knew and when it knew it. Still, the message was loud and clear. The producers had left no stone unturned in exploring the citizens' suspicions of a government cover-up of America's worst domestic terror attack, and it showed. After the broadcast, Thrasher and Roger were ready to go hunting again, this time for bigger game.

⅄

A week after the *20/20* broadcast, the producers flew to Oklahoma City and on to Denver to vet the Carol Howe story. When they arrived at Stephen Jones's transplanted law office in Denver, where the bombing trial would take place, they were traveling perilously light, bringing with them only the *Tulsa World* newspaper story about the FBI raid on Viefhaus and Howe. Everything else was in their heads or in Roger's notebooks: a stark reminder of how much they needed the lawyer's help.

Jones and his defense team occupied an entire floor of a Denver high-rise, some thirty stories in the air. In his private office, the lawyer listened intently. "This is fucking radioactive," he declared and summoned his most trusted lieutenant to scour his circle of Tulsa contacts "right away." Roger told me he could still see the amazed look on the second lawyer's face as he read the newspaper story, handed it back to Jones, and then bolted from the room.

It only took a few hours to nail down the source of the raid story. Viefhaus's lawyer reported that Carol Howe called him after her boyfriend's arrest and made two stunning disclosures. She said the ATF had been investigating Dennis Mahon as a suspect since right after the bombing. This information was puzzling: Why was Mahon—a nonfactor on the surface of the McVeigh prosecution and never even interviewed about the case by the FBI—looming so large behind the scenes?

Howe also told the lawyer that she wasn't indicted after the raid because the government didn't want her role as an informant against Mahon to go public. The signal to Howe was loud and clear: Keep quiet or face indictment.

Though this intel was intriguing, it didn't solve the producers' dilemma. Had Carol Howe warned the government about the bombing or not? Without a credible answer, their story would be dead on arrival at ABC. As Thrasher put it on a call with J.D.: "There's zero doubt the girl was a CI. What's in doubt, when did she go on payroll?" They needed to interview Howe, and J.D. set it up in late January. She called the Wilburns' home and spoke to Thrasher for forty minutes.

Howe told Thrasher that she attended a meeting at Elohim City in late 1994, during which Strassmeir said the group should be blowing up federal buildings instead of just talking about it. She said she filed seventy-five reports on her spy mission with her handler, ATF Agent Finley. Within hours after the bombing, Howe noted, Agent Finley contacted her and drove her to Oklahoma City for three days of extensive debriefing.

Recalling viewing the FBI composite sketches of John Doe 1 and John Doe 2 during those debriefing sessions, Howe told Thrasher: "There's not a doubt in my mind Brescia is John Doe 2." A week later, the ATF sent Howe back to Elohim City for follow-up surveillance. Soon after, she was warned to stay away. Her cover was blown.

Finally, almost two years after the bombing, Carol Howe was on the record. The ABC team had her story. However, vetting it would still depend on McVeigh attorney Stephen Jones, who was about to live up to the nickname the producers had given him: the "Sly Fox from Enid." A closed-door hearing in the chambers of US District Judge Richard M. Matsch, who presided over the McVeigh trial, began on familiar ground on January 29, 1997. Over the past year, Jones's complaints that the government was hiding documents had risen to a boil. Now, he stood before the judge to charge that prosecutors had concealed the astounding fact that the government had an informant inside Elohim City.

To this charge, prosecutor Beth Wilkinson had a ready answer, countering that the government had dutifully given Jones the FBI's report on the informant's debriefing. It was up to Jones to find it, somewhere in the mountain of discovery documents prosecutors had turned over. But at least Jones now had a precious clue about where to look when he returned to his office and launched a massive computer search.

Jones wasn't ready to have this hearing end, however. Before it did, he made sure the judge understood the magnitude of this so-far unnamed witness's story. Jones told the judge that "someone"—meaning Thrasher—had listened to an audiotape—meaning the one J.D. played for the producers at the Wilburns' home—on which an unnamed government informant said that they had heard Elohim City's Andreas Strassmeir threaten to bomb federal buildings.

Also, in a blind-side challenge to prosecutors' repeated claim that Strassmeir had never been a bombing suspect, Jones presented to the judge a secret State Department Protective Intelligence Bulletin featuring four photographs of Strassmeir bearing the State Department's unique file number for the bombing case. Jones later recalled this triumph, which Roger recorded in his notebook, as nearly causing "the old judge's eyeballs [to] fall out."

When the dust settled on the contentious session in Judge Matsch's chambers, Stephen Jones had scored a victory that went beyond the particulars of his feud with prosecutors over hiding documents or Strassmeir's still hidden potential role in the bombing. The judge now knew about Carol Howe, though not by name, and knew she might have an important story to tell in the coming

McVeigh trial. With a push from Jones, the wheels were turning for Carol Howe to go public.

Still, Jones and the ABC team could hardly claim total victory on January 29, 1997. The opposing forces had gained at least as much with a move that perhaps signaled that the government knew exactly where Carol Howe's revelations would lead next: to a revival of the John Doe 2 mystery. That same day, the Justice Department unsealed papers formally stating that John Doe 2, as originally described by mechanic Tom Kessinger at Elliott's Body Shop, had never existed.[98] Prosecutors had been leaning this way for more than a year. But as of January 29, the far-fetched scenario of how Kessinger somehow time-traveled an innocent soldier into a mistaken John Doe 2 sighting became a permanent part of the official story of the bombing.

In another development that day, so pointed that it almost seemed scripted, after months of public speculation about John Doe 2 look-alike Michael Brescia's whereabouts, the FBI finally arrested the man Carol Howe claimed *was* John Doe 2 at his parents' home in Philadelphia. However, Brescia faced charges only for his role in the Aryan Republican Army's Midwest bank robbery spree, not in the bombing.

Prosecutors scoffed at the possibility that Brescia was a suspect, but the timing of his arrest was tricky to chalk up to coincidence. In federal custody and dependent on federal prosecutors as he negotiated a remarkably lenient plea deal for the bank robberies, Michael Brescia would probably not be talking to the news media about the Oklahoma City bombing anytime soon.

That momentous day, January 29, 1997, saw an almost perfect standoff between those seeking to protect the official story of the bombing and those seeking to challenge it. However, fortune appeared to smile on the challengers the very next day. Roger and Thrasher visited Jones in his office for an update on the document outlining the FBI's debriefing of Carol Howe, which Jones had found in a search of his computer database.

"Just between the three of us, this is a highly explosive document," the lawyer confided. That was an understatement.

Howe's debriefing report—by FBI Agent James R. Blanchard—of what she saw and heard on her spy mission inside Elohim City in the months leading up to the bombing was staggering. It was all there on the page.[99] Howe's FBI interviewer took notes as she described Strassmeir talking of assassinations, bombings, and his commitment to direct action against the US government. Howe told her interviewer that Dennis Mahon specifically named the Oklahoma City federal building on a short list of bombing targets. She told of accompanying Mahon and Strassmeir on one of their three alleged trips to Oklahoma City, perhaps to case the Murrah Building.

Timothy McVeigh wasn't John Doe 1, Howe told her FBI interviewer. Instead, to her, Strassmeir's friend and Elohim City resident Peter Ward resembled the man known as Robert Kling, who had rented the bomb truck.

Agent Blanchard's consistent misspellings were so atrocious it was hard not to side with Stephen Jones's bitter charge that evading his computer search system was the goal of the nearly perfect mangling of so many proper names. Still, the lawyer finally had the buried document in his hand. And the producers finally had what they needed from the government's own account of the spy mission to deliver their story to ABC.

Curiously, the FBI debriefing document differed sharply from what Carol Howe told J.D. and Thrasher on two points. Regarding

John Doe 2, Agent Blanchard reported that Carol Howe named Tony Ward, Peter Ward's brother, as her candidate for John Doe 2—and not Michael Brescia. According to the debriefing report, Howe described Tony Ward as "not well-liked at [Elohim City]," but someone who "would do as his brother directed." On the contrary, to J.D. and Thrasher, Howe positively identified Michael Brescia as John Doe 2.

The other discrepancy concerned Dennis Mahon. According to the FBI report, Howe had tried unsuccessfully to track down Mahon after the bombing. However, in her interview with Thrasher, Howe said she did find Mahon at his parents' home in Illinois. Both crucial points needing clarification. But when would anyone be able to interview Carol Howe again about Mahon, John Doe 2, or anything else? She had gone into hiding, reportedly in fear for her life.

The names Carol Howe had revealed in the FBI debriefing underscored a troubling question. While the FBI was undertaking the most extensive criminal manhunt in US history, why didn't it pursue the specific leads it received from the government's own informant inside the bomb plot?

What about Tony Ward, Howe's John Doe 2 candidate as mentioned in Agent Blanchard's FBI notes? If correct, Howe's identification of John Doe 2 could potentially have ended the FBI's global manhunt almost as soon as it got off the ground. Yet the FBI did not interview Tony Ward for six more months. Even then, in November 1995, on a visit to the extended Ward family in New Mexico, the FBI asked Tony only a few perfunctory questions before moving on.

Also notable from the FBI's brief New Mexico visit: Peter Ward—Howe's consistent John Doe 1 candidate—was missing from the family circle. His relatives admitted that Peter had been in Elohim City at the time of the bombing, but they said they did not know where he was now. That was that: The FBI had their John Doe 1—Timothy McVeigh.

Roger uncovered a baffling clue in the Ward brothers mystery while researching his 2012 book, *Oklahoma City: What the Investigation Missed—And Why It Still Matters,* coauthored with Andrew Gumbel. The clue involved the brothers' last-known interaction with federal law enforcement. In September 1996, almost a year after the New Mexico FBI interviews, Oregon police arrested Peter and Tony Ward, along with another brother, Sonny, for stealing gas and driving a stolen car.

When Roger dug into the story, a local law enforcement source told him that an FBI agent mysteriously appeared at the Oregon jail and finally interviewed Peter Ward, in very general terms, about the bombing.[100] To FBI Agent Kerry Larsen's questions about Elohim City, Peter Ward portrayed the compound as a peaceful, nonviolent community without weapons, and said that he had never met Timothy McVeigh. Agent Larsen apparently did not inquire about Peter's whereabouts at the time of the bombing.

However, the most remarkable feature of this FBI encounter was what happened next. According to Roger's law enforcement source, the FBI bailed all three Ward brothers out of jail in an unprecedented move—Peter's bond alone was $3,000. Free again, the Ward brothers jumped bail and quickly disappeared. Under normal circumstances, this would have produced additional criminal charges. However, in 2018, Roger told me that a licensed private investigator had searched public databases for possible criminal records on Peter Ward and found none. Had someone erased his felony charges? Like Michael Brescia, the Wards were now out of the reach of curious journalists, notably J.D. Cash. The Ward brothers were among the few interviews J.D. was missing from Andreas Strassmeir's circle of Elohim City associates.

As for Strassmeir and Mahon, ringleaders of the Elohim City bomb plot, according to Carol Howe, they also had curiously attracted practically no heat during the FBI's massive bombing investigation.

The FBI never interviewed Strassmeir during 1995, even when TV cameras captured him shortly after the bombing parading around Elohim City with a pistol on his hip. In early 1996, after he had returned to Germany, and was for all practical purposes out of reach of US law enforcement, DOJ attorneys finally contacted Strassmeir by telephone. Based on two perfunctory calls, they ruled him out as a bombing suspect.

Following conflicting reports that Dennis Mahon was or was not a suspect and was or was not at his parents' home in Illinois in the days following the bombing, the FBI had not bothered to interview the ex-KKK imperial dragon as of late 1996. Mahon was at home in Tulsa, disseminating white separatist propaganda, uninterrupted.

For a prosecution that prided itself on its narrow focus on one man and was now ready to try him as a lone-wolf terrorist, the web of Elohim City connections was bewildering. The federal government had paid Carol Howe to spy on the neo-Nazis of Elohim City. But her ATF handlers ignored her warnings that they were planning a terror attack. Stranger still, the FBI bombing investigators also ignored Howe's leads. She was the logical first and best choice to rely on, and they had her FBI debriefing report. Didn't they want to solve this case?

Before Roger and Thrasher left Stephen Jones's office to return to Oklahoma City, the lawyer issued a stern warning. "There are people in ABC News that don't like the two of you and have it in for you," Jones told them. "The DOJ is working against you inside ABC."

The caution wasn't a complete surprise, but Thrasher and Roger were no strangers to pushback. Armed with their fully vetted source, the producers liked their chances of getting their huge story on the air. After all, barring someone bringing the full weight of the federal government down on them, what could go wrong?

CHAPTER 7

TRUTH TO POWER

WHAT HAPPENED NEXT would be unbelievable, except that Roger Charles lived it and took meticulous notes. Ever since his training at the US Naval Academy, when instructors drilled midshipmen on the importance of getting coordinates right for a search-and-rescue mission, Roger took notes on whatever was said on the job. Even on his way out the door to a dinner party, where choice gossip was sure to flow in Washington circles, Roger's wife would sometimes jokingly ask him: "Do you have your notebook?"

While investigating the Oklahoma City bombing, Roger filled more than forty of these skinny tablets with telegrammatic revelations. The entries came fast and furious, beginning in mid-January of 1997, covering the climactic finale of the producers' race to break the Carol Howe story on the ABC network.[101]

They had to hurry. Rival network NBC was chasing the story, too, with help from J.D. Cash, who was hedging his bets by assisting both network news teams. Roger wasn't happy when he found this out, but J.D. was a force of nature under no one's control. He wanted the story told, period. At that moment, J.D. was conveniently hiding out, working on one of his biggest scoops: McVeigh's alleged bank robbery activities with the Aryan Republican Army.

"Don't tell Jones," J.D. cautioned when he called Roger with a Howe update. "He'll be suspicious." With good reason: Some of the information J.D. was secretly harvesting from Jones's discovery files would not be helpful to the McVeigh defense.

As Roger and Thrasher strategized to beat NBC to air, Tom Jarriel weighed in from Washington on January 30, 1997, with a powerful idea. Knowing that it would take several weeks to get a magazine segment booked on *20/20,* Jarriel proposed this: "We could write a hard story...and lead *World News* [ABC's evening news program] with it." It was a great idea. Thrasher could have a script ready for Jarriel to read later that day.

An obligatory phone call to Justice Department press representative Leesa Brown would yield the official government comment for the story. Thrasher was ready with a dozen points he asked Brown to confirm or deny. His last question—whether Andreas Strassmeir had ever been the subject of investigation—seemed to fluster Brown. She tried to deflect, only to be run over by Thrasher's relentless logic:

> LB: If you go beyond the story of an informant in a white supremacist compound hearing these stories...that happens all the time. What else have you got? If all these things are accurate—what does it add up to?
>
> DT: 168 people dead.

In the end, the press rep had to surrender. The Carol Howe story was accurate in all its parts. "This is not an official response, but we're not going to be able to deny it," Brown told Thrasher the day before the story was slated for broadcast on ABC.

By 5:30 p.m. in Oklahoma on February 5, 1997, Thrasher and Roger were in the lobby of KTUL, Tulsa's ABC affiliate. They had delivered the last footage for the story to New York by satellite. *ABC World News Tonight* was on the air. The producers knew their story would play third in the lineup. They watched eagerly as anchorman Peter Jennings covered the latest twist in the O. J. Simpson case. Next up: reaction to President Clinton's State of the Union Address. Finally, in the third slot: Wait. What was this? A car chase in New Zealand?

At that moment, Thrasher's phone rang. It was Tom Jarriel, calling to tell him that the ATF had called the network at the last minute saying the story wasn't true, even though the Justice Department had confirmed it. ABC decided to hold the story.

Early the following day, February 6, Jarriel called again about a plan by Christopher Isham, ABC's evening news senior producer for investigative projects, to get the story on the air that night. The producers would scramble to add interviews with an Oklahoma state legislator and a bombing survivor. Meanwhile, Isham, who had been talking with the Justice Department, called Thrasher and Stephen Jones to report a breakthrough: Jones would be allowed to review some of Carol Howe's confidential informant reports, including her alleged warnings to her handler before the bombing from inside Elohim City. "But only him," Isham cautioned. Thrasher would not be allowed to see the crucial documentation.

Later that day, Jones recounted his side of this remarkable episode for Thrasher. Jones said he had received an early morning phone call from Larry Mackey, one of the prosecutors on Joseph Hartzler's team. Mackey said Carol Howe was expected to go public in a press conference in Denver that very afternoon. Jones reported that prosecutors now had a bizarre request for him. Would he side with them publicly, against Howe, and join them in "a controlled statement that there was no prior knowledge of the bombing on the part of a US government agency?"

According to Jones, Mackey warned: "If it comes out that the government and the ATF had prior knowledge, it will bring the country down."

Jones hadn't heard political doomsday talk like this since his days as a young lawyer working for a president. "Larry, I think you've lost your mind," Jones said he told Mackey. "You just said to me the craziest thing I've ever heard since I was working as the president's lawyer, and Richard Nixon said, 'I'm not a crook.'" Mackey would later disavow this phone call to Jones, but still later Jones would again insist it happened.[102]

In any case, the afternoon press conference did not take place. It was a hoax that originated who knew where or how. But in the process, Jones seized a prize opportunity to be the first one outside the government to read some of Carol Howe's confidential ATF reports. FBI agents hand-carried them to the lawyer's office, then stood guard as Jones read them to ensure he didn't take notes or make copies.

Meanwhile, after a day spent coordinating interviews in the legislative chambers of Oklahoma's state capitol, Roger delivered additional videotape footage to a studio at the University of Oklahoma where ABC paid $7,000 to transmit it to New York and Washington by satellite. When Roger returned to the Medallion Hotel in Oklahoma City later that afternoon, the door to Thrasher's room was open. But to Roger's amazement, Thrasher now gave him the thumbs-down sign. He was on the phone with Tom Jarriel again. A little while later, Thrasher described to Stephen Jones what happened:

DT: ABC has killed the story.

SJ: Really?

DT: Yep. Absolutely one hundred percent buckled under. Actually, what they said is they simply don't think the girl is credible. I said, well, that's great. She's passed every polygraph.... Every single thing she told me is absolutely confirmed in documents....They simply buckled under to the Justice Department. Plain and simple.

SJ: How did they get that done?...

DT: I have no idea. That's way beyond my level.... But when you don't see it on the air tonight, I think you should raise holy hell.

Through Jarriel, the producers heard that the Justice Department had unleashed a perfect storm of phone calls to ABC. Roger told me he could still remember every detail of those reported calls. It wasn't just public affairs people. Principals were calling the network. The callers didn't ever say the story wasn't true. The argument they used was this: If you air this, it will lead to the abolishment of the ATF, and there will be machine guns on every corner. As Roger summed it up: "The executives in New York just couldn't handle the possibility that they would be responsible for that. End of story."

When he learned what had happened, the usually decorously polite Roger Charles was shocked. "My wife doesn't like this next moment," Roger told me. "She has heard me recount it more than a few times when Marine buddies stopped by our house over the past two decades. She thinks it reflects badly on me."[103]

Roger called Christopher Isham's number on his hotel phone:

RGC: What hand are you holding your phone with?

CI: What does that mean?

RGC: Reach between your legs with your other hand and see if you can find your balls.

CI: Oh, Roger.

RGC: Fuck you.

Later that night, the producers went to the hotel bar to drown their sorrows. Thrasher's restless mind was still racing a hundred miles an hour. He had an idea for how they could salvage their story. Thrasher knew that Colonel David Hackworth, *Newsweek*'s esteemed senior military affairs correspondent, was Roger's journalism mentor, sometime story partner, and close friend.

Hackworth had interviewed Timothy McVeigh in prison in June 1995 for a *Newsweek* cover story. Thrasher knew Hackworth had clout. "Isn't Hackworth a regular on the Don Imus show?" Thrasher now asked Roger. "Why don't you call Hackworth and see if he can get you on the show if you're willing to go?"

Roger was more than willing. His tour of duty in network journalism was probably over anyway after the call to Isham. Besides, unlike Thrasher, Roger had his Marine Corps retirement to rely on. In what came next, he may have acted more as a Marine than a journalist. He and Thrasher were on a mission they needed to finish for the Wilburns and, frankly, Roger thought, for the country.

A round of phone calls and faxes followed with Hackworth and the producers of the bitingly topical *Imus in the Morning* radio broadcast, simulcast on MSNBC from New York City. The following day, February 7, 1997, Roger went on the show from his room in the Medallion Hotel. Probably out of respect for

Hackworth, Imus's producers let Roger take his time and present the story straight. They didn't interrupt once as he reported on what he and Thrasher had learned:

> Here we've got...this great story.... The government... admitted that this girl's information was right, that she was telling her ATF handler that these wackos out there are talking about blowing up federal property...buildings...installations...in either Tulsa or Oklahoma City... months before the attack on the building in downtown Oklahoma City.... What we would call a strategic warning.... And interestingly enough, the Justice Department's spokesperson has admitted this, that our facts are right, that the girl, what she has told us is reflected in the documents that she was providing the government, because any information that she provided the government they'd write up in reports. And it appears that there was tactical warning, in the sense that there were bomb squads on the street that morning that were not normally there.

This last detail brought Imus up short. "Bomb squads?" he asked incredulously. His follow-up question allowed Roger to highlight the most troubling discrepancy in the federal government's official version of the crime:

> We had that on the show on January 17. There's no question that unusual activity was taking place.... We spoke to Joe Hartzler, the chief prosecutor, and he denied to us before that program went on the air that there was any general warning or any specific warning [or] a threat of any kind to Oklahoma City.

Roger gave a plug to NBC's story on Carol Howe, set to air that evening on the *Nightly News*. Afterward, the producer of that story told Roger that NBC, facing the same pressure as ABC, was going to kill the story until Roger praised the network's anchorman Tom Brokaw on the *Imus* show for having the courage to air it.

For the occasion of the *Imus* interview, Roger borrowed a phrase he had recently read that Don Imus used while talking on air to CBS newsman Mike Wallace. As Roger's interview wrapped up, Imus's producer tossed him one last question, pointedly using his Marine Corps rank: "What's your bottom line there, Colonel?" Roger was ready. "Well, as a great American said fairly recently to another journalist: Peter Jennings and ABC News folded like a cheap suitcase."

Roger's appearance on *Imus* triggered reactions and revelations that would continue illuminating the story, its fate, and the still-unfinished bombing investigation. The executive producer of *20/20* called on the day of the *Imus* broadcast and fired Roger, though gently. NBC reportedly yanked its producer off the Oklahoma City bombing story while ABC redeployed Thrasher into general coverage of the coming McVeigh trial.

Tom Jarriel phoned a week later, calling Roger's appearance on the Imus show "terrific," a wake-up call saying what needed to be said.

ABC's senior correspondent didn't hold back in his assessment of the network. "I assumed both days up 'til airtime that we were on," Jarriel told Roger. "I think we were blindsided. We were set up. I'm disgusted. I've never in all my life seen something like this."

Roger never found out conclusively who at the network killed the story, but he had a strong suspicion. Years later, in 2011, while researching a collection of FBI files, Roger found a document marked "PROTECT IDENTITY" to flag its classified status. The document revealed that in 1995 and 1996, the FBI used "a senior official employed by ABC News for over fifteen years" as a confidential informant on the Oklahoma City bombing story.[104]

Roger told me this was the only unreleased secret government document he had ever seen in his years of document research. That told Roger he was probably looking at what the intelligence world calls a "Black Valentine," a message leaked anonymously by someone inside the government who wants secret information to be known. Roger gave the document to Jesse and Associated Press reporter John Solomon, who broke the story, triggering some sharp criticism of the information-sharing practice by reporters.[105]

After two publications named Christopher Isham as the alleged FBI mole, he fired back angrily, calling the allegation "outrageous and untrue."[106] Still, Isham defended the practice of trading information with law enforcement on a high-profile story as part of a journalist's job. He did not deny passing the FBI confidential information on the Oklahoma City bombing—not on Roger's story, however, but for an earlier 1995 story relating to alleged foreign sponsorship of the bomb plot.

The controversy over the mole memo reawakened Roger's questions about who spiked the Carol Howe story fourteen years earlier and why. During the struggle to save the story, Roger had watched as Christopher Isham appeared to open up extraordinary access for Stephen Jones to read Carol Howe's confidential government informant files. That begged a question never answered: What did the government receive in return from ABC?

In hindsight, one thing was clear. Roger and Thrasher weren't imagining disaster as their story went down in flames. Or, as Thrasher once sniped in frustration at DOJ press representative Leesa Brown, they weren't seeing black helicopters on the Grassy Knoll. The fix had been in. The Justice Department, with the cooperation of ABC News, had suppressed the biggest news story of that new year. And so it was, most improbably, that the story broke not on television network news, but on tabloid radio in New York City.

After Roger finished the interview in his Oklahoma City hotel room that morning, he visited Glenn Wilburn's home. Tragically, Glenn was dying of pancreatic cancer after being diagnosed just a few months earlier. Kathy Wilburn would always believe that grief and stress over the murder of their grandsons, Chase and Colton, had claimed her husband.

Glenn spent most of his time in bed now, not seeing visitors. But he wouldn't have missed the *Imus* broadcast for the world. When Roger dropped by, Glenn opened the front door and hugged him. "Here's this great guy standing before me who's dying," Roger told me. "He has spent the last months of his life trying to expose some truth for the sake of his dead grandsons. For that moment, for me, it was all worth it."

⅄

Luckily for J.D. Cash, one news organization that would not bow to government bullying remained. The sole taker for a shocking journalistic rewrite of America's worst domestic terror attack was the *McCurtain Daily Gazette*. On February 11, 1997, five days after

ABC killed the Carol Howe story, the tiny Oklahoma newspaper published J.D.'s 3500-word story under the headline, "Informant Who Warned of Bombing Now Fears for Her Life: Government's Lie Detector Tests Showed Her Reports Truthful."

Carol Howe was now facing criminal indictment on federal bomb threat conspiracy charges. Her allies saw this move as a hardball play by the Justice Department to silence Howe or destroy her credibility if she went public with her spy story. But she was still talking to the journalist she had come to trust. Now, reporting from a McDonald's restaurant somewhere on the Turner Turnpike between Oklahoma City and Tulsa, J.D. unpacked Carol Howe's incredible saga in the *Gazette*.

Recent events had transformed the reporter's petite and immaculately dressed interview subject into a woman on the edge. Howe spoke to J.D. in whispers while sipping iced tea and keeping a close eye on two men who entered the restaurant and chose a table fifteen feet away.

"Those are the guys I told you about...they've been following me ever since I left Tulsa," Howe confided, referring to two men in jeans and flannel shirts sharing a bag of French fries at their table.

"This is the way it's been since they raided my house in December," she said. "I'm constantly under surveillance." With that, Howe opened her leather purse to reveal two semiautomatic pistols.

"I won't be easy to kill," she said.

Howe studied a photo lying on their table. "That's Pete Langan, okay, the bank robber," she said. "He was one of the leaders, but when I knew him, his hair was long and stringy... and reddish."

Howe took note as one of the men in flannel moved to a nearby water fountain where he could steal a glance at the photo of the Aryan Republican Army's coleader Peter Langan. She pointedly met the stranger's gaze. "He knows I've made him," Howe offered. "They'll probably be leaving soon." Sure enough, minutes later, the two men exited the restaurant, leaving behind their bag of fries.

"Sometimes I think this is all just a game to them," she said.

To Carol Howe, the cloak-and-dagger scenario was deadly serious and with good reason. J.D.'s ninety-eight-pound source was carrying weapons while dodging federal law enforcement tails and national media attempts to interview her. One month before Timothy McVeigh's trial would open in Denver, just enough of Howe's spy mission had leaked from NBC's news story and Roger's radio appearance to blow her cover and potentially turn the McVeigh trial upside down.

The Justice Department had now confirmed that Howe was the federal government's paid neo-Nazi infiltrator inside Elohim City, watching, listening, and reporting that terrorists were plotting to bomb federal buildings and go to war with the US government. She was in a world of trouble, and she knew it. Her gravest concern was that someone might want to kill her before she could tell the rest of her story to the public. Maybe if J.D. Cash would report it in the *Gazette*, it might remove that incentive. J.D. was more than glad to oblige.

"Until just days ago, details of Howe's work for the BATF and her firsthand knowledge of the Oklahoma City bombing conspiracy remained buried from public view by an agency whose very existence [may] now be threatened by the evidence she once provided it," J.D. wrote.

Laying out the details of his secret interviews with his source, the reporter chronicled her spy assignment inside Elohim City, including her warning to her ATF handler that the Murrah Building was on a short list of buildings targeted for destruction. J.D. also documented the polygraph tests she passed regarding her ATF reports, and her specific warnings that the Elohim City plotters were zeroing in on three Oklahoma federal buildings—and preparing for a bombing.

"She now believes that on April 19, 1995, those same subjects—with the aid of others—bombed the Murrah Federal Building, the worst act of terrorism in US history," J.D. wrote.

"Today, Howe wonders what went wrong," he told his readers. "With all the information she gave the agency, why didn't the BATF stop the bombing? It is a haunting question shared now by many Americans, including those who are now, for the first time, hearing in the national media serious allegations of what Howe says is the indisputable truth that the government had 'detailed prior knowledge' of the plot to bomb the building, but somehow failed to stop it."

Writing those words must have been a surreal experience for J.D. Cash. The suppression of Roger's story and the blow to Howe's credibility that would follow her impending indictment had dealt a crushing blow to his reporting. It practically ensured that the glaring disconnect between the informant's claims and the government's lone-wolf terror case against Timothy McVeigh would survive the reporter's best efforts to expose it nationally.

Undeterred, J.D. filed his sensational account of what his source revealed for the *Gazette*'s faithful few thousand readers. J.D. reported that in the first of their recent series of clandestine interviews, Howe had told him of her involvement with members of the radical underground group calling itself the Aryan Republican Army. Later, she admitted to him her role as a government informant inside Elohim City and made allegations prominently featuring Andreas Strassmeir, the community's paramilitary trainer.

"I kinda had a relationship with him for a while," Howe told J.D. "[Strassmeir] was real quiet and reserved...and when he did speak, you could hardly understand him because of his accent."

"We talked about relationships once, and he said he wasn't interested in settling down with a woman. All he wanted to do was blow up federal buildings!"

Howe said Strassmeir's best friends at Elohim City were Peter Ward and the ARA's Kevin McCarthy and Michael Brescia, and that a close Tulsa friend was Dennis Mahon.

"Dennis brought me out to Elohim City in the summer of 1994 and introduced me around," Howe told J.D. "After that, I started hanging around with the people there, and in December, I moved into a travel trailer he kept out there. But when it got too cold, I moved in with one of the families. I stayed for about five weeks that time."

Not for the first time in J.D.'s reporting, Michael Fortier, soon to be the government's star witness against McVeigh, made a surprise appearance in Carol Howe's telling of the bomb plot. According to her, McVeigh and Fortier visited Elohim City together in December 1994, a few months before the bombing.

"Sometime before Christmas, a lot of guys showed up at EC," she told J.D. "One that I recall was Tim...[and] a guy who used the name Fontaine, a person I now recognize as Mike Fortier."

About Timothy McVeigh, Howe said: "I never even spoke to him. He was considered a 'good soldier' by members of the

ARA but not a leader; he was just someone you sent out on jobs because he was reliable."

"I never knew much about Fontaine," she added. His name was mentioned a lot by the guys when they would be talking in other parts of Andy's house—you know, making plans they didn't want me to hear the details of."

By their third interview, Howe revealed to J.D. how her government informant role developed.

"I was contacted by Dennis Mahon after I ordered some literature from this group called the White Aryan Resistance," Howe said. "He wanted to have a closer relationship than I did, and later, he threatened me when I tried to get away from his group. I went down and obtained a protective order from the Tulsa County Court.

"Shortly after I got the court order, I was contacted by Special Agent Angela Finley from the Tulsa BATF, and she wanted to know if I wanted to get even. Angie said she would pay me to set up Dennis.... I went along with it."

On Finley's instructions, Howe enlisted Mahon to introduce her to Elohim City residents who could help her gather information on Strassmeir and other radicals.

"I started going to as many of their meetings as I could and met a lot of people who were very secretive," Howe said. "But sometime in November there was a meeting, and Strassmeir and Mahon said it was time to quit talking and go to war."

"I reported all this to Angie," Howe said.

Howe said Finley wanted her to get Strassmeir handling grenades on film, which led to the Halloween-themed dinner party at Howe's Tulsa apartment in the fall of 1994, which J.D. had described to Roger Charles a few weeks earlier in a phone briefing.

"He brought in Pete Langan and Kevin McCarthy, the bank robbers. In no time I had them painting the grenades in front of the surveillance camera, and I later gave the film to Angie," Howe told J.D.

However, she grew increasingly disenchanted with her work. "In March of 1995, I got fed up with the whole thing because of my negative feelings about Reverend Millar and some of the other people at Elohim City," Howe said.

J.D. quoted her account of Reverend Millar's alarming message before the bombing. "Reverend Millar was working the people up into a frenzy about a holy war that he said would come by the anniversary of Waco" on April 19, 1995, J.D. quoted Howe as telling the FBI in her post-bombing debriefing session. Further, she said, Reverend Millar warned his followers that "they had to strike first, or they would end up like David Koresh and his [Branch Davidian] followers."

Howe's mission was going nowhere, it seemed. As she summed it up for J.D., "Angie hadn't made any arrests, either, and that was frustrating, so I quit going out there...until the [Murrah Building] got blown up!"

She wasn't quite done, however. Of her return to Elohim City after the bombing, she recalled: "I spent about four days at EC, then returned and was debriefed about the situation." She told J.D. her final reconnaissance mission held one surprise: "Strassmeir was missing from the compound!"

⅄

Andreas Strassmeir and doubts about her credibility as his accuser were still lurking in the shadows of Carol Howe's life as she sat for the interview with J.D. Cash in February 1997. A few weeks later, the government would indict her, as expected, on conspiracy charges stemming from the recorded bomb-threat message at the home she shared with James Viefhaus. Howe's attorney, Clark Brewster, had charged that the prosecution was an effort to smear, discredit, or silence Howe as to what she saw and heard about the bomb plot in Elohim City.

Appearing to agree, her jury would acquit Howe on all charges six months later, in August 1997, in only six hours. However, the trial would force her to revisit traumatic passages from her spy mission, including her March 1995 transport to a mental health facility with injuries J.D. reported that Tulsa police believed were self-inflicted cuts.[107]

As for the racist beliefs that had helped Howe fit into Elohim City's white separatist culture, she testified that she only truly held those beliefs for about six months during a painful period of her life. Her father read from a letter to her family that Howe had given a friend in case she had to go into witness protection. She said her informant mission was a chance "to do something for someone else." Similarly, after the verdict, Howe said she wanted to "do something" for the Oklahoma City bombing victims.[108] Then, without another word, she vanished from public view.

Carol Howe had not died. However, her disappearance from Tulsa at age twenty-six after such high-profile involvement in the bombing saga was, in its way, as mysterious as the trail of deaths in the years following the bombing. Almost all those deaths, like Howe's disappearance, had silenced witnesses with knowledge about what really happened on April 19, 1995, in Oklahoma City. Wherever she had relocated, doubts about Carol Howe's credibility would trail her forever, especially relating to the charges she had leveled against Andreas Strassmeir.

For J.D. Cash, Howe's trial would bring few surprises. He already knew that another disappearance, this one by Strassmeir, would remain the elephant in the room regardless of the verdict in Howe's trial. The rest of J.D.'s February 1997 story in the *Gazette* gathered up the threads of the enigmatic Strassmeir puzzle as J.D. knew them so far. Who was this rabble-rouser who rallied the neo-Nazi troops at Elohim City in late 1994 to bomb federal buildings but managed to attract no interest from FBI bombing investigators?

After tapping his best sources in local, state, and federal law enforcement, J.D. knew how big a gap there was between the aristocratic pedigree Strassmeir had inherited in Germany and his US persona as a vagabond Civil War reenactment buff, one with no permanent paying job who only wanted to find an American wife. Strassmeir's father, an influential conservative political operative, had been chief of staff for Germany's Chancellor Helmut Kohl. *Der Spiegel* magazine called Gunter Strassmeir the "architect of German reunification." Before coming to America, Andreas had received intelligence training while at an elite military academy and served as an officer in a mortar company of the German Army. Elohim City was not even a lateral move for Strassmeir.[109]

The shadowy immigration status of "Andy the German" included missing data and unusual codes that may have carried diplomatic immunity from the US legal system. A law enforcement source informed J.D. that authorities had stopped Strassmeir's vehicle and impounded it for traffic violations near Elohim City. A tow truck driver later told J.D. that phone calls from high-level Oklahoma and Washington, DC, offices had flooded local police with instructions to release the vehicle.

In a sidebar, a curious law enforcement officer investigated the briefcase Strassmeir had left in the vehicle. Inside were records documenting his efforts to broker Boeing 747s to a buyer in Luxembourg on behalf of his Washington, DC, patron, retired US Air Force Colonel Vincent Petruskie. The colonel, an old friend of Strassmeir's father, Gunter, was widely believed to have used his Air Force career to cover a CIA career in counterespionage, a claim Petruskie denied.

As J.D. looked ahead to where the Elohim City story would likely lead next, his reporting, common sense, and the FBI's striking lack of interest in Strassmeir told the reporter that he was probably someone's intelligence asset. A year before, J.D. had reported on FBI Director Louis Freeh's high-profile 1993 visit to Germany to address that nation's concerns that neo-Nazi groups in the US were exporting racist violence and neo-Nazi activity to Germany.

The two nations had agreed on the need for a joint intelligence operation—a mission that included spying on American citizens.[110] Freeh had named Larry Potts, then assistant FBI director for criminal investigations, to handle the bilateral intelligence initiative between the US and Germany.

By the time of Freeh's trip to Germany, Andreas Strassmeir had traveled back and forth to America for five years, beginning in 1988. His hope that Colonel Petruskie could get him a job with the Drug Enforcement Administration fell through. He stayed at the home of Kirk Lyons, the attorney representing high-profile radical white power groups. He also worked as a low-level runner for Lyons's associate David Holloway, a former CIA pilot, in Texas. While there, Strassmeir reportedly attended meetings of a militia group calling itself the Texas Light Infantry Brigade (TLI) whose members came to suspect Strassmeir of being a government operative. One of them spoke to J.D. on the condition of anonymity in a tape-recorded interview:

> Andy was coming to our meetings in 1989 and 1990.... Some of the members of our group began following that guy at night. We were suspicious of him and who he really was. He told us he was wanted by the Immigration Service because he said he was here illegally. Once, we followed him to a federal building and watched him use the keypad to enter the offices at night. Then, we knew he was a federal agent of some kind.[111]

William Mueller, the murdered gun dealer, told a reporter that he, too, believed Strassmeir was a federal agent, with ATF, after their hostile encounter at a gun show.[112]

There were so many clues that Strassmeir's humble profile as Elohim City's paramilitary trainer was a cover. But for what hidden role? J.D. had now identified the ATF spy inside Elohim City, and it was Carol Howe. How likely was it, J.D. wondered, that someone had planted Strassmeir there also? As he wrapped up his exclusive coverage of Carol Howe's spy mission, that question still needed to be settled in J.D.'s mind, so he posed it to a former undercover agent.

Was it likely? "Yes. The reasons are obvious," the agent advised. "First, there is no way a law enforcement agency is going to risk exposing the life of one of their assets should the other 'resource' succumb to torture or decide to double-cross the agency. And, of course, the monitoring of information can best be verified if neither resource knows who the other is. That's the only way this game works, and it's the only way it succeeds."

J.D. Cash needed a creative solution for his own game now. Discovering Strassmeir's actual role in the bomb plot was crucial. But attorney Stephen Jones had been right when he called the Carol Howe story radioactive. Now the question was: With the dead end at ABC, where would the widely and willfully ignored story go from here? The clock was ticking. It was mid-February 1997, just weeks before Timothy McVeigh's trial as the lone-wolf bomber was scheduled to begin in Denver.

As J.D. would soon learn, the "Sly Fox" wasn't leaving anything to chance. Stephen Jones was planning an ambush.

CHAPTER 8

BLIND JUSTICE

"WE COULD USE SOME HELP OUT HERE." Ten days after ABC fired Roger Charles, Stephen Jones called Roger's home in Virginia, the one person on the planet with a shot left to uncover the real story of the Oklahoma City bombing. Just like that, Roger was back on the case, bringing Timothy McVeigh's defense team the added firepower of what he knew about Carol Howe and the Elohim City bomb plot.

As often happens in high-stakes trials, the most consequential action would occur behind the scenes of the courtroom. Roger took up his new post in Denver just in time for a devastating surprise. On February 28, 1997, the *Dallas Morning News* broke the story that Timothy McVeigh had allegedly confessed his guilt in the bombing to a member of his defense team and offered an incendiary detail: McVeigh allegedly ignited the bomb in broad daylight to "increase the body count."[113]

Next, *Playboy* published its version of the McVeigh confession, detailing how he allegedly lit a five-minute detonating wire while driving the bomb truck to the targeted Murrah Building.[114] Stephen Jones's attempts to dismiss these stories as hoaxes didn't gain much traction, even when J.D. Cash stepped forward to volunteer that he knew what must have happened. J.D. recalled a defense investigator reading him excerpts from a fictional McVeigh confession, scripted to entice a would-be source to agree to an interview.

J.D. laughed off the "confession" and its contrived flourishes, which read like a Mickey Spillane pulp fiction paperback. But the claims went unresolved, and the damage was catastrophic. McVeigh's defense team was in serious trouble with the trial date looming. Jones knew this better than anyone and responded with an urgent plan to make Carol Howe a star witness in the coming trial. Roger Charles would be pivotal in that effort.

Startling fresh secrets flowed from J.D. Cash to Roger over drinks and dinner in Denver days before the opening gavel. The reporter told his trusted friend how he had harvested incriminating disclosures about Dennis Mahon and members of the Aryan Republican Army in face-to-face interviews and phone conversations with Mahon during 1996. J.D. had yet to write about this exclusive information.

Over dinner, J.D. regaled Roger with details of his first visit to Mahon's Tulsa home in January 1996.[115] The reporter had won over the former KKK imperial dragon by showing him a copy of *Jubilee*, a Christian Identity journal of the far right. The magazine featured a photo of J.D. with Louis Beam, the towering eminence of the white supremacy movement. The strategy worked. Mahon opened up to a reporter he assumed shared his extreme political beliefs.

In J.D.'s telling, the interview at Mahon's home took a startling turn when J.D. dropped a confidential hint that Mahon's friend

Andreas Strassmeir had operated as a government informant at Elohim City. This news spooked Mahon, who immediately placed two urgent phone calls. The first was to warn ARA members Mark Thomas and Michael Brescia, who were now staying at Thomas's farm in Pennsylvania.

In a second call to Germany, Mahon ordered a contact there to find the recently returned Strassmeir, force a confession from him, and then kill him. All this happened while the stunned reporter looked on.

Before the five-hour interview at Mahon's home ended, J.D. revealed to Mahon that he had won approval from Stephen Jones for a private interview with Timothy McVeigh. Mahon then recorded an audiotape, asking J.D. to hand-deliver it to McVeigh. Oh, and there was one other thing Mahon wanted to share before J.D. left, possibly truth, possibly bombast.

Michael Brescia, Mahon confided, was John Doe 2.

This interview was one to remember, even for J.D. Cash, who quickly contacted Stephen Jones, giving the lawyer Mahon's taped message to McVeigh. On it, in characteristically cryptic style, Mahon thanked McVeigh for "hanging tough" and reassured him that he, Mahon, believed McVeigh was innocent because of "entrapment." In closing, Mahon urged, "Remember all the good soldiers who have fallen on the field of battle in their fight for the cause.... Justice will be done, Tim."[116]

Coming from an international terrorist implicated in the bombing by government informant Howe, Mahon's message was alarming. His words could be interpreted as praise or a threat to a captured soldier from higher-ups in a terrorist cause. J.D. gave a sworn statement to Jones, covering Mahon's disclosures during their interview.

Jones informed the FBI of Mahon's threat against Strassmeir and filed J.D.'s statement, including Mahon's disclosures implicating himself and ARA members Michael Brescia and Mark Thomas in the bombing, as a sealed document with the McVeigh trial court.[117] The whereabouts of the audiotape and whether the FBI heard it or read J.D.'s statement are unknown. As far as J.D. knew more than a year later, Mahon's attempts to open communication with the imprisoned McVeigh never triggered investigative curiosity by the FBI.

Over dinner in Denver, J.D. and Roger couldn't help but wonder: Did Dennis Mahon enjoy protected status in the bombing case, along with Strassmeir, now safely returned to Germany? Was Mahon, the lifelong radical white separatist, a government operative? Stephen Jones was delving into those same questions. But for Jones, the stakes, literally his client's life or death, were even higher.

⅄

On March 25, 1997, a few days after Roger's dinner with J.D., the lawyer went above Judge Matsch, presiding over the McVeigh trial, to seek access to long-withheld documents Jones believed the government should have turned over. In a petition for a writ of mandamus, Jones asked the US Court of Appeals for the Tenth Circuit to order the government to turn over the documents, notably relating to Carol Howe's disclosures revealing a broader conspiracy in the bombing.

In blistering language, Jones's petition recounted two long years of slow-walking, double-talk, evasion, and, the lawyer claimed, outright lies by the government in response to some thirty requests for prosecutors to share details of their global investigation involving multiple federal intelligence agencies. "This is a solemn criminal case, not Alice in Wonderland, where definitions mean only what 'the Queen thinks,' and what she thinks is not known to anyone else," Jones wrote.

His petition zeroed in on Howe, Strassmeir, Mahon, and the neo-Nazi crew at Elohim City. Jones made the case that after Waco, anti-government activists at Elohim City were fomenting a preemptive strike against the federal government. He argued that Howe, a paid informant, really did warn the government about the bomb plot. Strassmeir, the neo-Nazi-espousing militia trainer, really was a suspect in the bombing despite repeated denials by the government. And according to Jones, white power propagandist Mahon was a member of the Aryan Republican Army gang and a prime suspect in the bombing.

Stephen Jones was out on a limb with this petition, not only because it risked alienating the judge who was about to open the McVeigh trial. The petition was also a gamble on Carol Howe's credibility. Jones still needed to read the full documentation of her pre-bombing reports to her ATF handler. Only the government knew everything in those documents. But did the Sly Fox from Enid have another back-channel motive for his petition?

As the respondent to the writ of mandamus, Judge Matsch would read every word. Jones could count on that. So, when the higher court swiftly rejected the petition and ordered it sealed in just three days, all was not lost. Jones's preview of what Carol Howe would say on the witness stand had reached the judge. No one could un-ring that bell.

On April 1, 1997, J.D. followed Jones's mandamus filing with a long story about Dennis Mahon in the *Gazette*, including fresh revelations from Mahon. J.D. recounted for readers Mahon's three-day visit to J.D.'s rural cabin in Battiest, Oklahoma, in the fall of 1996. Fueled by one hundred–proof vodka and Jeep rides along backcountry roads, it had summoned up a vision of an Aryan paradise for the visiting propagandist.

Granting that anything said by Mahon might be deflection or even deliberate disinformation, J.D. reported to his readers that "many pieces of Mahon's information were checking out." To J.D., Mahon's new candor during this visit seemed to signal his intuition that the bombing investigation was closing in on him. Most of the ARA gang members were now behind bars for the bank robberies. Mahon was next, he predicted. As J.D. reported, "'Every day,' Mahon told me, 'the feds put another fence post around me. It won't be long before I go down with the rest of the guys.'"

Mirroring Carol Howe's account, Mahon laid out the bombing conspiracy at Elohim City for J.D.: twenty-some conspirators operating separate cells of three to five men. The goal: to rob, pillage, and murder in the name of the white race and a coming revolution. According to Mahon, Timothy McVeigh, a former armored car driver, helped plan some of the ARA gang's bank robberies.

Adding to Carol Howe's assessment of McVeigh as a "good soldier," Mahon told J.D. that McVeigh "from the beginning wanted to be the fall guy in the bombing, securing his place in history as a patriot hero."

When asked to look at some artists' sketches of the two bombing suspects, Mahon said that the man who took delivery of Chinese food in room 25 of the Dreamland motel the night of the bomb truck rental was not McVeigh. According to Mahon, it was Peter Ward, Strassmeir's close associate, who Carol Howe had speculated to J.D. and the FBI might be John Doe 1.

But when asked if Ward rented the bomb truck, Mahon pointed in another direction, telling J.D.: "Well, you know his brother, Tony, has a pocked complexion. Maybe you ought to go to Belen, New Mexico, and get a picture of him, too."

J.D.'s April 1997 story delivered a final zinger loaded with incriminating allegations involving McVeigh, the ARA's Michael Brescia, and the November, 1994, robbery of Arkansas gun dealer Roger Moore, which prosecutors believed helped finance the bombing. J.D. told Mahon that the story came straight from Elohim City's patriarch:

"Rev. Millar told me a year ago that you used to bring McVeigh down to Elohim City to use the gun range," J.D. told Mahon. "He also told me on tape that Brescia helped with the Hot Springs gun robbery of Roger Moore."

To this, according to J.D., Mahon replied: "Oh, that son-of-a-bitch! That dumb son-of-a-bitch doesn't know when to keep his mouth shut!"

Roger told me that following the publication of this story, J.D.'s editor, Bruce Willingham, feared that his reporter, whose story referenced recorded interviews, was about to be indicted for obstruction of justice. That didn't happen. But no doubt those were intense hours for a journalist whose source of a lifetime, Carol Howe, might be about to vanish down the rabbit hole of her criminal prosecution without telling her story to an audience wide enough to trigger a reckoning for the bombing.

⅄

Still, for J.D., there was one upside to the moment. Following his cameo role in the McVeigh confession story, the national news media finally woke up to his reporting on the bombing case, vaulting him from obscurity into his fifteen minutes of fame.

J.D. Cash was the talk of the town in *The New Yorker* that spring of 1997. *The Wall Street Journal* featured him in a front-page story about his unlikely collaboration with Glenn Wilburn. *Newsday* published a profile of J.D. by a writer who coincidentally journeyed from New York back to his hometown, Idabel, to report the story. In Washington, DC, JFK Jr.'s *George* magazine and *The Washington Post* grappled with the paradox of a journalist labeled a conspiracy theorist who reported so much that was true.

On March 25, a month after *The Dallas Morning News* story broke, Bruce Willingham reflected on his maverick reporter's newfound fame. *Good Morning America* and *Newsday* were in town that day to interview J.D. A BBC reporter from London called for directions to Idabel for his TV crew. An Arkansas woman arrived by car, delivering a bouquet of tulips for J.D. The reporter's role in the McVeigh confession story had finally delivered the recognition that had eluded him for nearly two years.

For a story in the next day's *Gazette*, Willingham ticked off J.D.'s greatest hits, including the Carol Howe interview; Jennifer McVeigh's admission to the FBI that she helped her brother launder bank robbery money; McVeigh's visit to Lady Godiva's night club with Strassmeir, a third man, and at least one Ryder truck eleven days before the bombing; and McVeigh's phone call to Strassmeir at Elohim City two days before the blast.

The harshest criticism of J.D. Cash by fellow journalists involved his cozy relations with extremists in the militant wing of the white separatist movement. J.D. wrote about the bombing investigation for *Jubilee* magazine and even gave a speech at a 1996 magazine event two months after his exclusive prison interview with McVeigh. There J.D. delivered cringeworthy praise: "I have never met a young man that I have such positive feelings for as I did for Tim McVeigh."[118]

To the *Newsday* reporter, J.D. was unapologetic about his methods. "In my dealings with the people I think are involved in the bombing, I've used hidden wires, I have played to their beliefs," J.D. said. "I have used the contacts I have in the neo-Nazi movement." He added: "Clearly when you are dealing with people at Elohim City, which is almost a mind-control atmosphere under the Millar family, it is excruciating. Oftentimes, I go out there and spend eight hours and get one sentence of what I thought was the truth."

The lady from Arkansas who came bearing tulips didn't need convincing. "If you ever need any patriotic help, call me," she offered. As *Newsday* reported, J.D. thanked her, quipping, "You're the first lady to bring me flowers," and adding, "That's our job, to watch the government."

Soon, however, the reporter would be mostly watching from the sidelines as the government told the American public a story of good and evil that J.D. believed to be anything but patriotic. As March turned to April of 1997, the preliminaries were over. The stage was set for the bombing trial, which would take place some 700 miles from the scene of the crime because of the change of venue Timothy McVeigh's lawyer had won.

⅄

Compared to the O. J. Simpson trial in Los Angeles, which had transfixed the nation in 1995, the McVeigh trial was far quieter. Despite the horrific toll of lives he stood accused of taking, McVeigh wasn't a celebrity. Newsmagazines didn't put the opening of his trial on their covers, and there were no cameras in Denver's Federal District Court. Presiding Judge Richard P. Matsch strove to avoid a media circus, even ordering a wall constructed to hide the jury from news media in the courtroom.[119]

However, if decorum and order ruled there, behind the scenes, drama and chaos swirled. On April 24, 1997, the day the bombing trial opened in Denver, one such offstage drama unfolded in Carol Howe's Oklahoma trial. A closed-door pretrial hearing that day in Tulsa in Howe's prosecution on terror and weapons charges might make or break Stephen Jones's plan to bring Howe as a witness in McVeigh's trial.

At stake in the Tulsa hearing was the government's control over the reports Howe had filed with her ATF handlers while on her spy mission in Elohim City. Howe's attorney, Clark Brewster, sought permission from US District Judge Michael Burrage to obtain copies of those reports. The government wanted the court to keep them sealed.

Behind closed doors, with a court stenographer taking it all down, the unauthorized story of the Elohim City bomb plot spilled out to the handful of participants in the Tulsa hearing. On the witness stand was the story's most unimpeachable source yet: Carol Howe's ATF handler, Angela Finley—now using her new married name, Finley-Graham—answering questions to help the judge decide the records dispute.

Under skillful prodding by Howe's lawyer, Brewster, Finley-Graham confirmed that Howe had spied for the ATF on Mahon, Strassmeir, and others in Elohim City in the months before the bombing. The agent also confirmed that Howe reported to her as many as seventy times and that after the blast, Finley-Graham dispatched Howe back to Elohim City to look for bombing suspects and clues.

Attorney Brewster made sure to zero in on Andreas Strassmeir, which sometimes caused his uncomfortable witness Finley-Graham to squirm:

> Q: Now, you were interested in knowing as much as you could about Mr. Strassmeir, weren't you?
>
> A: Yes
>
> Q: And what kind of guns he had?
>
> A: Yes.
>
> Q: And the kind of threats he made about—to blow up Federal buildings? You were interested in that, weren't you?
>
> A: I was interested in anything I could find out about any violation.
>
> Q: And Ms. Howe told you about Mr. Strassmeir's threats to blow up Federal buildings, didn't she?
>
> A: In general, yes.
>
> Q: And that was before the Oklahoma City bombing?
>
> A: Yes.
>
> Q: Now, Ms. Howe actually took some of these people from Elohim City at your direction to Oklahoma City, didn't she?
>
> A: She went with them. I don't know if she—she probably did drive.

When it came time to debate the central issue—access to Howe's ATF files—the hearing took a notable turn. The government's attorney adamantly opposed giving Howe access to the files, not because of her case but because of the McVeigh trial. "I'm sorely afraid that they may be acting consciously or unconsciously as a stalking horse for the defense in the trial in Denver," the government's lawyer told the judge.

Surprisingly, this argument won the day. Judge Burrage, who earlier had wondered aloud why the ATF needed to keep the files from a closed surveillance operation secret, now pivoted toward the prosecution:

> THE COURT: A lot of this makes for good conversation, like the trip to Oklahoma City, you know, before the bombing and so forth, and it makes for sensationalism, and I don't know that it really has anything to do with the Oklahoma City bombing, but I saw where you were coming from. With that McVeigh trial going on, I don't want anything getting out of here that would compromise that trial in any way.
>
> MR. BREWSTER: What do you mean by compromise? Do you mean shared with the McVeigh lawyers?
>
> THE COURT: Yes, or something that would come up—you know, we have got evidence that the ATF took a trip with somebody that said buildings were going to be blown up in Oklahoma City before it was blown up or something of that nature and try to connect it to McVeigh in some way or something.

Attorney Brewster made one more effort. He acknowledged knowing that the McVeigh defense team hoped to call his client as a witness. He repeated his promise not to share files with them. In closing, though, the lawyer diplomatically registered his profound dissent from the lack of transparency the government was asking the court to approve:

> MR. BREWSTER: Your Honor, I'm kind of a believer in that the cross-examination method really works in a courtroom, and if there is anything in those documents—well, if Your Honor tells me not to share them with those lawyers, that's fine. I'm interested in one person in this courtroom, and that's Ms. Howe, but if there is a document in there that would tend to suggest that someone is not telling the truth or tend to suggest that there is something more than just Mr. McVeigh being the person that blew up the Oklahoma City Federal Building, I think that would be good to have in their hands because then they could prove the truth. So, I'm a great believer—I don't think it really causes confusion as much as it spreads light.

Brewster's argument failed. Judge Burrage ordered Howe's ATF reports and even the hearing's transcript sealed. Months later, on July 22, 1997, after the transcript was unsealed, J.D. Cash would finally report on the hearing, but by then, Timothy McVeigh's trial was over.

⅄

The *United States v. McVeigh* trial lasted thirty-six days and produced few surprises. In presenting the government's case, Joseph Hartzler's team of federal prosecutors would boil down 25,000 FBI witness interviews, 100,000 pieces of evidence, more than

500 audio and videocassettes, 30,000 photos, and 160,000 documents into a radically streamlined case.[120] They were not aiming for "Trial of the Century" status. They wanted a conviction. According to the Associated Press, most of the jury pool were white and well-educated, with ties to the military. "They said they believed in God, family and the justice system, but distrusted big government and the news media," the AP reported.[121]

Emotions ran high throughout the trial as prosecutors wove the agony of hundreds of bombing victims and their families into the testimony and frequently circled back to the trial's central storyline of raw grief, injury, and irreparable loss.

Michael and Lori Fortier, star witnesses against McVeigh, held up well, even under harsh cross-examination. They had every incentive to do so: total immunity for her and a lenient plea deal for him. The Fortiers came to court with makeovers transforming their scruffy appearances as drug-using hippies into freshly scrubbed, clean-cut yuppies.

They told of McVeigh's rage against the government for the Waco massacre and of how he confided incriminating details of his plot, even arranging soup cans on their kitchen floor in Kingman, Arizona, in the same configuration as the plastic drums he planned to use for his crime. The Fortiers admitted that they had helped McVeigh wrap blasting caps in Christmas paper and that Lori helped him create a fake Robert Kling driver's license using her iron.[122]

Covering the trial for the *Gazette*, J.D. Cash noted the fury in the courtroom following Lori Fortier's testimony. "I want the (expletive) to die," said a woman whose relative had been killed in the blast. "She is guilty of murder! I want her (expletive) hung!" another woman told J.D.

The third key witness for the prosecution, McVeigh's sister Jennifer, also testified under a grant of immunity. She confirmed receiving letters from her brother revealing his anti-government rage. She verified a letter he wrote on her computer referring to the ATF as "tyrants" for its actions in Waco. "Die, you spineless cowardice [*sic*] bastards," the file read. Recalling her interrogation after the bombing, Jennifer broke down while testifying that prosecutors showed her a federal treason statute and threatened to charge her under it.

Stephen Jones had anticipated hundreds of witnesses, but the prosecution case only lasted twenty-three days. In his memoir of the case, *Others Unknown*, Jones recounted with a mixture of admiration and blame the prosecution's radically truncated witness list—141 compared with the 327 witnesses Jones was expecting.[123]

To persuade the jury of the twin foundations of their case, that McVeigh rented the Ryder truck and delivered the bomb by himself, prosecutors surgically excised dozens of eyewitnesses. They didn't call people who saw McVeigh in the company of John Doe 2 to the stand. They didn't call witnesses who saw a Ryder truck at the Dreamland motel or Geary Lake State Park before the bomb truck was rented or others who saw a second Ryder truck.

Prosecutors did not call Tom Kessinger or Vicki Beemer from Elliott's Body Shop; Lea McGown, proprietor of the Dreamland motel; Jeff Davis, the deliveryman from the Chinese restaurant; or dozens more eyewitnesses in Kansas, on the road to Oklahoma City, or along the downtown route to the Murrah Building.

"It was daring, it was high-risk," Jones wrote in his book. "Who would ever have guessed that a case, already highly circumstantial, in which the federal government was asking the death penalty, would leave the jury *without a single witness* to Tim McVeigh's whereabouts between Junction City, Kansas, on Monday, April 17, and Perry, Oklahoma, at 10:30 AM on April 19?"[124]

⅄

When the defense opened its case on May 22, 1997, Stephen Jones leaned into the evidence of a broader bombing conspiracy. It was a challenging task targeting suspects who were nowhere to be found. Still, Jones got off to a strong start with testimony about the unidentified severed leg recovered from the Murrah Building rubble that was never matched to any known bombing victim.

That mystery had continued unfolding since August 1995, when Oklahoma's medical examiner, Dr. Fred Jordan, announced that the leg appeared to belong to an unknown victim. Further investigation revealed that 21-year-old Lakesha Levy, an Air Force airman first class killed in the bombing, had been buried with a left leg belonging to someone else.

Even exhuming Levy's body and retrieving the unknown leg did not solve the mystery, however. For decades, journalists and bombing survivors have unsuccessfully sought access from the FBI and Oklahoma authorities to a DNA sample from the leg which they believe could identify one of Timothy McVeigh's terrorist accomplices through genetic research. Privacy policies have so far blocked those efforts.

Stephen Jones launched the long-running forensic investigation into the leg's identity when he flew to Europe in the spring of 1996 with a locked briefcase containing postmortem photos of all the bombing victims. Memorably, Jones made the transatlantic flight with the briefcase handcuffed to his wrist and a court order to protect the evidence he would present to Northern Ireland's former chief medical examiner, Dr. Thomas K. Marshall.

On the stand a year later in the McVeigh trial, with experience autopsying 200 bombing victims of terror attacks in Ireland, Dr. Marshall was persuasive. "This is an extra left leg," he testified. "Until shown otherwise, this must be a 169th victim." Further, Dr. Marshall offered his opinion that the limb might have belonged to a bomber who stood so close to the Ryder truck as to have been vaporized except for his leg.

On redirect examination, the pathologist left a lasting impression when asked if the leg might have belonged to an innocent passerby. "When nobody misses them, it reinforces the suggestion that the deceased was involved in the bombing," Dr. Marshall testified.

With seeds of doubt planted, the defense turned to two eyewitnesses prosecutors had not called. Jeff Davis delivered an order of Chinese food in the name "Kling" to room 25 of the Dreamland motel on April 17, 1995, hours after the rental of the bomb truck. Under dogged cross-examination by a prosecutor, Davis stuck by the story he had told for two years: The man in room 25 who paid for the moo-goo gai pan was not Timothy McVeigh.[125]

Vicki Beemer from Elliott's Body Shop also testified for the defense. Despite standing at the counter across from the man calling himself Robert Kling and processing his paperwork, Beemer could not identify Timothy McVeigh as the man who rented the bomb truck. Beemer confirmed that she told the FBI that the man, who called himself Robert Kling, stood five feet, ten inches tall, nowhere near Timothy McVeigh's height of six feet, two inches. As for John Doe 2, Beemer was sure he was there: "There were two men present who came in that afternoon to rent the truck," she testified.[126]

However, another witness who was supposed to flesh out the John Doe 2 narrative hurt the defense instead. Daina Bradley, the only eyewitness to the delivery of the bomb to testify, was the young mother who had been people watching, in her words, from the Social Security office on the ground floor of the Murrah Building when the bomb exploded. It killed Bradley's two toddlers and her mother and trapped her in the rubble underneath a heavy construction beam. That night, Bradley became one of the last victims to emerge alive, but only after a doctor had to amputate her leg without anesthesia to pull her out.

From her hospital bed, and then consistently until the trial, Bradley told what she saw through the Murrah Building window: an olive-skinned man wearing a baseball hat with wings on the sides. She said he had exited the passenger side of the Ryder truck and walked quickly away from the vehicle right before the blast. She told the FBI that the man she saw resembled the John Doe 2 poster. But now, in one of the most dramatic moments of the trial, the young woman wobbled in her testimony.[127]

Under cross-examination, Bradley testified that she saw two men exit the bomb truck, not one as she had previously recalled. In another shift, she now agreed that the suspect driving the truck could have been Timothy McVeigh. Bradley's admission of mental health issues in her past didn't enhance her credibility. Her flawed testimony of the Ryder truck facing the wrong way on the one-way street in front of the Murrah Building was a well-executed trap by the prosecution, and it worked.[128]

Time was running out for the McVeigh defense. With every witness who stepped off the stand, the trial sped toward its irrevocable end. For those in the defense team's orbit, suspense was building by the hour for the arrival of the one witness who could change everything. Finally, on Sunday, May 25, 1997, over a working brunch, attorneys Stephen Jones and Clark Brewster agreed on the ground rules for Carol Howe to testify without breaking any restrictions placed on her by her criminal case.

Among the documents that Brewster handed to Jones that day was a note in Angela Finley-Graham's handwriting that revealed just how deep Dennis Mahon's expertise with explosives went. According to this evidence, which Jones was seeing for the first time, Howe had told Finley-Graham that Mahon once used a 500-pound ammonium nitrate bomb to blow up a truck in Michigan.

Another piece of evidence Jones saw for the first time revealed the ATF's February 1995 discovery of the FBI's investigation in Elohim City. What exactly was this FBI investigation? Who were its sources? What did it reveal? At this late date, answers to most or all of these vital questions were unknown, as they still are today.

Nonetheless, the race to go public with the informant's story was on—again. Tapped by Jones to write the first draft of the formal "proffer" for Judge Matsch, Roger Charles returned to Jones's offices from the brunch. For the rest of the day, he drafted the document previewing what Carol Howe would say under oath for the judge.

"She will confirm that, as stated in the indictment of Mr. McVeigh and his codefendant, there truly were "others unknown" involved in different aspects of the broader conspiracy that planned, supported, and conducted the bombing of the Alfred P. Murrah Federal Building," the proffer stated. "She will attach names and faces to some of these 'others unknown,' and she will do so with credible testimony that is supported by voluminous documentation."[129]

Two days later, on Tuesday, May 27, all the pieces were in place for a grand courtroom finale. The beautiful mystery witness was closeted somewhere in the Denver area, ready to make her dramatic entrance after being flown from Oklahoma in shackles aboard a Learjet and guarded by deputy US marshals. But the fate of Howe's testimony was still up in the air at an 8:00 a.m. hearing before Judge Matsch.

In his book, Stephen Jones recounted the closed-door hearing, in which the judge pressed Jones for proof of the guilt of the Elohim City suspects Howe would accuse. For his part, Jones believed he had offered as much evidence against the alleged Elohim City conspirators as the government had brought against McVeigh in its mammoth investigation. But the judge remained unpersuaded. Behind the scenes, behind closed doors, where so much of the real story of the bomb plot still lay hidden, Judge Matsch wasn't going to trust the jury or the American public with Carol Howe's explosive testimony. He made a ruling that would decide the trial.

Jones recalled the moment:

> Suddenly, I realized what was coming. It was devastating. Two years of effort, of expense, of struggle to get information, evidence, were about to be brushed away by the flick of a hand.
>
> "Well," Judge Matsch said, "we've had a number of disclosures concerning Mahon, Strassmeir, Elohim City, and now some additional information from Carol Howe. But my ruling is that it's excluded, not sufficiently relevant to be admissible."[130]

That one phrase, "not sufficiently relevant," was the only explanation the judge would ever give for his decision. Outside the courtroom, to reporters, Howe's attorney Brewster said he guessed that the judge believed her testimony "might have confused the jury." In the *Gazette* on May 29, J.D. wrote: "Legal analysts around the country were quoted in the aftermath of the shocking decision, calling Matsch's ruling totally wrong and saying it likely laid the foundation for a new trial should McVeigh be convicted."

When the trial resumed, testimony by FBI whistleblower Frederic Whitehurst about the likely contamination of physical evidence from McVeigh's clothing couldn't make up for the loss of Jones's star witness. Neither could the audiotapes Jones played in the courtroom from the FBI wiretap of Michael Fortier's Kingman home. They featured Fortier bragging that he would make money off the tragedy. "I'll do some talk shows because I can tell a tale.... I've found my calling 'cause I can tell a story."[131] Jones rested his case the day after the judge barred Carol Howe as a witness.

McVeigh hadn't testified, and his lawyers had offered no alibi to support his not-guilty plea. On June 2, 1997, to no one's surprise, the jury convicted him. In the dirge-like death penalty hearing that followed, laying bare again the wounds inflicted on the dead and their families, his legal team had to reverse course awkwardly, admit that he committed the crime, and plead that he was politically motivated. It was a doomed effort.

"The jury recommends that the defendant Timothy J. McVeigh shall be sentenced to death," Judge Matsch told the hushed courtroom on June 13, 1997. *The Washington Post* reported that McVeigh appeared unshaken, mouthing the words "it's okay" to his family and giving a wave and a nod to the jury as bailiffs escorted him out of the courtroom.[132] Justice was served.

Or was it? Roger Charles was heading home again, knowing that the questions he and J.D. Cash had helped uncover in Denver would soon wake him up at 3:00 a.m. A political scandal was buried inside Elohim City. Roger was sure of that now. He and J.D. had gotten a piece of it but didn't get it all. That was going to be hard to live with.

CHAPTER 9

LABYRINTH

Maybe the millennium, with its alchemy of cultural change, had something to do with the message from federal death row that Timothy McVeigh sent Jesse Trentadue in the year 2000. Or maybe it was folklore justice, which pledges that "murder will out." If not through some higher power, the message from McVeigh, of all people, that began to unravel the mystery of Kenneth's death for Jesse is hard to explain.

Most of America's prison inmates probably didn't need trials, investigations, or hearings to tell them what happened to Kenneth Trentadue. It was a bloodbath in cell 709A of the Federal Transfer Center, and it hit too close to home no matter where prisoners were confined. "Getting Trentadued" caught on as slang for every inmate's worst nightmare: a sudden invasion into a prisoner's cell by a SWAT team in the dead of night, flashes of batons and boots, overpowering violence, no help coming, and then the darkest of endings: a beaten dog's death at the hands of strangers in uniform.

The news of Kenneth Trentadue's murder spread widely through America's vast prison population and beyond. *Prison Legal News*, the nation's longest-running newspaper written for and by prisoners, covered the Trentadue family's civil lawsuit challenging suicide as his cause of death for almost a decade. Amnesty International wrote Attorney General Janet Reno to express concern that an independent forensic pathologist it asked to review Kenneth's autopsy had concluded that his many injuries "very strongly suggest the use of physical force against him." Amnesty's regional program director added: "[W]e believe that the very serious questions raised by this case require the most thorough investigation."

Within months of Kenneth's death, that belief brought a brilliant, unconventional ally to Jesse's cause. Notorious prison inmate David Paul Hammer had earned his reputation as a criminal mastermind through a series of dazzling con jobs, hostage-taking, and prison escapes. According to one published account, Hammer was a model for Hannibal Lecter in *The Silence of the Lambs*,[133] though he took offense when I asked him about that.

Hammer first read about Kenneth's death in the *Spotlight* newspaper, the same publication from which McVeigh had purchased the phone card that would eventually lead to his conviction in the bombing case. Captivated, Hammer called Jesse from a federal prison in Pennsylvania, where he was serving three consecutive *400-year* sentences. "But I can cut that in half with good behavior," Hammer quipped with his deadpan humor, which endeared this criminal to many supporters of his various benevolent causes over the years.

Even when committing crimes, Hammer operated with flair, as when he obtained a minister's license to raise money for his "church," contracted a helicopter company to fly Santa Claus into a shopping mall and then absconded with the money or stole the warden's credit card number and used it to send flowers to the prison secretaries—or so he said.

Two Catholic nuns became Hammer's spiritual advisers on death row, and he devoted himself to their benevolent causes from his prison cell, creating artwork for their charitable holiday cards and helping to raise $92,000 for poor, at-risk children like himself. Still, there is no denying the depravity of Hammer's criminal violence. He committed armed robbery, kidnapping, and hostage-taking, and he strangled two fellow inmates. One of his former prosecutors called him "a classical con man, second rate killer and an awful human being."

In prison, Hammer was known as a jailhouse advocate, helping other inmates pursue their legal rights. The high-profile Kenneth Trentadue case was a natural for Hammer, and he had information to offer Jesse. During a recent transfer between prisons, he had spent time on the same cellblock where Kenneth died. Hammer told Jesse he was sure the prison's suicide scenario was bogus. "Your brother couldn't have strung himself up using that air vent," Hammer declared. "The ceilings in those cells are twelve feet high. There's no way he could have climbed up there."[134] Sure enough, an inspection of the air vent revealed no fingerprints or blood on the air vent—only dust.[135]

David Hammer became Jesse's inside man on prison logistics during the preparation for the Trentadue family's wrongful death case. This inmate, with time on his hands, had spent most of his forty-some years inside prisons, beginning at age nineteen. He knew the system and its players, down to critical details about where and how the prison kept video surveillance records and prisoner movement logbooks. From his very different station in life, Hammer saw Kenneth's case much the way Senator Orrin Hatch did from Capitol Hill: as a probable murder and cover-up.

Hammer never veered from his belief, and nothing would please him more than to help Jesse prove it.

Meanwhile, by 1998, the story of Jesse's quest to find his brother's killers had gathered a devoted prison following nationwide. For once, inmates were on the righteous side of a popular cause. They were rooting for Kenneth's champion, a man who was their champion too. Among those following Jesse's campaign was Timothy McVeigh, whose next stop after his trial on the way to execution was the federal supermax prison in Florence, Colorado.

McVeigh's neighbors on a cellblock nicknamed "Bomber's Row" were Unabomber Ted Kaczynski and 1993 World Trade Center bomber Ramzi Yousef. With plenty of time to read, it was probably in solitary confinement in Colorado that McVeigh learned of the controversy surrounding Kenneth's death. In February 1998, McVeigh wrote journalist Phil Bacharach a letter, published in *Esquire* in June 2015 and excerpted here:

> Hey Phil,
>
> Clearly, the BOP and DOJ are covering up. Murder? Well, that is only inferred because of the obvious cover-up—but there's really no other reason for such an effort, is there?
>
> I think that the Trentadue family is learning something I've seen for a long time: There is no justice when the government is asked to police their own.... I refer you to (a vaguely recalled) opinion by a DC court recently: "Government officials never seem to learn that the cover-up is oftentimes worse than the underlying conduct."
>
> Regarding all these "camera malfunctions," amazing coincidence, huh? Personally, I have a camera in my cell (which is said to be "for my own protection"), even

> though the hall outside my cell is watched by "crisscrossing" cameras on either end.
>
> With all these systems, I have no doubt that, were I ever killed (not suggesting such an atmosphere exists, but there's always a "renegade" in every crowd) there would be a system-wide "malfunction" that day.
>
> To tell me that they videotaped the Trentadue scene, but there was a "camera malfunction" defies belief.

The summer of 1998 brought a fateful crossing of paths between McVeigh and Hammer. Since volunteering to help Jesse, Hammer had received the death penalty for murdering a cellmate, which led to his transfer to McVeigh's prison in Colorado. From there, in July 1999, Hammer and McVeigh were both transported to Indiana as members of the "Terre Haute Twenty," the first inmates on America's newly designated federal death row.

In his 2010 prison memoir *Deadly Secrets,* Hammer wrote about the wisecracking that lightened the tension and launched his prickly friendship with McVeigh the day they met. On July 13, 1999, they boarded a US Marshals Service "Con Air" plane to fly to their new prison. "Hey Hammer, I hear you're from Oklahoma," McVeigh yelled from a distance. When Hammer yelled back that he was, McVeigh replied, "Hope there are no hard feelings."

Later, as they awaited processing in a holding cell in Terre Haute, Indiana, the prisoners passed the time musing about the death penalty. Pressed by Hammer for his thoughts, McVeigh quipped: "All I have to say is that the official score is 168 to 1. I'm up." Hammer had the last word this time: "Huh, well, I guess they can't kill you more than once."

After getting acquainted, Hammer showed McVeigh the file he had compiled on the Trentadue case. McVeigh knew of the case, but it may have been his first close look at Kenneth's photograph. Hammer showed McVeigh the pictures the Trentadue family had taken of Kenneth at the funeral home. "The first time I saw a picture of Trentadue and learned of his death, I knew instantly that someone thought he was Richard Guthrie," Hammer would quote McVeigh as saying in *Deadly Secrets*.

As Hammer already knew from McVeigh, Guthrie was the coleader of the Aryan Republican Army gang. But McVeigh had disclosed more to Hammer, telling him that Guthrie was one of McVeigh's accomplices on the bombing run. That connection made McVeigh's new piece to the puzzle unique. McVeigh was strongly hinting to Hammer that Richard Guthrie was John Doe 2, the terrorist suspect who rode beside him in the Ryder truck on April 19, 1995.

Their exchange in the prison recreation yard possessed almost surreal millennial potential. Two notorious death row criminals were collaborating in crime solving at a high level, a pastime that was about to break out as a cultural phenomenon when CBS launched its TV crime drama *CSI* later that year. Even on federal death row, America was morphing into a nation of armchair murder sleuths who soon would know the ins and outs of forensic science from ballistics to bones.

McVeigh asked Hammer to pass his information about Guthrie along to Jesse, which Hammer was glad to do. In January 2000, he phoned Jesse, filling him in on the Aryan Republican Army, its bank robbery spree, and its notorious leader Richard Guthrie, whose name meant nothing to Jesse—not yet. There might be a lot to unpack here. However, Timothy McVeigh, as a source, was ridiculously compromised: a compulsive liar with a solid motive to undermine federal law enforcement authorities. Jesse thanked Hammer and set the lead aside.

Jesse was now engaged in an all-consuming *CSI* mission of his own. The Trentadue family's wrongful death trial would begin later that year, in November 2000. Jesse's trial preparation had armed him with a prodigious amount of forensic knowledge about the dark art of murder. Wasn't scientific certainty what made forensics such a powerful courtroom weapon? Jesse intended to use forensic science to attack what he believed was political manipulation behind the federal grand jury's decision in 1997 not to bring criminal charges in Kenneth's death.

An investigative diary Jesse kept from the day Kenneth died until 2003 records his investigation of the physical evidence in the case, starting with the same telltale clue that first caught Timothy McVeigh's attention: the crime scene videotape.[136] While Kenneth's death was under multiple investigations—by the prison, the FBI, the medical examiner, the Oklahoma City Police Department, the federal grand jury, the Oklahoma County district attorney, the inspector general, and Congress—the videotape and photos of the death scene mysteriously disappeared, then reappeared in dizzying fashion. Yet the result seemed methodical. The story the crime scene images told investigators, especially grand jurors weighing criminal charges, was always incomplete. They were never allowed to see the whole picture.

The first entry in Jesse's diary, for August 21, 1995, covers the video and photos. Three different guards videotaped and photographed the death scene. The video camera supposedly documented Kenneth hanging from a ceiling vent in his cell, his feet suspended (in a physics-defying scenario) above the level of a wall-mounted sink from which he supposedly jumped to hang himself. The camera also supposedly documented two other guards cutting Kenneth down. However, according to the Bureau of Prisons, the guard's camera malfunctioned, producing only two-to-three seconds of forensically useless footage.[137]

Compounding the damage caused by the incomplete video footage, all the Polaroid photographs, all the film negatives, and half of the 35mm photos of the death scene went missing the morning Kenneth's body was discovered in his cell.

With such scant visual evidence, the federal grand jury relied on the word of prison guard Roger Groover, who shot the video, to understand how Kenneth died. Undoubtedly, the guard's sworn testimony that he videotaped Kenneth hanging and the guards cutting him down figured heavily in the grand jury's decision to accept the suicide scenario and not indict anyone for a crime.

But the guard's story wasn't true, as Jesse's investigation for the wrongful death trial would reveal. Here is guard Groover's U-turn in his trial testimony on November 16, 2000:[138]

> Q: Mr. Groover, you testified under oath before the Federal Grand Jury, you testified under oath before the Office of Inspector General, and you testified under oath in the BOP Affidavit that you saw Mr. Trentadue hanging, correct?
>
> A: Yes...
>
> Q: Then, on August 21, 1995, did you see Kenneth Trentadue hanging in that cell?
>
> A: No...

Q: Mr. Groover, you never videotaped Kenneth Trentadue hanging, correct?

A: Correct. I did not videotape Trentadue hanging.

Q: Because you never saw Kenneth Trentadue hanging, correct?

A: I did not see Trentadue hanging.

This testimony was astounding. The guard had lied. The grand jury had believed him and believed that Kenneth hanged himself.

There was more to the story of this videotape, as Jesse's diary reveals on October 5, 1997, four days *before* the announcement of the grand jury's decision not to indict anyone. That day, FBI attorney Kathleen Timmons, chief of the bureau's Color of Law Unit in Washington, DC, wrote a memo to her FBI superiors. In it, she revealed that she had viewed the supposedly nearly blank videotape but discovered that, to the contrary, it was loaded with incriminating footage. Jesse's diary quotes from Timmons's memo:

> There is a potential perjury issue regarding a Bureau of Prisons paramedic who indicated he administered CPR [cardiopulmonary resuscitation] to the deceased Trentadue, and the evidence of a videotape does not indicate CPR was administered.[139]

Again, astounding. The memo reveals that the videotape existed, and it recorded an entirely different death scenario from the one the grand jury relied on. The FBI lawyer's memo also reveals that the FBI knew about this other copy of the videotape in time to correct the grand jury's course, which the DOJ would not announce publicly for four more days, on October 9, 1997.

The videotape continued to concern Timmons. Jesse's diary reports that she followed up with another memo to her superiors, worrying that the prison paramedic on duty might face state criminal charges because of the "lack of efforts to resuscitate the victim who was left hanging for an extended period after being found."[140]

Undoubtedly, the filing of state charges would have reflected adversely on the FBI. But the lawyer's memo begs another question by omission: Why wasn't the paramedic facing federal charges? Who was looking out for justice for the prisoner in federal custody left to die without CPR?

No one has ever shared how, when, or from whom the FBI lawyer obtained this crime scene videotape that Kenneth's grand jury never saw or what happened to the tape next. The paper trail ends with lawyer Timmons at FBI headquarters in Washington. However, one more glaring irregularity involving this problematic video shot by guard Roger Groover was still to come.

By 1999, the Justice Department's Office of the Inspector General (OIG) was conducting its review of the grand jury's decision. In June of that year, the OIG retained forensic video expert Norman Perle, well-known from the Rodney King police brutality case in Los Angeles, to examine the videotape. Their response shocked Perle when he previewed his findings, telling OIG investigators the video had been tampered with and erased. They suddenly took back the tape, terminated Perle's work on the project, and switched to a new expert.[141]

Sometime later, while Jesse was preparing for the wrongful death trial, Norman Perle called him and recounted his strange, aborted analysis for the OIG. Nothing like that had happened in his career, and it still upset him. Perle offered to testify at the trial and, undoubtedly, would have made a compelling witness if he had lived to tell his story. Tragically, Norman Perle, age sixty-two, died of unknown causes in a hotel in Monterey, California, while on a business trip in February 2000. As a result, the highly doubtful story of the malfunctioning video camera would stand unopposed at Jesse's trial.

⅄

The missing crime scene photographs were another crippling loss. The original Polaroid and 35mm photos documented the "bloodbath" described by the inmate eyewitness who mopped up the death cell. They also documented the impact of the baton and boot marks on the walls and floor of Kenneth's cell, and his bloody handprint on the wall, described by witnesses, as he reached for the panic button. All that horror was hidden from view when the originals went missing.

Also missing: 35mm negatives depicting the suicide note Kenneth supposedly wrote on his cell wall in pencil. The note reportedly read: "My mind is no longer its friend." This writing on the wall became another deep forensic controversy in the case. Without negatives to enlarge to show detail, the FBI crime lab couldn't establish whether the handwriting was Kenneth's, a supposition Jesse flatly rejected.

Early on, prison investigators reported that the note on the wall was signed "Love Paul." However, the medical examiner's chief investigator, Kevin Rowland, saw the note before the prison painted it over, ignoring his instruction to have the FBI analyze the handwriting first. Rowland reported that the note was signed "Tom Linx."[142]

The Office of the Inspector General's examination turned in a different direction after the disclosure that Kenneth hadn't used the alias Vance Paul Brockway—the only possible rationale for him to sign the suicide note "Paul"—since the 1980s. Supposedly based on new handwriting samples provided by the Trentadue family, the OIG now reported that the suicide note was signed not "Love Paul," but "Love ya familia," possibly a farewell to Kenneth's Hispanic wife, Carmen. Helpfully to the new finding, the OIG now concluded that the handwriting—which the FBI crime lab had previously said could probably never be identified—positively matched Kenneth's. One thing was clear: Forensic science wasn't always infallible as practiced in the Trentadue case.

The questionable handwriting evidence had a profound impact. In July 1998, the medical examiner, Dr. Fred Jordan, finally changed Kenneth's official cause of death from "unknown" to "suicide," saying that the note on the wall weighed heavily on his change of mind.

Dr. Jordan said the other game changer was the evidence that Kenneth had been alone in his cell and not the victim of an assault by someone else. However, as Jesse's diary reveals, this forensic finding was just as suspect as Kenneth's authorship of the suicide note. The missing crime scene photos could have proven that to the medical examiner and the grand jury.

Blood spatter was by now a flashpoint in the case—a physical marker, if present, of a violent assault on Kenneth inside his solitary confinement cell or an indication, if absent, that he died alone. Without the benefit of seeing the missing Polaroid originals or enlargements, Dr. Jordan and the grand jury didn't see blood spatter, leading them to conclude that Kenneth died alone. Later, however, after the announcement of the grand jury's no-bill decision and after Dr. Jordan changed his ruling, some of the missing original Polaroids would surface. Jesse's April 2, 1998, diary reports what they revealed: "[W]hen the original photographs are enlarged, they show blood spatter in cell 709A."[143]

So, where had the missing pictures been all this time, blinding the grand jury and the medical examiner to crucial forensic evidence? In 1998, while assisting the inspector general's investigation, FBI Special Agent Tom Linn, the lead agent on the Trentadue case, found the missing Polaroid photos in the possession of another FBI lawyer in Washington, DC. Amazingly, this attorney, Rita M. Sampson, was working on the Justice Department's defense against the Trentadue family's lawsuit.[144]

The optics of missing pictures squirreled away at FBI Headquarters in Washington were terrible, conjuring up an obstruction of justice. Still, it might have been even worse for the government at trial time if all the crime scene photos had gone missing for good. Or maybe, as Jesse had come to suspect, someone's single-minded priority in the opposing camp had been to prevent criminal prosecutions in Kenneth's death at all costs. If so, the grand jury's no-bill announcement in October 1997 had, in all probability, accomplished that goal.

Besides, bad optics never seemed to yield consequences. When it mattered most, the FBI demonstrated an almost Houdini-like facility to escape accountability for lost and missing photo evidence. In early 1998, Senate hearings in Washington on Kenneth's death were on the line. That January, three months after the grand jury's no-bill decision, Senator Orin Hatch went on television, telling Fox News that he was "disappointed in the grand jury result" and promising Judiciary Committee hearings because the Trentadue case had the "aroma of cover-up."[145]

In a counter move a week later, however, the bureau dispatched the first of two contingents of FBI agents to Oklahoma City to meet with the state's influential Senator Don Nickles. On January 23, 1998, Nickles, obviously troubled by swirling rumors, asked FBI agents on hand if photographic evidence in the case had been lost. Jesse's diary reports their reply that, "There had been no mishandling or loss of evidence, especially photographic evidence, because 'the Government has possessed and utilized [that photographic evidence] throughout this investigation.'"[146]

⅄

Jesse's forensic discoveries while preparing for the trial extended far beyond the missing pictures and videotape. Delving into the blood evidence, he learned that analysis had revealed stains of two different blood types on Kenneth's bed in the death cell: Kenneth's blood and someone else's. However, the FBI never attempted to identify the second blood sample. The reason given was that "there were no suspects," even though the identities of six guards who worked the afternoon and night shifts on Kenneth's cellblock the day of his death were readily accessible.

From a little-known branch of forensic science, fabric expert J. Douglas Perkins at the Oklahoma State Bureau of Investigation had weighed in with an analysis that undermined a cornerstone of the hanging scenario.[147] The rope around Kenneth's neck had always been a problematic element in the suicide scenario. For one thing, it was beyond belief that Kenneth could have torn a bedsheet into strips and then patiently braided them together into a rope strong enough to hang himself in well under twenty-four minutes. That was all that the timeline allowed for him to accomplish the many steps of self-injury and hanging supposedly involved in his death.

The rope raised other problems. Kenneth's neck measured nineteen inches, but the rope was only twenty-three inches long, leaving only four inches to knot it securely to the ceiling vent. Also, when the FBI crime lab deconstructed the rope, the analysis showed it was woven from only half a bedsheet. No one ever found the other half or explained where it went. No bedsheet fibers were found on Kenneth's body, as they would have been if he'd torn up the sheet to make the ligature.

In the run-up to the trial, Jesse found Perkins's report in the massive pile of evidence the government had turned over to him in discovery. There, he read about the expert's microscopic examination of the rope fibers for the first time. According to Perkins, the noose had never been cut, making it far likelier that someone staged the hanging after strangling Kenneth to death—as his broken hyoid bone and broken blood vessels in his eyes also indicated.[148]

If the hanging was staged, how then did Kenneth die? Perkins's analysis set the stage for a stunning discovery Jesse made among the autopsy photos late in the trial. Surprisingly, in an investigation marked by so many evidentiary zigzags, it would turn out that someone on the medical examiner's team had taken one photograph during the autopsy that might tell the complete story of Kenneth's murder.

The evening before Kevin Rowland, the medical examiner's chief investigator, would testify, he helpfully brought his collection of autopsy photos to a preparation session with Jesse, who had never seen the originals, only degraded copies. One photo in particular stood out, leading Jesse, Rowland, and a pathologist friend who had come to the session to puzzle over its significance.[149]

The photo showed a deep furrow injury around Kenneth's neck, supposedly made by the bedsheet rope, even though fabric expert Perkins disputed this idea. He pointed out that there was no way a rope woven together from these wide, soft fabric strips could make the narrow furrow injury they could see around Kenneth's neck.[150]

While the three men considered what might have caused the distinctive furrow, the visiting pathologist suddenly had an insight. "Here's your answer," he said, pointing to the photo. "Plastic handcuffs." As Jesse looked closer, the visitor pointed out a distinctive pattern of tiny cross-tie impressions in the injury around Kenneth's neck, consistent with the locking mechanism on plastic handcuffs.

There was the answer Jesse had been searching for, right before his eyes. At last, he believed he knew how Kenneth died. If this discovery had been a television drama, it would have set up a grand courtroom reveal, reversing a grievous injustice. But this was the wrong courtroom for that. US District Judge Timothy D. Leonard refused to allow Rowland to link the furrow depicted in the autopsy photo to plastic handcuffs. It was too late in the trial to take that path.

In May 2001, Judge Leonard awarded the Trentadue family a million-dollar judgment for extreme emotional distress.[151] Still, to Jesse's unending fury, that judgment left the stain of suicide on Kenneth's name, probably forever. The civil trial had established that the Department of Justice had concealed a critical videotape and photographs that could have proved Kenneth's murder.

However, none of that mattered to the federal grand jury that never saw the evidence.

"You can rip our hearts out and spit in our faces, but we're not going to quit," Jesse told me, underscoring his family's determination to see justice done for Kenneth, no matter how long it took.

⅄

Jesse emerged from the trial stunned by the two parallel realities of Kenneth's death: one where he hanged himself and the other where he was tortured and murdered. "[But] for the commonality of names and dates, a reasonably intelligent person, having read the OIG Report about the circumstances of my brother's death and attended the trial to hear witnesses testify about my brother's death, would not have recognized that both…concern the same event," Jesse wrote in a letter to Justice Department Inspector General Glenn Fine on April 13, 2001.

Kenneth's case now resembled an X-File as much as it did a homicide file. Jesse's march through the justice system's labyrinth would be done the Marines' way: Never say die. One by one, he intended to hold personally accountable the political heavyweights he believed had turned a blind eye to Kenneth's murder.

Over the next three years, Jesse fired off probing, sometimes accusatory letters, including more than a dozen to the Justice Department's Inspector General Fine in March and April 2001. The autopsy photo from the trial showing Kenneth's neck wound was still tormenting Jesse. He included copies of it with his first letter to the inspector general on April 2. "The red arrow on the 8x10 photocopy points to the tooth or railroad tie marks left by the plastic handcuffs with which my brother was slowly strangled," Jesse explained. "That is right: plastic handcuffs!"

Jesse suspected foul play inside the Justice Department and said so on April 4 in another letter to Inspector General Fine: "Those wide, soft strips of bed sheet...did not produce the handcuff tooth marks in this furrow," Jesse wrote. "But you undoubtedly already knew this, and so did the FBI and the Civil Rights Division attorneys. You all knew this because you had this photograph, whereas my family did not."

If the officials in charge of the several investigations that had led nowhere believed they had discharged their duty, Jesse intended to set them straight. On April 23, 2001, he signed off his final letter to the inspector general with a personal indictment: "The record of corruption, dishonesty, and abuse of power in my brother's case is clear, and someday somebody just may pick up this well-documented trail and follow it right back to you and your staff and put some very hard questions to you," Jesse wrote. "At least that is my hope and why I write these letters."

Jesse's face-off with the inspector general would escalate into a battle royale over the coming years. Meanwhile, the Justice Department's Public Integrity Section (PIS), led by Noel Hillman, reviewed Kenneth's case again. In letters of appeal to Hillman in 2002 and 2003, Jesse bluntly invoked the mission of Hillman's office to expose public corruption, writing on March 17, 2003: "In terms of perjury, subornation of perjury, destruction of evidence, fabrication of evidence and other acts of obstruction of justice by DOJ employees, my brother's case is unequaled in American jurisprudence, which brings me to my final question... [Is] the *PIS* really going to put lipstick on this pig?"

Not that Jesse was letting go of the raft of forensic evidence he had uncovered pointing to Kenneth's murder. A two-and-a-half-page, single-spaced catalog of questions opened that letter to

Hillman and featured enough forensic clues to keep a *CSI* writers' room busy for a season. But Jesse, the lawyer, was shifting gears into deposition mode. He wanted his questions heard for the record, including:

> Why the crime scene was sterilized or cleaned in violation of Oklahoma State Law and federal policy after the medical examiner's investigator had spoken with Acting Warden Carter and told her that he was calling the FBI to process the cell?
>
> Why my brother, who resided in San Diego, whose crimes were committed in San Diego, and who was sentenced in San Diego, was sent to Oklahoma City for a parole revocation hearing when his co-defendant, who had been violated numerous times, had his hearings in San Diego?
>
> Why the DOJ would obtain a Confidentiality-Protective Order to prevent me from going to prosecutors or congressional oversight committees with evidence of crimes committed by DOJ employees?
>
> Why the medical examiner was never told that BOP employees had observed blood spatter and cast off in that cell, which would be indicative of a fight?
>
> Why the DOJ would threaten so many witnesses, both inmates and non-inmates, including the medical examiner?

Hillman's office offered one last path for Kenneth's case to reach the criminal justice system. Maybe this watchdog would finally bark. Jesse grabbed at the chance, and Michael Hubbard, Senator Hatch's former top investigator and Jesse's trusted former Capitol Hill ally, offered to assist. Hubbard, who had been loaned to the Senate Judiciary Committee by the Environmental Protection Agency, had returned to the EPA in 1997 and now was running its criminal office in Boston. But Hubbard had kept up with Jesse's campaign and knew his options were running out.

In 2003, Hubbard contacted Hillman and visited him at his Justice Department office in Washington to discuss Kenneth's case. Hillman had reviewed it and told Hubbard he was "impressed."

"Is there anything we can do here?" Hillman asked Hubbard.

The question was promising enough, but what followed was astonishing. "Everyone knows it was a murder," Hillman said.

With that assessment, the high-ranking Justice Department official seemed to wave off all the investigations, the hundreds of man hours, the millions of dollars spent on the suicide narrative, and the Trentadue family's agony over a colossal miscarriage of justice.

"How can we pursue this?" Hillman asked, adding: "I would like to do it, but I'm hamstrung because [Attorney General] Ashcroft has already published that voluminous report," referring to Inspector General Fine's sealed 1999 review of Kenneth's case.

Still, Hillman was a problem solver and delegator. "I need your help," he told Hubbard.

"It would take subpoenas," Hubbard countered.

"I was federal law enforcement," Hubbard reminded me later. "I had a gun, a badge, and a hard-on for this case. I would have served those subpoenas myself. This was so wrong."

Now, it was Hillman's turn again.

"Can you get Grassley or Orrin Hatch to weigh in?" Hillman asked, referring to Senator Orrin Hatch and Senator Charles Grassley, Hubbard's former bosses on the Senate Judiciary Committee.

Here, as Hubbard well knew, Hillman's trial balloon had reached the end of its brief flight. While Hubbard worked on the Judiciary Committee, Senator Hatch had backed away from hearings on the Trentadue case after Senator Nickles weighed in against them. Grassley wouldn't cross Hatch on an issue that belonged to the chairman.

Hubbard knew that Hillman's idea was dead on arrival and confirmed that assessment later with a senior Grassley staff member. This meeting wouldn't advance Jesse's cause. But more than almost anything said on the record in eight years of wrangling over Kenneth's death, it spoke volumes about the vulnerability of a justice system at the mercy of politics.

"It was so obvious he was murdered, and yet, nothing was ever done," Hubbard told me. "That's what sticks in my craw more than any other case from my time on the Hill."

Sure enough, when public pressure—including blistering letters from Jesse—finally led Hatch to seek accountability on Kenneth's case from FBI Director Robert Mueller in 2003, the senator did so in a whisper, hardly a roar. He handed the FBI director five written questions about the Trentadue case at an oversight hearing before his Judiciary Committee. He even allowed Mueller to reply in writing without the challenge of live or follow-up questions.

Neither Hatch nor Mueller would give Jesse a copy of the questions or, more importantly, Mueller's answers. When Jesse obtained them through a Freedom of Information Act request, they showed that Senator Hatch had given FBI Director Mueller softball questions, inviting him to confidently declare that he was "not aware of any credible evidence" running counter to the finding of suicide in Kenneth's death by multiple authorities, which the senator listed.[152]

⅄

No credible evidence. Coming from the FBI director, that pronouncement had the ring of finality. Yet, the contest wasn't over. Help for Jesse was on the way, but not from the justice system or the watchdog news media that had fallen silent in Kenneth's case. Help would come from a maverick news reporter chasing the colossal, seemingly unrelated story that obsessed him. A television news network had killed it once, and a federal judge had killed it a second time at the trial of Timothy McVeigh.

In the spring of 2003, around the time Senator Hatch and FBI Director Mueller were having their say on Capitol Hill, Jesse's phone rang at his law office in Salt Lake City.

It was J.D. Cash, skipping pleasantries as usual, though the two men had never met.

"Are you sitting down?" J.D. asked.

CHAPTER 10

THE CROSSING

"Do you think he did it alone?" On December 10, 1997, ten months after the network spiked Carol Howe's story, ABC's Diane Sawyer sat down with Howe in an exclusive on-camera interview for its newsmagazine *Primetime Live*. Millions of viewers saw Sawyer ask the former government informant the lone-wolf question about Timothy McVeigh.

"No," Howe replied. She didn't think he acted alone. "Because I know of too many people that were talking about that building, talking about Oklahoma City, talking about doing something on that date using a truck bomb. It cannot be coincidence to use that many specifics."

When asked if she took seriously the Elohim City talk about truck bombs and targets, including Oklahoma City, Howe answered just as firmly, "Oh, they did mean what they were saying. They meant it. I was driving on the highway when I heard it on the radio. The first thing I thought is: 'They did it. This is it. This is the war.'"

In Sawyer's interview, she and Howe talked about Andreas Strassmeir's threats, Dennis Mahon's racist and anti-Semitic slurs, Reverend Millar's alleged preaching about inciting a holy war, and even the day Howe believed she saw Timothy McVeigh with Strassmeir at Elohim City.

So what caused the network's sudden U-turn, allowing the informant to tell her story now? One thing had changed: The jury had convicted Timothy McVeigh. The lone wolf had been captured and locked away awaiting execution. No president, attorney general, newspaper editor, network news anchor, or federal judge would now follow the terrible logic of Howe's words through to its conclusion: If she was telling the truth, terrorists had walked free after the Oklahoma City bombing. However, the influencers who had shaped the narrative had moved on. Carol Howe's story was no longer radioactive.

"And this is one of the most perplexing stories we think you'll ever hear," Sawyer said by way of introducing a report that was more balancing act than bombshell. "There is a question at the center of it," Sawyer added. "Is Carol Howe a very brave informant, betrayed horribly by the US government, or is she a dangerously mixed-up young woman—or both?"

Earlier that day, Howe had testified at Terry Nichols's federal trial to some of what she was telling Sawyer now. Her appearance in the courtroom was another U-turn. Something had changed Judge Matsch's mind from his previous ruling to bar Howe as a witness in McVeigh's trial. Again, the likely X factor was that the lone wolf was gone. But the judge attached a string the size of a rope to that permission. Howe was forbidden to tell the jury that she went to Elohim City as an informant—or about the alarming plans and threats to blow up a federal building in Oklahoma City or Tulsa that she heard there and warned her handler about.

Even without the lone wolf in the courtroom, that story might have been radioactive for the Nichols jury. They convicted him but deadlocked on the death penalty, leading to his sentence of life in prison. Afterward, the jury's members said that they believed there had been others involved in the bombing who were not facing prosecution. The muzzled witness Howe was free to talk but couldn't say anything too alarming or anything that might call the federal government's actions into question.

Roger Charles had graciously returned to the network that had fired him, working on preproduction of the Sawyer interview. For Roger and J.D. Cash, however, the bombing story was a comet trail now, not the comet. With both federal bombing trials over, the *McCurtain Gazette*'s extensive case coverage would naturally wind down, leaving J.D. with a diminished platform. He and Roger were left to watch from the wings.

Luckily, however, or unluckily, depending on your point of view, investigative journalism can be an addiction, capable of eclipsing everyone and everything but the elusive story. The pursuit had become primal. J.D. and Roger had uncovered evidence that government insiders in Washington were not telling the truth about the bombing, not to journalists and not to the public.

Quitting wasn't an option for the journalists despite truth-seeking's occupational hazards. With the bombing case officially closed, J.D. and Roger knew they would have to wear the mantle of conspiracy theorists now, dismissed by other journalists for beliefs so far from the mainstream that they seemed to border on crazy.

⅄

Sitting outside Jesse's law office almost ten years later, listening to J.D. and Roger's story, I felt a keen connection to their journey. I had walked this walk myself long ago. As a rookie journalist, I broke a conspiracy story in Chicago that led to the exoneration of a death row inmate. It was one of the nation's first significant death row innocence cases. The story would trigger a cascade of overturned death sentences in years to come, along with soul-searching over the fairness of our justice system's ultimate punishment.

As managing editor of a tiny legal newspaper in Chicago, I answered a letter from a young death row inmate, a proverbial message in a bottle. Dennis Williams claimed that he was innocent. I admit I had doubts. Friends counseled me to drop this story before it ruined my career prospects. But I couldn't. An almost eerie obsession drove me.

The crime was horrific. Black youths abducted a young white couple at the gas station where the man worked. As the official story went, the abductors took the couple to an abandoned townhouse. They gang raped and shot the woman in a nightmarish thrill killing in a pitch-black room, illuminated only by the flame of a Bic cigarette lighter. Then, they marched the man outside to a creek bank and shot him in the head.

I tracked down a prison inmate who said he knew who the real killers were. My newspaper, *Chicago Lawyer*, published the inmate's account of the crime.[153] My brilliant editor, Rob Warden, broke the case open by demolishing the official story presented to the jury. The manufacturer of the Bic lighter confirmed that it would be way too hot to hold for the duration of the crime. The star witness, who supposedly held the lighter, recanted her testimony.

Over the next decade, everyone involved in the case would learn about the near impossibility of undoing a miscarriage of justice once it's on the books. For the condemned prisoner and

April 19, 1995, 9:02 a.m. A massive explosion tore the front off of Oklahoma City's Federal Building, killing 168 people, including 15 children in their daycare center. The tragedy stands as America's deadliest domestic terror attack.

Two days later, the FBI took 26-year-old Timothy McVeigh, a decorated Gulf War veteran, into custody as the suspected terrorist.

Minutes before the bomb truck's rental, McVeigh was a mile away at McDonalds, wearing different clothes than the man who rented the truck.

Four minutes before the blast, a surveillance camera captured the Ryder bomb truck heading toward the Murrah Building, a half-block away.

Within 90 minutes of the bombing, McVeigh was stopped by an Oklahoma state trooper for driving without a license plate. McVeigh was carrying a .45 caliber Glock, an extra ammo clip, and a knife, but surrendered peacefully when arrested.

Within hours of taking Timothy McVeigh into custody, the FBI arrested his former Army buddy Terry Nichols. In doing so, it exposed an almost mythical accomplice, a killer whose identity remains a mystery.

Nichols was 250 miles away on the day of the bombing, looking nothing like the FBI's sketch of a muscular, tattooed suspect who rode beside McVeigh in the bomb truck. McVeigh was identified as John Doe 1, but who was John Doe 2?

John Doe 1 John Doe 2

Kenneth Trentadue

Jesse Trentadue

On August 21, 1995, three days after a mysterious transfer from a California federal prison to Oklahoma City, parole violator Kenneth Trentadue was found dead in his cell. Mistaken for John Doe 2?

Prison officials declared it suicide by hanging, despite evidence of torture and murder. So began attorney Jesse Trentadue's 30-year quest for justice for his brother.

Oklahoma's J.D. Cash scooped the national news media on the bombing story.

Sources told Cash the reclusive religious compound Elohim City was being used as a paramilitary training camp. McVeigh reportedly visited.

German national Andreas Strassmeir, a weapons trainer, fled the US for Berlin after the bombing.

Months before the bombing, undercover informant Carol Howe warned her ATF handlers of right-wing extremist plans to blow up federal buildings, but they failed to act.

April 19, 1993. Two years to the day before the Oklahoma bombing, the Branch Davidian compound in Waco, Texas, erupted in flames, ending a 51-day siege that claimed 86 lives. Timothy McVeigh had visited the standoff, fueling his anti-government sentiments as part of a growing, nationwide movement against deadly federal overreach.

Timothy McVeigh

Terry Nichols

Richard Guthrie

Roger Moore

On death row in 1999, McVeigh named members of Richard Guthrie's Aryan Republican Army gang as his support squad on April 19, 1995, and fingered one of them as John Doe 2.

At Colorado's supermax federal prison in 2007, Terry Nichols claimed gun dealer Roger Moore was an undercover government operative who supplied McVeigh with explosives.

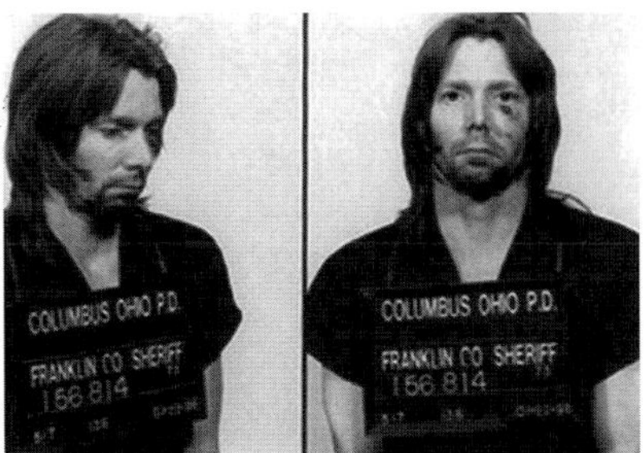

From prison, where the ARA gang's co-leader Peter Langan is serving life, he charged that Washington is covering up the terror gang's ties to the bombing.

"The federal government has gone to extreme lengths to keep those fragments of the truth from coming out and coming together into a coherent story," he said.

Demanding the true story of the bombing, a first responder on Oklahoma's Team 5 scrawled this plea on a damaged wall.

After criminals with insider knowledge deliver bombshells about the mystery in *Blowback*, the plea still stands.

The truth was buried in the rubble 30 years ago. Can America finally uncover it?

his codefendants, known as the Ford Heights Four, it led to two more trials, ending again in *more* wrongful guilty verdicts. Another investigation, this one by college journalism students, finally solved the case. Newly available DNA technology proved that all four men were innocent and identified the real killers.

A conspiracy inside the justice system of Cook County had railroaded the Ford Heights Four. The county paid them $36 million, the highest settlement ever at that time in a wrongful imprisonment case. My editor and I won journalism prizes in Chicago for our coauthored story, "Will We Execute an Innocent Man." *Newsweek* later featured it in a cover story on the death penalty.[154] That battle had stayed with me, and I could see that J.D. Cash and Roger Charles were on that same risky path. I was rooting for them.

⅄

The two castaways from the Oklahoma City bombing story soon washed up on a fertile journalistic island to continue telling their story. In the aftermath of Timothy McVeigh's trial, then during the run-up to his 2001 execution and beyond, *Soldier of Fortune* (*SOF*) magazine scored a brain trust in J.D. Cash and Roger Charles. There, they broke more original exclusive stories, adding to their body of evidence that the bomb plot extended far beyond the man executed for the crime.

In the November 1997 issue of *SOF*, drawing on ATF files that had surfaced for Carol Howe's trial, Roger broke the news of a missed opportunity by the FBI to stop the bombing two months before it happened. In late February 1995, Howe's ATF handler, Angela Finley, had been laying the groundwork for a weapons raid on Andreas Strassmeir at Elohim City. While Finley was on a reconnaissance flight over the compound, a highway patrol trooper piloting her plane told her something extraordinary.

Calling it the "most explosive revelation" of Carol Howe's trial that summer of 1997, Roger quoted from a report by Finley: "On 22 February 1995, this agent met with OHP Trooper Ken Stafford to exchange certain information regarding this investigation," Finley wrote. "Trooper Stafford indicated that the FBI also had an ongoing investigation regarding Elohim City."

So, there were two federal undercover investigations ongoing inside Elohim City at the same time. "Finley was no doubt shocked," Roger noted in his *SOF* story. "The ATF's imminent raid of Elohim City to arrest 'Andy the German' would interfere with an ongoing FBI undercover investigation at [Reverend] Millar's neo-Nazi compound." Roger detailed what happened next. That same day, Finley's boss, "in a highly unusual exception to bureaucratic protocol, met with the US Attorney for the Northern District of Oklahoma to discuss the newly identified threat of an 'intramural firefight' between FBI and ATF agents in what was now recognized as a comingled investigation."[155]

An urgent round-robin of phone calls and meetings between FBI and ATF officials quickly produced results. First and foremost, the FBI pushed the ATF out of Elohim City. A month later, on March 27, 1995, the ATF deactivated informant Carol Howe on Agent Finley's recommendation that "CI-183 was no longer loyal or competent to operate as an informant for ATF."

What amounted to a hostile FBI takeover left the bureau's spy operation inside Elohim City as the only one standing. That operation seemingly included at least one undercover operative for the Southern Poverty Law Center, who reported on the April

17, 1995, phone call from Timothy McVeigh to Elohim City—attempting to reach Andreas Strassmeir.[156]

When and to whom the SPLC informant made that report remains cloaked in secrecy, raising grave accountability questions for the catastrophe that followed. Considering that an ATF raid on Strassmeir almost certainly would have upended the bomb plot, how did the FBI power play in late February benefit public safety on April 19, 1995?

Inexplicably, in the eight weeks remaining before the blast, the FBI took no known action on Carol Howe's warnings to her handlers. It was as if she had never made them. Years later, in 2011, Roger's coauthor Andrew Gumbel interviewed the FBI's Bob Ricks, former special agent in charge of the Oklahoma City field office, about the curious disconnect. Ricks said the ATF told him "nothing" about Howe, Mahon, or Strassmeir during the FBI takeover.[157] If so, that still begs the question of why Ricks didn't press the ATF for a full briefing on its spy operation. Disastrously, with the ATF off the case, plans for a terror attack proceeded at full speed in Elohim City.

Another surprise for Roger and J.D. in the Howe trial was the outing of Elohim City's patriarch, Reverend Millar, as an FBI confidential informant. "[Senior] FBI Special Agent Peter Rickel stunned everyone when he reluctantly admitted that the man Elohim City cult members call 'Grandpa' is really a cooperating source for the FBI," J.D. wrote in the July 1, 1997, *Gazette*. He buttoned his story by observing: "When Rickel disclosed this startling information, a senior FBI agent present and several US Attorneys bolted from the courtroom in an agitated state."

Reverend Millar took issue with the informant label, saying that it implied he "runs to law enforcement authorities to tell them things." J.D. duly noted Reverend Millar's objection the next day in the *Gazette*, along with instances when he reportedly did initiate contact with the FBI to report on Andreas Strassmeir and a "situation involving the federal government and the white separatist movement."

⅄

J.D. had interviewed Timothy McVeigh off the record with Stephen Jones's approval in February 1996 at the federal prison in El Reno, Oklahoma. He wrote about the interview for the first time in *Soldier of Fortune* in July 2001 in a wide-ranging book review of *American Terrorist* by journalists Lou Michel and Dan Herbeck.[158] "I came away impressed by only one thing," J.D. wrote. "Mr. McVeigh was no leader. I found him to be immature and easily manipulated. His hot buttons were fringe right-wing ideology and fantasies involving women. Push those buttons, and Sergeant Mac will be your boy. The perfect patsy."

J.D. panned the McVeigh-authorized biography as "self-serving aggrandizement of a delusional meth addict and psychotic killer." He took his fellow journalists to task for not delving into McVeigh's mysterious money trail and what it said about the involvement of others. "How does someone with nothing on the asset side of his balance sheet but a trashed car survive on the road for over two years with no evidence of income beyond a couple of minimum wage jobs that last only a few weeks?" J.D. asked.

By his math, McVeigh's nomadic, road-warrior lifestyle during the bombing conspiracy would have cost over $50,000 against his roughly $5,000 in known income. That gaping deficit brought J.D. to the matter of the Aryan Republican Army gang's bank robberies. The authors ignored information on the record, including Jennifer McVeigh's admission that her brother wrote her a "Robin Hood" letter in praise of bank robbery and asked her to launder money he said was his share of bank robbery loot. But even so, they reported fresh information that McVeigh gave his father $4,000 in hundred-dollar bills. Was this the money trail of a lone wolf?

⅄

In the same July 2001 issue of *Soldier of Fortune,* Roger surfaced fresh information from his prime quarry, Andreas Strassmeir. Interviewed by British journalist Ambrose Evans-Pritchard, Strassmeir revealed his knowledge that two yellow trucks were involved in the bombing and that someone had covertly outfitted one of the trucks with a tracking device.[159]

Multiple credible sightings of a second yellow truck were on record with bombing investigators. Still, prosecutors had airbrushed this evidence from their case when faced with a fatal timeline discrepancy: Timothy McVeigh drove a yellow truck into the Dreamland motel's parking lot on Easter Sunday, April 16, 1995, the day *before* the bomb truck was rented at Elliott's Body Shop.

Also, multiple credible witnesses saw a yellow truck parked at Geary Lake State Park, where prosecutors said McVeigh and Nichols built the bomb on April 18. However, the witnesses were sure that those sightings happened the week *before* Easter. All this truck-related activity occurring before Timothy McVeigh even arrived in Kansas was highly problematic, so prosecutors ignored it.

Strassmeir's mention to Evans-Pritchard of a tracking device on one of the bomb trucks intrigued Roger. He reported that multiple witnesses had seen agents holding hoop-like devices over their heads on the streets and highways around Oklahoma City in the hours before the bombing. From his military career, Roger recognized these devices as transponder trackers, causing him to wonder in *SOF* how Andreas Strassmeir knew about the transponder that correlated with these sightings, if not via insider information.

Roger had spotted another clue pointing to transponder tracking in the bombing investigation. On April 28, 1998, *The Washington Post* ran a front-page story pegged, curiously, to the Oklahoma City bombing three years earlier. The story reported on a study citing the FBI's number one hardware need for combatting domestic terrorism: a "reduction in size of tracking devices, currently difficult to install covertly due to large size."[160] Much was left unsaid in the story, but from his career in intelligence, Roger theorized that federal law enforcement had installed a monitoring device on the yellow truck, but the terrorists had disabled it.

Five years after his *Soldier of Fortune* story, in 2006, Roger would have a breakthrough in his pursuit of the real Andreas Strassmeir. True to the cloak-and-dagger vibe the investigation had taken on, the breakthrough came in Roger's chance meeting in a suburban Washington, DC, parking lot with a longtime CIA source. The source revealed that he had seen a document revealing that Elohim City's paramilitary trainer was "a German government asset whose information was shared with the FBI."[161]

▲

In two jointly bylined *SOF* stories in September and October 2001, J.D. and Roger advanced their investigation into McVeigh's ties to the Aryan Republican Army. Most of the colorful history of the criminal partnership between Richard Guthrie and Peter Langan was already on record. Still, J.D. had gathered a few choice nuggets from fellow journalist Bob Ruth of *The Columbus Dispatch,* including how Secret Service agents had leaned on a Georgia district attorney, in a most unusual move, to extract Langan from jail so he could become their informant.

The goal in freeing Langan was to capture Richard Guthrie after witnesses to a Pizza Hut robbery in Georgia overheard him threatening to kill President George H. W. Bush. But there was an unintended consequence to this Secret Service–sanctioned jailbreak. It freed a criminal who, as J.D. and Roger reported in *SOF,* was "on record bragging to an undercover former police officer that he intended to bomb a federal building if he ever got out of jail."[162]

Breaking some new ground in their exploration of McVeigh's ties to the Aryan Republican Army, J.D. and Roger zeroed in on the fall of 1993 when the path of new partners in crime Guthrie and Langan crossed neatly with that of new partners in crime McVeigh and Nichols. All four men turned up almost simultaneously in Arkansas near Elohim City.[163]

"Guthrie and Langan were looking for like-minded men with military backgrounds to help carry out a race-based revolution that would use small cells of operatives to strike at the heart of the enemy they called ZOG (Zionist Occupied Government)," J.D. and Roger reported. "Dead broke, Terry Nichols tells his family he is going to Arkansas *to look at real estate*." Nichols checked into a motel room in Fayetteville. The following morning, Timothy McVeigh got a speeding ticket about an hour away from Fayetteville and minutes away from Elohim City, the ARA's reputed paramilitary training camp.

Days after the Arkansas trip, as J.D. and Roger reported, McVeigh and Nichols ordered *The Spotlight* newspaper's prepaid phone card they would use for bomb-related transactions. They were in the domestic terror business now. A few weeks later, McVeigh wrote his sister Jennifer, extolling the virtues of robbing banks because he believed Jews ran them.[164] Now, McVeigh was seemingly a believer in the ARA's core ideology.

Soon after, the ARA's series of twenty-two bank robberies began. From investigative records of McVeigh's movements, J.D. and Roger picked up on an intriguing statistical pattern: Days before most ARA robberies, McVeigh would disappear. Afterward, he would suddenly reappear hundreds of miles away. The journalists capped off their speculative link between McVeigh and the ARA with a tantalizing clue from an unpublished manuscript by Richard Guthrie chronicling the bank robbery spree.

In it, Guthrie wrote that the gang called its getaway driver "Speedie" for his excellent skills, but according to J.D. and Roger's sources, Guthrie confided to his brother Nick that Speedie's real name was Tim.[165] After Guthrie's untimely death in July 1996, the FBI produced interviews in which Guthrie agreed that "Tim" was the ARA's Michael Brescia. That claim didn't hold water, however. Besides Brescia's name being Mike, Brescia was indicted for only one ARA bank robbery—and none in 1994. As J.D. and Roger noted, the question remained wide open: "Who was the getaway driver for the gang in 1994?"

⅄

In mid-2002, J.D. completed his *Soldier of Fortune* saga with a three-part overview of his years on the bombing case. The essay, written in the freewheeling style of a reporter's notebook, laid out J.D.'s still-evolving theory of the crime. By now, he had come to suspect members of the Aryan Republican Army, never investigated for the bombing, as being its prime movers. "The BATF had a snitch inside the gang and the gang was financed by bank jobs," J.D. wrote. "The key players operated out of Elohim City and various safe houses in the Midwest. McVeigh was a mule. The key men were radical revolutionaries, experienced with explosives, who had been casing the OKC target for months."[166]

So, what really happened in Oklahoma City on April 19, 1995? With a disclaimer that his theory was a work in progress, J.D. laid it out in *Soldier of Fortune*, portraying Elohim City as the crime's springboard. "The date and target were chosen as payback for the execution in Arkansas of patriot martyr Richard 'Wayne' Snell," J.D. wrote. "The men who pulled it off were members of a gang of bandits calling itself the Aryan Republican Army (ARA). And the government tried to stop them but failed. Enter the cover-up team."[167]

After seven years on the case, J.D. Cash's bottom line on the bombing was counterterrorism. He wrote that his working theory as of 2002 mirrored his first takeaway, when he landed in Oklahoma City and discovered evidence of the federal government's prior knowledge. "The totality of this tremendous amount of evidence suspiciously pointed to a busted counter-terrorist operation," J.D. wrote. "Somehow, the bad guys had pulled this off—in spite of advance warning."[168]

⅄

J.D. wrapped up his reporter's notebook with a two-month countdown to the bombing, focusing on evidence of government foreknowledge. On February 21, 1995, J.D. placed the FBI's Weldon Kennedy suddenly showing up in Arizona's Camp Verde desert, near a location where the ARA gang was conveniently camping. They were within driving distance of Kingman, where Timothy McVeigh was living at the time, and where a small ammonium nitrate/fuel oil bomb had just exploded.[169]

A year later, in the *Gazette*, J.D. would flesh out the story of this little-known Arizona bombing just weeks before the Oklahoma blast. In what was believed to be retribution for a business deal gone bad, J.D. reported that the Arizona bombing had used virtually the same ingredients as the Oklahoma bomb to blow a crater in the backyard of Kingman resident Francis "Rocky" McPeak's home.[170] The blast broke windows, ripped interior doors from their hinges, and smashed dishes on the kitchen floor.

J.D.'s reporting in the 2003 *Gazette* story would expose the fact that multiple key figures from the Oklahoma City bombing case were allegedly involved in the Arizona crime. According to an unnamed source of J.D.'s, Clark S. Vollmer, the local drug dealer convicted in the crime, admitted to the FBI that he had hired Timothy McVeigh and Michael Fortier to carry out the bombing of McPeak's home. "During negotiations with Vollmer, McVeigh was a peripheral figure," J.D.'s source said. "Mike was the leader in the talks. He was there at the beginning, fully involved."

For good measure, J.D. tagged his *Gazette* story by noting that Michael Fortier possessed bomb-making components similar to those used in the Oklahoma City bombing.

J.D. reported that Vollmer's codefendant was mining blaster Dennis Malzac, the roommate of McVeigh associate Steven Colbern in Oatman, Arizona, 30 miles from Kingman. Memorably, when confessing to his part in the Arizona crime, Malzac admitted that he had coconspirators but said he couldn't remember who they were.

J.D.'s 2003 reporting would radically reframe the lead-up to America's worst domestic terror attack. Two months before the Oklahoma City bombing, the Aryan Republican Army gang was camped out near McVeigh in the Arizona desert, a perfect place to practice setting off bombs.

There, the gang had seemingly attracted the notice of FBI Agent Kennedy, who, after the bombing, would lead the FBI's massive investigation. But already in late February, there was Kennedy, chasing around the desert near Kingman mere hours after the ANFO bomb went off in Rocky McPeak's backyard, a crime that authorities would quietly link to McVeigh and Fortier, but never breathe a word publicly when it came time to solve the Oklahoma City bombing.

Was Agent Kennedy clairvoyant? Or did the FBI have the Kingman crew—McVeigh, his chemist associate Colbern, Colbern's mining blaster roommate Malzac, and even possibly Michael Fortier—under surveillance in Arizona weeks before the bomb exploded in Oklahoma?

Rocky McPeak testified before the federal grand jury in Oklahoma City that indicted McVeigh, saying that he believed McVeigh had been involved in the Arizona blast. According to a grand juror's secret notes, McPeak, who said McVeigh was a friend, told the grand jury that he drove by Clark Vollmer's house after the bomb exploded and saw McVeigh and another man standing on the porch.[171]

⅄

Continuing his two-month countdown to the bombing in the September 2002 issue of *Soldier of Fortune,* J.D. picked up the trail of the FBI's Danny Coulson, a commander on the coming bombing investigation, in March 1995. That month, Coulson brought reformed domestic terrorist Kerry Noble to Quantico, Virginia, for a meeting of the FBI's Critical Incident Response Group. On the agenda, a month after the ATF was forced to stand down from its planned raid of Elohim City, was the topic of how to negotiate with a cult group under barricade conditions. Was it just another coincidence? Or was the FBI readying for trouble in Elohim City a month before the Oklahoma City bombing?

By the day of the blast, J.D.'s timeline reported that a massive mobilization of strategic forces had assembled in Oklahoma City. The groups included the Oklahoma Highway Patrol's Tactical Team and Bomb Squad, agents from the Oklahoma Bureau of Investigation, and members of Oklahoma's Department of Civil Emergency Management. They attended a gathering at the National Guard Military Academy, whose records and communications would all disappear after the bombing.

Later, after the publication of J.D.'s 2002 story, he uncovered hotel records indicating that the FBI's Danny Coulson may have been in Oklahoma City too, having checked into the Embassy Suites Hotel eight hours *before* the bombing,[172] an allegation Coulson has denied. In his biography, *No Heroes,* he recounted driving to Oklahoma from Texas after hearing the shocking news of the bombing.[173]

Still later, in 2012, Roger's book *Oklahoma City* added two more names to the roster of the untold stealth mobilization. In mid-April 1995, Air Force bomb disposal experts Cliff Mogg and Dan Humphries were under orders to drive 500 miles from Kirtland Air Force Base in New Mexico to Oklahoma City on a mission that was never publicly disclosed. They were in the city on standby until the blast. But if they were part of a plan to defuse the Oklahoma City bomb, tragically, they never got that call. They departed as mysteriously as they had come.

In 2003, with the Aryan Republican Army in the crosshairs of his investigation, J.D. reached out to inmate David Hammer on federal death row. The connection proved to be pivotal. J.D. knew that Hammer was working on a book about his exclusive prison interviews with Timothy McVeigh and that the book would heavily feature the ARA. Possible links between their bank robberies, McVeigh, and the bombing were top-of-mind for J.D. and Hammer both.[174] The two had much to talk about, starting with the clue from McVeigh that Hammer had delivered to Jesse Trentadue two years earlier: that the FBI had mistaken Kenneth Trentadue for the ARA's Richard Guthrie.

From his sources, J.D. knew how vital the bank robbery angle was from the very beginning of the FBI's bombing investigation. On June 21, 1995, he reported in the *Gazette* that FBI agents had pressed Michael Fortier about McVeigh's bank robbery connections. Fortier did not confirm any connection, but the FBI had revealed its thinking.[175] The month prior, FBI agents extracted Jennifer McVeigh's admission that she had laundered bank robbery money for her brother.[176]

Right away, then, unidentified fugitive members of the Midwest Bank Robbers—as the Aryan Republican Army was known to the FBI—had become prime suspects in the bombing case. The two case names signaled their close link in the eyes of the FBI: OKBOMB and BOMBROB.

According to J.D.'s sources, next came a computer search for all convicted bank robbers across the United States with similar styles to the ARA gang. Telltale behaviors fed into the database included the speed of the gang's operation, avoidance of injuries, sometimes stationing only one robber inside the bank, and their signature command, "Get down, get down."

Kenneth Trentadue's one-man robberies were a close match, including his use of purposely disabled firearms and the orders: "Get down, get down. This is a robbery. Let's not make it a homicide."[177] According to J.D.'s sources, the FBI's computer search, keying in on fugitive members of the Aryan Republican Army, flagged Kenneth Trentadue, a.k.a. Vance Paul Brockway, as a bombing suspect.[178] After comparing notes with Hammer, J.D. was ready to share what he knew with the man who needed to hear it most.

⅄

"The FBI mistook your brother for John Doe 2," J.D. said when Jesse picked up the phone in his law office that day in 2003. Kenneth Trentadue and Richard Guthrie each stood about five feet, seven inches tall, weighing about 175 pounds with muscular builds, full heads of hair, and mustaches. Perhaps fatefully, both men also fit the FBI's profile of John Doe 2, the escaped terrorist and possible bank robber with a bodybuilder physique and full head of hair who rode alongside Timothy McVeigh in the bomb truck. Kenneth was an even closer match to the John Doe 2 profile because of his distinctive dragon tattoo and the brown pickup truck he drove.

When J.D. mailed photos of Guthrie to Salt Lake City, Jesse found himself staring in amazement at a dead-ringer image that could have been his brother. J.D.'s information was already triggering memories for Jesse rippling back to 1995 and the anonymous phone tipster who told of a bank robbery connection and of Kenneth fitting a profile.

Was it possible that the ARA's Richard Guthrie was McVeigh's accomplice in the bomb truck? Then, four months later, relying on the physical and behavioral profile of John Doe 2, was it possible that the FBI confronted Guthrie's look-alike, the prisoner in cell 709A of the Federal Transfer Center in Oklahoma City, and brutally interrogated Kenneth Trentadue for admissions about the bombing he was tragically unable to make?

It wasn't the notoriously unreliable Timothy McVeigh now who was floating this possibility. J.D. Cash was a reporter Jesse had to take seriously. Horrific though it was to imagine his brother cornered, beaten, and having his throat cut in a prison cell through a case of mistaken identity, still, after eight long years, Jesse finally had a coherent scenario for what might have happened that terrible night of August 21, 1995.

If only the FBI had known his brother's actual identity as Kenneth Trentadue and his marriage to a Hispanic wife, Jesse believed Kenneth would never have been interrogated for information about his suspected role in a neo-Nazi bank robbery gang. Tragically, the FBI only knew the prisoner in cell 709A as Vance Paul Brockway, a convicted bank robber without a family to protest his death.

Jesse had a thousand questions for Richard Guthrie but would never get to ask even one. J.D. filled him in on the incredible rest of the story. Guthrie wouldn't be telling any tales. Like Kenneth Trentadue and Alden Baker, who witnessed Kenneth's murder, Guthrie was dead: the victim of a third mysterious supposed jail cell suicide by hanging while in federal custody.

As Jesse finished telling me his story that morning in Salt Lake City, he was still calmly smoking his cigar. I was transfixed by what I'd heard. Before I left Utah, Jesse handed me a CD and told me to watch it when I returned to Los Angeles. "It's a recruitment video for the Aryan Republican Army," he explained. There they were again: the ARA. Everything in this case seemed to lead back to the neo-Nazi bank robbers and their hideout Elohim City. I was glad to get this assignment. It meant I was holding my first concrete clue in my hands. I wanted to join this search party.

CHAPTER 11

HEAVILY REDACTED

TERRY NICHOLS, a man of endless contradictions, wasn't on Jesse Trentadue's mind as he strategized his next move. Why would Nichols be? In 2004, Timothy McVeigh's coconspirator emerged from the forensic microscope of two mass-murder trials almost as much a phantom as John Doe 2. Wisely taking his lawyers' advice to keep his mouth shut, Nichols never took the witness stand or gave a single media interview. Except for his anguished apology to victims after his trial in Oklahoma, the public never heard from him about his part in the terrible crime. Two juries convicted Nichols. Still, they both deadlocked on the death penalty, seeming to embrace his lawyers' account of the hapless accomplice who couldn't say no to an overbearing partner.

Timothy McVeigh's legal team circled the globe in search of evidence that Nichols was a driving force, not the unwitting coconspirator, in the bombing. That investigation, centered in the Philippines, where Nichols found his second wife, turned up explosive clues. Investigators learned that Nichols frequently flew to Southeast Asia, placed countless phone calls to a Cebu City boardinghouse frequented by Islamic terrorists, and reportedly once brought along a book about bomb-making to the Philippines.

According to one account from a Philippine terrorist turned police informant, Nichols attended a meeting in the early 1990s with 1993 World Trade Center bombing mastermind Ramzi Yousef on the island of Mindanao. Yousef was known to have been in the Philippines plotting a terror attack during Nichols's last extended travel there in late 1994.[179]

Even Lana Padilla, Nichols's friendly first ex-wife with whom he shared a twelve-year-old son, who adored him, was shocked and suspicious about two envelopes Nichols left with her in Las Vegas in case of his death when he departed on that last Philippines trip. Alarmed, she opened both envelopes. The one marked for her contained $20,000 in cash. The other one, tagged for McVeigh, contained the incriminating coded message, "Go for it." When Padilla investigated the storage locker Nichols used at her Las Vegas home, she discovered assorted wigs, masks, and pantyhose, items that were difficult to explain except as criminal accessories. It all left Padilla with the same baffling question that confronted everyone investigating Terry Nichols: Who was this meek, mild, supposedly submissive stranger anyway?

J.D. Cash chased one obscure Nichols lead to the Memory Motel in Sedalia, Missouri, while digging into white supremacist connections to the bomb plot. The reporter was chasing a lead pointing to Nichols's possible link to the murdered Mueller family, discovered suffocated and dumped in an Arkansas bayou in June 1996. Willliam Mueller, like Roger Moore—McVeigh and Nichols's November 1994 robbery victim—was an Arkansas gun show exhibitor who reported a home robbery of tens of thousands of dollars' worth of guns, cash, and valuables. In the Muellers' case, the theft included thirty boxes of ammunition.

By a strange coincidence, Nichols had passed right near the scene of the Mueller crime on the drive to a Sedalia, Missouri, gun show. The Mueller robbery occurred sometime after three in the afternoon in Tilly, Arkansas, on February 10, 1995. That evening at around nine, 150 miles away, in Sedalia, Terry Nichols pulled into a motel and booked a room for two nights using his familiar alias, Joe Rivers. The soft-spoken Nichols asked for a discount, telling the motel owner he was attending the gun show. J.D.'s federal law enforcement sources doubted it. They had evidence placing Nichols in Manhattan, Kansas, at 1:30 p.m. that day, meaning he likely missed most or all of the first day of the weekend firearms event.

Early the following day, as J.D. reported in the *Gazette* on December 12, 1996, the motel's housekeeper peered into Nichols's camper shell. "[T]he truck was crammed full of stuff," she said, "including large boxes marked 'ammunition.'" Later, on a housekeeping mission to Nichols's room, she recalled, "When I opened the door, I couldn't believe it! The floors and bed were covered with all these crates of ammunition. I couldn't clean the room because of all the heavy boxes and tarps he had moved in there."

Though investigators in the bombing case subpoenaed sales records from the Sedalia gun show, targeting the names and aliases used by McVeigh, Nichols, and Michael Fortier, the search came up empty. No connection ever materialized between Terry Nichols and the Mueller robbery. When the Muellers disappeared and were murdered the following year, Nichols was in custody and charged as Timothy McVeigh's co-conspirator in the bombing. Yet Nichols's specter-like figure seemed to flit around the edges of violent events that might somehow be related to the terror attack.

As the only journalist to interview Terry Nichols face-to-face in prison after the bombing, I wish I could have solved the riddle of his identity. However, I couldn't penetrate the secrets held by this frail man dressed all in white, sitting in an interview cubicle in Colorado's federal supermax prison in January 2007. He appeared almost doll-like and fragile, conspicuously out of place among the worst of the worst criminal monsters. When the subject of his family came up toward the end of the interview, Nichols began twisting the gold wedding band on his ring finger while tears streamed down his face. Divorced from two wives and the rest of the world, Terry Nichols struck me as a man shrunken by an agony of guilt that far exceeded his admitted deeds. So the question remained: What else, what more, was tormenting this man?

The second life sentence Nichols received in June 2004 in his Oklahoma state trial removed the death penalty threat hanging over his head, possibly freeing up information he had to protect. A few months later, Nichols broke his decade-long silence about the bombing. He wrote a letter to US Attorney General John Ashcroft, offering to reveal new information if Ashcroft met certain conditions.[180]

"Otherwise," Nichols wrote, "I am prepared to go public about the above facts after September 30, 2004. If you want this to work in a positive way, then I strongly suggest that you contact me as soon as possible. Time is short, don't wait till the last minute."

In a nutshell, Nichols wanted to help expose Arkansas gun dealer Roger Moore, depicted in all three bombing prosecutions as the innocent victim of a robbery of $60,000 worth of guns, valuables, and cash. Did McVeigh and Nichols use this money to finance the bombing? Not so, according to Nichols in his letter to the attorney general. Instead, he dropped heavy hints that Moore provided the explosives used in the bombing and was "connected with the Federal Gov't in some capacity."

Thus, another candidate, Roger Moore, joined the crowded ranks of potential undercover government operatives in the Oklahoma City bombing conspiracy.

On one hand, this outreach by Nichols was a golden opportunity that had eluded investigators, prosecutors, judges, and the American public for a decade. Many still believed that there was more to the bombing story and that Terry Nichols knew some of it. "By the way, I'm not looking for any favors," Nichols pledged to Ashcroft. "I am simply wanting the full truth to come out. Thus, I am willing to disclose publicly all I know, including how I was involved in the OKC bombing."

On the other hand, Ashcroft had plenty to lose by starting a dialogue with a convicted criminal who was proposing to tie the federal government to the bomb plot. "Should you choose to deny, manipulate or remain silent it will be clear evidence to me and others that you want to ignore, deny and cover up the truth and suppress it from the public, not to mention the survivors and victims," Nichols wrote.

When I interviewed him in prison a few years later, Nichols shared an intriguing backstory to this letter. While in jail in late 2003 and early 2004 awaiting his Oklahoma state trial, Nichols said that Michael Selby, a lawyer he had never met before, visited him to offer an extraordinary plea deal from the federal government—extraordinary because this was a state murder trial in which the feds were not even a party.

According to Nichols, Selby was previously a Missouri state trooper who served on Gov. John Ashcroft's security detail. Now, if the remarkable story Nichols was hearing was true, Selby had come to Oklahoma as the unofficial envoy of Attorney General Ashcroft's Justice Department in Washington. According to Nichols, Selby said the DOJ didn't employ him. However, as Nichols later stated in an affidavit for Jesse, Selby "was speaking for and with the authority of the United States Department of Justice, and from the highest level within the Department of Justice."

Selby said the offer was "off the books," designed to give the DOJ deniability if anyone found out about it.[181] According to the go-between lawyer, the DOJ could keep Nichols from receiving the death penalty by not releasing evidence to state prosecutors or not allowing FBI agents and other federal employees to testify.

On Nichols's side of the bargain was an odd to-do list, with only one item that Nichols could deliver.[182] The DOJ was asking him to disclose the whereabouts of a box of explosives stolen in the Roger Moore robbery. Because he knew these explosives could tie the gun dealer Moore into the bomb plot, Nichols assumed the government was preparing to prosecute Moore. Nichols told the lawyer that he was happy to assist: "I could give [Selby] Roger Moore." But Nichols had misunderstood. Suddenly, the negotiation went sideways.

"Mr. Selby's reaction to my offer, however, was not what I had expected," Nichols stated in the affidavit for Jesse. "Mr. Selby essentially said no deal. Mr. Selby told me that Roger Moore was 'untouchable.'" If Nichols was telling the truth, the government's emissary had seemingly come not to expose Roger Moore but to protect him by recapturing a box of explosives that could incriminate him in the bombing. From Nichols's point of view, the spectacular unfairness of this collapsed negotiation would stay with him for a long time.

Jesse told me that afterward, Nichols's former attorney confirmed that the plea deal conversations had occurred. The lawyer said he eventually concluded that the proposal must have been a hoax, but he had no idea how attorney Selby might have benefited from such a deception. The other requests to Nichols posed by Selby offered no clue about what drove the strange proposal. Would Nichols incriminate his brother in criminal activity? Would he claim responsibility for a phone call made to the FBI on April 18,1995, warning about the plan to bomb the Murrah Building? Nichols refused both requests, telling Selby he made no such phone call and that the accusation against his brother was not true.

Jesse told me that when the Nichols affidavit went public, Selby called him in a state of high agitation. "You fucking got me killed!" he declared. That was an exaggeration, but the angry lawyer did report that someone had ransacked his office.[183]

After the trial, as Nichols entered prison for life, he was still seething over Roger Moore's Teflon-like shield from an investigation that had crushed Nichols. He signed off his letter to Attorney General Ashcroft with this ultimatum: "If you are going to deny or try to manipulate the facts that Roger Moore had absolutely no part, directly or indirectly, in the Oklahoma City bombing and that he has no knowledge of explosives (particularly Kinestik), nor possessed any, or is not in any way connected with the Federal Gov't in some capacity, then please do not waste your time or mine in contacting me."

Ashcroft took that advice. Ignoring the letter's thinly veiled threat of a public relations backlash, he never responded to Nichols. Once again, the shocking possibility of federal government involvement in the bombing was left dangling in limbo.

⅄

In Nichols's state trial in McAlester, Oklahoma, his defense team had made an aggressive attempt to revive the ghost of John Doe 2 to deflect some of the blame for the bombing from Nichols. They scored points by producing striking new evidence from Secret Service records: an investigative log referencing surveillance videotape recovered by the FBI showing "suspects"—plural—getting out of the bomb truck 3.6 seconds before the explosion.[184]

A Secret Service agent had created the log entry while taking notes on an interagency task force conference call that took place days after the bombing. If the log was accurate, this meant that the FBI was holding at least one videotape of the apocalyptic blast but had never allowed the American public to see it.

On the witness stand at Nichols's trial, a Secret Service official tried to downplay the report, noting that the agent who created the log only took notes; he hadn't *seen* the video.[185] But this defied common sense. The agent's time reference to the bomb's exploding appeared to track the timecode caption on the tape down to a split second. Also, the video sequence that Secret Service Agent McNally described matched independent testimony from an eyewitness who saw the bomb truck parked in front of the federal building. Quoting from the Secret Service log:

> A witness to the explosion named Grossman claimed to have seen a pale-yellow Mercury car with a Ryder truck behind it pulling up to the Federal Building. Mr. Grossman claimed to have seen a woman on the corner waving to the truck. [Agent] McNally noted that this is significant because the security video shows the Ryder

truck pulling up to the Federal Building and pausing seven to ten seconds before resuming into a slot in front of the building, speculating that the woman was signaling the truck when a slot became available.

Another factor called into question the Secret Service's effort to downplay the credibility of the tape log. The agency had a considerable stake in containing the story of its responsibility for extracting the ARA's Peter Langan from jail to serve as its informant. That action launched Langan into his role as coleader of the Aryan Republican Army and, possibly, one of McVeigh's suspected accomplices, indicted along with him as "others unknown."

The Secret Service log was robust evidence coming from the government. Still, when Nichols's lawyers argued that the log proved prosecutors had concealed the videotape, Judge Steven W. Taylor dismissed the idea. "This would only conjure up visions of the prosecutors sitting across the street in their office at night watching a videotape of the Ryder truck pulling up in front of the Murrah Building and people getting out of it and the building blowing up, and the prosecutors watching the videotape and not telling anybody about it," the judge said, repeating back almost verbatim the defense attorneys' argument while summarily rejecting it.[186]

Nichols's lawyers tried to bring in the ARA's Peter Langan and McVeigh's death row cellblock mate, David Hammer, as witnesses to implicate members of the Aryan Republican Army in the crime, but Judge Taylor balked. "As to the BOMBROB case, this is a dry hole," he ruled. "There is absolutely no evidence of any overt act by the bank robbers in bombing the Murrah Building, nothing at all to link the bank robbers to the crime that is being tried before this court."

In some ways, this moment was an echo of seven years earlier, when Judge Michael Burrage in the Carol Howe case worried about allegations of the Elohim City bomb plot infecting the McVeigh trial and when Judge Matsch barred informant Carol Howe from a mainstream telling of what she had witnessed in Elohim City. But something had changed. It could be the sheer accumulation of evidence over a decade. A watershed moment was here. A long-simmering, suppressed news story was threatening to break out.

⅄

Roger Charles, whose document research skills approached wizardry, led the way with two discoveries he reported with J.D. Cash in the *McCurtain Daily Gazette* on December 13, 2003, a few months before Nichols's Oklahoma trial opened. While poring over confidential files from FBI whistleblower Frederic Whitehurst, Roger discovered two teletypes from FBI Director Louis Freeh. Even decades later, the significance of the secrets revealed by these memos—and especially the degree to which the FBI was concealing McVeigh's suspected ties to Elohim City and the Aryan Republican Army—cannot be overstated. Heavy FBI redactions in documents deemed too sensitive to share with the public hid portions of these teletypes. But Roger, J.D., and Jesse were skilled in the arcane art of redaction decoding. They could fill in some of the blanks.

A January 6, 1996, memo from Director Freeh, eight months after the bombing, reported on fresh intel about Andreas Strassmeir's possible connection to McVeigh. The teletype, sent to several FBI field offices, referred to someone whose name was redacted as allegedly having a "lengthy relationship" with McVeigh. Strassmeir's name and nickname both contained the exact same number of letters as the blacked-out letter spaces in the memo.[187]

For the first time, the director's 1996 memo revealed that McVeigh called Strassmeir at Elohim City on April 17, 1995, two days before the bombing—as well as having placed an earlier known call there on April 5. The memo emphasized that the April 17 call came at a time when McVeigh "was believed to have been attempting to recruit a second conspirator to assist in the OKBOMB attack." April 17 was also renting day for the bomb truck in Junction City, Kansas. That call thus bookended McVeigh's April 5 call, right after he phoned a Ryder truck rental agency in Arizona, possibly researching what truck size would be needed to carry the bomb. In any case, the strategic timing of the two calls to Elohim City looking for Strassmeir made it highly unlikely that McVeigh was phoning a casual acquaintance to chat.

Far from the man who, by his account, claimed he only met McVeigh once at a gun show or, by the Justice Department's account, was never a suspect in the bombing, Andreas Strassmeir appeared to be a priority bombing suspect in the director's memo, which rendered what followed stunning. At the time of his memo, FBI Director Freeh knew Strassmeir's recent North Carolina whereabouts and knew, as his memo stated, that Strassmeir "[planned] to leave the US via Mexico, in the near future," which he *did* a few days later. Still, knowing all this, the director did not marshal his vast FBI enforcement resources to find or stop Strassmeir. To Roger and J.D., the only explanation for this failure to act was that Strassmeir was somebody's informant, and the FBI was protecting him.

The source of the new intel on McVeigh's April 17 call to Elohim City was another surprise. According to the director's memo, the Southern Poverty Law Center, a high-profile Alabama-based civil rights advocacy group targeting white supremacy, had an informant inside Elohim City before the bombing. That informant had supplied the information about McVeigh's April 17 phone call to Strassmeir and their alleged long-standing relationship.

After Roger's discovery, J.D. chased this new Southern Poverty Law Center lead doggedly, with mixed results. He learned that Morris Dees, the group's founder, estimated that McVeigh had made "dozens" of visits to Elohim City, far exceeding Carol Howe's testimony at Nichols's federal trial that she saw McVeigh there only once with Strassmeir. Presumably, Dees was sourcing his guess from the Southern Poverty Law Center informant. However, when J.D. pressed Dees at an academic conference about what the SPLC was doing in Elohim City, Dees replied cryptically: "If I told you that, I'd have to kill you."[188]

⅄

Roger's second discovery was another teletype from FBI Director Freeh, sent to the bureau's Philadelphia field office on August 23, 1996. This memo, sourced mainly from FBI interviews of the ARA's Richard Guthrie after his capture in January 1996, underscored the significant terror threat posed by the Aryan Republican Army.[189]

In the memo, FBI Director Freeh explored the critical linkage between the ARA, Elohim City, and Timothy McVeigh—and between the FBI's two intertwined major case investigations: OKBOMB and BOMBROB. Both citations appeared in the teletype, indicating that the FBI director knew or suspected that the crimes were linked at least by August 1996—seven months before the McVeigh trial. Again, the document's redactions obscured some critical content. However, Roger and other insiders were able to fill in most of the blanks, including the intel that on April 5, the day of McVeigh's first known call to Strassmeir, the ARA's Kevin McCarthy and Scott Stedeford were both staying at Strassmeir's home in Elohim City.

Eleven days later, on April 16—three days before the bombing—the teletype reported that someone placed a call from Strassmeir's home to a residence in the Philadelphia area. Though redactions cover the name, it may have been ARA gang member Mark Thomas, who was also present in Elohim City on April 16. Was Thomas phoning home to his farm near Philadelphia, where he had recruited the two youths, McCarthy and Stedeford, into the ARA? Both would spend the summer after the bombing at Thomas's farm, performing in the white power rock band Cyanide.

Also on that day, FBI Director Freeh reported that McCarthy and Stedeford left Elohim City to join Guthrie and Langan right after the bombing at the ARA's safe house in Pittsburg, Kansas, a few hours' drive from Oklahoma City.

Despite heavy redactions, the memo revealed that more than a year after the bombing, while Justice Department prosecutors were cementing the lone-wolf terror narrative for their case against Timothy McVeigh, the FBI director was heading in a different direction. He was looking hard at phone evidence suggesting that McVeigh may have mobilized the movements of

ARA gang members at Elohim City with his phone call there on April 5, 1995.

Were the ARA and Timothy McVeigh coconspirators in the Oklahoma City bomb plot? That was the unspoken question behind the teletype's call to action. Urgently, FBI Director Freeh pressed the Philadelphia field office to open a full domestic terror investigation into the Aryan Republican Army. The memo underscored the ARA's qualifying acts, including threats of political assassination, genocide, bombings, and bank and armored car robberies. "ARA members advocate the violent overthrow of the US government; are known to be well-armed; use explosives; and in the past have fired weapons at agents to avoid capture," the FBI director advised. This bombing story was not what the government was telling the American public.

That August 1996, when the director wrote his memo, was the same month when Roger Charles had landed in Oklahoma to investigate the bombing story for ABC News. No mainstream national media coverage had yet challenged the government's lone-wolf terror theory. Yet Director Freeh's memo revealed that he was urgently and secretly mounting a full-scale terrorism probe of the ARA, triggered by McVeigh's phone calls to Strassmeir in Elohim City, where some ARA members had gathered in the run-up to the bombing.

⅄

In early 2004, soon after Roger and J.D. reported on the FBI director's memos, the AP's John Solomon made another discovery. On February 25, 2004, with Terry Nichols's state trial set to open in a few days, Solomon broke the news that the FBI had mishandled evidence possibly tying McVeigh to the Aryan

Republican Army. The story stemmed from the bureau's search of the ARA safe house in Columbus, Ohio, following the capture of Guthrie and Langan in January 1996.[190]

Solomon discovered blasting caps, a duffle bag, and two distinctive items described as a "Christmas package" in evidence records relating to the Ohio safe house. The whereabouts of the blasting caps that McVeigh and Nichols had stolen from a Kansas quarry but did not use in the bomb was a flashpoint for FBI investigators. They worried about the possibility of subsequent attacks. The FBI also knew from its cooperating witness Lori Fortier that she had helped McVeigh disguise boxes of blasting caps as Christmas presents. The packages rode in the trunk of McVeigh's car, along with a couple of duffle bags of bomb gear, on his drive from Arizona back to the Midwest in late 1994.

The bureau had gone so far as to track down the Walmart receipt for wrapping paper purchased by Lori Fortier. The Christmas packages were hard to miss as telltale clues connecting McVeigh to the Aryan Republican Army. Yet the FBI somehow overlooked them. Instead of alerting the bombing task force, FBI investigators allowed the Columbus Fire Department to destroy most of a precious cache of physical evidence, which might have settled the question of McVeigh's connection to Guthrie and Langan's terror group.

Solomon's safe house story ignited angry reactions from usually tight-lipped former FBI brass. Danny Defenbaugh, who headed the FBI's bombing investigation, said his team never learned of the evidence found in the ARA safe house. Defenbaugh blasted its destruction as a "total violation of the FBI's regulations and the rules of evidence," adding, "If there was Christmas wrapping paper, that should really have been a key to people. That should have keyed interest and caused them to be compared by the laboratory to see if these were from McVeigh."

In another discovery among Guthrie's possessions in the safe house, investigators retrieved a fake Arkansas driver's license in the name of Robert Miller. That name was the alias used on the gun show circuit by Roger Moore, the supposed robbery victim. Defenbaugh told Solomon this was the first time anyone had ever told his team about it. "If the license is the same as our Roger Moore, then I'm really concerned," Defenbaugh said. The bureau refused Solomon's repeated requests to check out the license.

Danny Coulson, a commander on the bombing task force, weighed in with an even more pointed reaction to Solomon's story. "A lot of things happened that were inappropriate," Coulson said about the FBI investigation: "I think it needs to be reopened, but I don't think it should be reopened by the FBI. It needs to be a special investigator, a lawyer, totally independent. He needs to have subpoena power and the ability to use a grand jury."

Strong reactions by these veteran FBI officials were understandable: Following the money is a cardinal rule of investigation. Yet the McVeigh case relied almost exclusively on political ideology to explain the crime, at least partly because investigators never got a handle on the bombing conspiracy's financing or logistics. Their thin storyline never could explain how the penniless McVeigh paid for his nomadic, yearslong motel lifestyle and seemingly endless miles of driving throughout America. Or how Nichols, also practically destitute, financed his many international round-trip flights to the Philippines.

An ARA connection, if it existed, could explain all that. Authorities never recovered the $250,000 from the gang's Midwest bank robbery spree. In FBI interviews following his arrest, Guthrie reportedly said he donated generously to white power causes. Yet in early 1996, at a time when the McVeigh investigation was front and center at the FBI, the bureau somehow managed to miss evidence that might have linked a terroristic bank robbery spree, eclipsing the proceeds of the Jesse James gang, to the nation's worst domestic terrorist attack. No wonder Solomon's reporting shocked Defenbaugh and Coulson. Far from the "dry hole" Oklahoma's Judge Taylor would soon deem them to be, the ARA's bank robberies stood out for journalists Cash, Charles and Solomon as a lead that could upend the bombing case.

In Oklahoma City, Jannie Coverdale, the grandmother whose phone call would later launch my journey into this mystery, was grateful for the FBI's promise to reinvestigate the ARA safe house evidence. "I have prayed and asked God this time to let the truth come out," Jannie said. "I did not believe what the federal government had said. I had spoken with too many people who had seen Tim McVeigh in Oklahoma City that morning, and not one saw Tim McVeigh by himself."[191]

⅄

Changing public perceptions of the bombing story raised hopes in Jesse Trentadue's circle for the prospects of his next move. In August 2004, just before Terry Nichols wrote his letter to the attorney general, Jesse filed a Freedom of Information Act (FOIA) lawsuit against the FBI in federal court in Utah. He sought access to any FBI files linking McVeigh, Strassmeir, Guthrie, Howe, and others to an FBI sting operation in Elohim City that Jesse believed led to his brother's murder.[192]

Drawing heavily on J.D.'s reporting and Roger's discovery of the FBI teletypes, the lawsuit alleged that the bureau and the

Southern Poverty Law Center worked together in an undercover surveillance operation targeting the neo-Nazis in Elohim City and their terror plot. Later, the lawsuit alleged, during a cover-up, the FBI tortured and killed Kenneth Trentadue in the mistaken belief that he was John Doe 2, a suspect capable of unraveling the whole disastrous operation.

Jesse's strategy had to be bold, and it was. Turning to the Department of Justice to investigate itself was out of the question because of its conflict of interest. Besides, Jesse had made many enemies and no friends at the DOJ through years of bitter and sometimes flamboyant contention. Journalist Andrew Gumbel's assessment that Jesse had been "all over the federal government like a bad case of lice"[193] might have offended some people. Jesse took it as a compliment.

Gumbel reported on an email Jesse wrote to FBI Director Mueller after a pivotal court ruling in the FOIA case. US District Judge Dale A. Kimball had ordered the FBI to turn over documents Jesse had requested relating to the alleged sting operation inside Elohim City. The subject line of Jesse's email read: "OH MY GOSH DARN BIGGEST FRIGGIN HECK!!!" The body of the email said this: "After you read [the judge's] order, you are going to need a case of Preparation H!!"

Irreverence aside, Jesse understood the stakes of the contest he was setting in motion. As a lawyer, he knew the federal Freedom of Information Act was the one higher power available to him in a private effort to expose government corruption, even murder. The FOIA, signed into law by President Johnson in 1966 to make government more transparent, carries the full weight of the federal judiciary. If a federal judge rules in favor of a private citizen in a FOIA contest with a federal agency over secret information, it must surrender damaging or even criminal files. Jesse's narrow way forward was this rare authority to bring an arm of the United States presidency—even the Federal Bureau of Investigation—to heel.

Initially, Justice Department attorneys treated Jesse's FOIA lawsuit as an unhinged fishing expedition. Judge Kimball must have also had his doubts at the outset. It was a wild story and, therefore, a case likely to end swiftly. Justice Department lawyers only needed to convince the judge that the government had no secret documents supporting the bizarre scenario Jesse had laid out.

Usually, this outcome was about as easy to accomplish as swatting a fly. For all its sweeping, democratic-sounding powers, the FOIA law grants significant advantages to government officials eager to keep their secrets. Nightmare war stories abound among researchers of high-profile mysteries, most notably the JFK assassination. The catch-22 is this: To see secret government files, off-limits except to insiders, you must first describe them precisely. Those without X-ray vision or leaked documents need not apply.

In the unlikely event that a petitioner manages to hit a bull's-eye with a FOIA request, all the agency usually needs to do to avoid turning over "responsive" documents is to invoke one of the law's many broad and generous exclusions—for national security, privacy, or an open investigation. In that case, it's usually game over. However, Jesse had a surprise for the FBI. He was a veteran trial attorney and former law professor who got his start clerking for a fiercely independent federal judge. This was not Jesse's first federal court showdown.

Roger once called "Hatfield cunning" one of Jesse's standout character traits. After J.D. Cash introduced the two men, both Marines from West Virginia, they discovered they had descended from the Hatfields and McCoys but on opposite sides of West Virginia's legendary family blood feud. The history sealed their friendship and, I'm sure, Roger's appreciation of the sleight of hand Jesse was about to use to turn the tables in the FOIA case.

When the FBI responded, empty-handed, to his FOIA request by telling the judge that it had no responsive documents about an Elohim City sting operation, Jesse marched into court and presented the teletypes Roger had discovered. The move blindsided the FBI's lawyers and prompted the judge to order the bureau to look again for documents.[194] After nine long years, Jesse had a victory to celebrate in his 2004 holiday letter to family and friends. "These documents show that the FBI had an informant in with McVeigh, that the FBI in all likelihood knew about the planned Oklahoma City attack but did nothing to stop it, and that Guthrie and about a dozen others were helping McVeigh," Jesse wrote.[195]

Before signing off, he closed his holiday letter with a revealing glimpse of the road ahead:

> My purpose in writing is to assure that we are not crazy! We realize that the Oklahoma City Bombing–John Doe 2 connection is a dangerous horse to ride for several obvious reasons, but it is the only one with the legs to take us where we need to go. I also want to say that despite what some may think and what the FBI has publicly stated, we do not enjoy this struggle. It has cost us and the ones we love most dearly, and we pray that it ends soon. Meanwhile, to you all–HAPPY MERRY

The struggle would not end soon, however. Judge Kimball's ruling set in motion a long contest over how many documents the judge would require the FBI to share and how many redactions he would allow. In the end, Jesse received eighty-seven pages of court-ordered files. Reporting on the document trove in the *Gazette* on July 31, 2005, J.D. and Roger zeroed in on the FBI's use of Morris Dees's Southern Poverty Law Center as a surveillance cutout passing information to the FBI about McVeigh's contacts with Elohim City before the bombing.

"Taken in their entirety, Utah attorney Jesse Trentadue's latest documents clearly place the role of the SPLC and its own undercover operatives at the center of unresolved issues about federal law enforcement's prior knowledge of the conspiracy to bomb a federal building in Oklahoma City on April 19, 1995," J.D. and Roger wrote.

As their story revealed, McVeigh's contacts with Elohim City went far beyond the one phone call there from McVeigh on April 5, 1995, that federal prosecutors acknowledged as they pressed their cases against McVeigh and Nichols—and even well beyond the April 17 phone call that Roger uncovered in the FBI director's teletype. The discrepancy mattered because every additional link uncovered between McVeigh and Elohim City further eroded the cornerstone of the bombing story as the Justice Department presented it to the public, in which Timothy McVeigh acted alone.

From the newly released documents and other sources, J.D. and Roger could report that Timothy McVeigh "traveled to Elohim City for meetings inside and outside the compound well over a dozen times, beginning in the fall of 1993." The Southern Poverty Law Center's Morris Dees tried to withdraw his statement to a *Denver Post* reporter that McVeigh had visited Elohim

City "on a number of occasions." Dees claimed that he was misquoted. However, J.D. checked in with the reporter, who confirmed the quote.[196]

The far-reaching clues in the redacted FBI teletypes that Roger had discovered were tantalizing but also frustrating for Jesse's investigation, revealing so much but hiding so much more. In a setback for his cause, Judge Kimball eventually sided with the FBI, upholding its right to keep all the redactions in place to protect the identities of its confidential sources. Still, in a consequential ruling, the judge ordered the FBI to turn over 108 pages of documents to him to review in private in their complete, unredacted state.[197]

Would this judge, within the limits of the FOIA law, back Jesse's further efforts to learn the rest of the story? The door was open for Jesse to seek more documents. But where was the untapped source that might lead to more hidden files? Who possessed the information needed to keep the FOIA case alive?

Enter Terry Nichols, still fixated on Roger Moore. In September 2006, Nichols wrote Jesse a letter sparking a provocative idea. "Roger Moore is a government provocateur who not only provided Timothy McVeigh with Kinestik explosives, but he also provided others with explosive components including those with the Midwest Bank Robbers," Nichols wrote, referring to the Aryan Republican Army by its other law enforcement handle. "This is why the DOJ doesn't want you to get access to the FBI's files, because it will reveal how the FBI uses corrupt means to further their agendas."[198]

Roger Moore. Explosives. McVeigh. The Midwest Bank Robbers. Could Terry Nichols connect the dots?

CHAPTER 12

THE INSIDER

JESSE TRENTADUE'S SEARCH PARTY was confronting a hard lesson in 2006: Conspiracies have a way of outliving their pursuers. Tragically, J.D. Cash was dying, and Roger Charles's probing reporting on the bombing case wasn't going to get him a ticket to visit Terry Nichols and two other inmates Jesse needed to interview for the FOIA case. They were sealed off by media lockdowns in America's most secure federal prisons.

After the September 11 terror attacks of 2001, the federal Bureau of Prisons imposed media lockdowns lasting for years. Jesse's inside guy David Hammer viewed the lockdowns as a strategy to keep the truth behind bars. Whatever Nichols, the ARA's Peter Langan, and possibly even Hammer knew about the bombing was buried alive with them, leaking out only in bits and pieces. Jesse thought he knew a way in.

He needed a stealth reporter to extricate the rest of what the criminals knew for the FOIA lawsuit. There I was, circling the investigation and hoping that my *America's Most Wanted* cred would be my ticket. It helped, but not as much as the fact that Jesse and Roger figured a woman would have the best shot at drawing out the criminals they needed to talk to. Jesse made me an offer.

If I would interview Nichols, Hammer, and Langan for his FOIA lawsuit, he would designate me as his paralegal, allowing me to bypass lockdowns and get interviews other reporters couldn't.

I was on the case.

⅄

Those who hoped that Terry Nichols's state trial would finally bring closure to the haunting mystery of John Doe 2 and the "others unknown" had been disappointed. Nichols would serve the rest of his life in prison. However, the words of Niki Deutchman, foreperson of Nichols's 1997 federal trial jury, still spoke for many. "I think the government perhaps really dropped the ball," Deutchman had said, adding: "I think there are other people out there, and decisions were probably made very early that Tim McVeigh and Terry Nichols were who they were looking for. And the same sort of resources were not used to try to find out who else might be involved."[199]

With Timothy McVeigh silenced by execution in 2001, would Terry Nichols unlock that mystery now that the threat of the death penalty was off his shoulders? America was still hungry for an answer to that question. However, Jesse and I were not the front-runners in the chase to interview Nichols. Kathy Wilburn, now Kathy Wilburn Sanders, had been corresponding with Nichols and was assisting *60 Minutes* as the show's producers tried to secure an exception from the media lockdown at ADX Florence. On Capitol Hill, Representative Dana Rohrabacher, investigating possible foreign connections in the bombing case, was pressing for a second face-to-face interview with Nichols.

That fall of 2006, however, Nichols pulled out of the Rohrabacher visit, claiming it was a waste of time if the congressman only wanted to pursue a Philippines connection. Nichols claimed there was none. Meanwhile, in a reversal that killed the *60 Minutes* story, the Bureau of Prisons shut down a scheduled phone call between Nichols and Sanders at CBS News headquarters in New York, with a producer standing by to record the call for broadcast. The prison then unceremoniously removed Sanders from Nichols's approved calling list, cutting the cord permanently between him, her and CBS.[200] Suddenly, Jesse and I had the Terry Nichols interview to ourselves.

Representative Rohrabacher's blistering report in December 2006 helped lay the groundwork for our interview. His investigation concluded that the FBI ignored credible eyewitnesses to John Doe 2, canceled the global manhunt too soon, failed to investigate Andreas Strassmeir before he left the country, and ignored the informant Carol Howe's warnings about Strassmeir casing the Murrah Building. The report mentioned Kenneth Trentadue by name, calling the circumstances of his death "very disturbing."[201]

Jesse told me that his mother's bus stop billboard campaign in Westminster, California, which was in Rohrabacher's home district, had been aimed at Washington, DC. The family hoped that the publicity would pressure the Justice Department to investigate Kenneth's murder. The billboards featured a larger-than-life-sized photograph of Kenneth's tortured body taken at the funeral home after the family stripped away the prison makeup hiding his injuries. When some commuters protested that the image was too disturbing, the city backed Mrs. Trentadue and left the billboards up. Rohrabacher was listening too.

Much of the congressman's report was familiar ground to us. Still, in one critical area, the Aryan Republican Army, Rohrabacher delivered sensational new evidence of the cover-up we believed we were confronting. His team of investigators, who interviewed the ARA's Peter Langan, Michael Brescia, and Scott Stedeford, found fresh cause for suspicion a decade after the crime. Langan, who had previously implicated fellow gang member Kevin McCarthy, now backpedaled and claimed to have no such knowledge. Thomas, who also had accused McCarthy but then recanted, kept his silence. The Rohrabacher team did not report specifically on the interviews with Brescia and Stedeford except to underscore that "their stories have been murky, if not contradictory, through the last decade. [202]

The congressman's bombshell, however, related to the ARA's Kevin McCarthy. Formerly accused by his fellow gang members of helping Timothy McVeigh bomb the Murrah Building, McCarthy was now missing and unaccounted for by Justice Department officials. Incredibly, they actively blocked the congressman's efforts to find and interview the paroled bank robber, as Rohrabacher detailed, step by embarrassing step, in his report.

It was a runaround on a grand scale. It might have been comical if congressional investigators hadn't been trying to solve America's deadliest domestic terror attack. McCarthy wasn't in Philadelphia, where he had been paroled after serving prison time for the bank robberies, and there was no record of him in the federal probation system. Next, a confidential law enforcement source told Rohrabacher's team that McCarthy was in Newtown, Pennsylvania. But their source bailed on them when they pressed for details, saying this matter was "above his pay grade." The head of the federal witness protection program confirmed to Rohrabacher that McCarthy had been in the program in the past but not anymore. The trail ran out when a private source told the congressional investigators that McCarthy was no longer attached to the Social Security number he had when he went to prison.

Understandably disappointed that his investigation had run into such a disturbing dead end, Rohrabacher blasted the Justice Department in his report:

> These facts raise questions about whether McCarthy is, in fact, still under some sort of federal protection, as well as why the Department of Justice was unable or unwilling to help find him. It is astonishing that officials from the Department of Justice and other law enforcement agencies were unwilling to permit congressional investigators to question a former bank robber with a possible connection to a large-scale terrorist attack.

Finally, someone in Washington had called out the Justice Department cover-up that had prompted Jesse to assure his family at Christmastime: "We ain't crazy." In a memo to the chairman of the House Committee on International Relations, who authorized his investigation, Rohrabacher wrote, "I have concluded that others were involved and that information about the bombing is being kept from the public and from the Congress."[203]

Independently, nearly a decade spent searching for those "others unknown" had led J.D. Cash and Jesse to the door of the Aryan Republican Army. Jesse knew he needed to dig for information to break down that door, starting with Terry Nichols, his next willing source. As Jesse's paralegal, heading out to meet Timothy McVeigh's convicted coconspirator, who claimed to hold a piece of the hidden story, I felt less crazy myself.

Rohrabacher signed off his report with words that would be a beacon to me for a long time: "This inquiry would have been significantly more complete with greater cooperation from federal law enforcement. Congressional investigators should not face such resistance in doing their job, which is to find the facts and determine the truth." Three weeks later, in January 2007, Jesse and I traveled to Colorado to interview Terry Nichols about the others unknown.

⅄

Florence, Colorado, would make a captivating end-of-the-world travel brochure, especially in January. It is a lonely, bitterly cold destination, with a sunless gray sky, a landscape defined by vast empty space, rugged mountains, and a forbidding supermax prison. If you're one of America's criminal monsters, this is the perfect place to spend twenty-three hours a day in a five-by-twelve-foot cement bunker until you die.

Fragments of the latest intriguing chapter of Terry Nichols's story had trickled out in 2005, around the time of the tenth anniversary of the bombing. Notes that Nichols exchanged with fellow prisoners had led the FBI to cardboard cartons of explosives buried under a crawl space of his former Kansas home. These were the same explosives that had been a bargaining chip in Nichols's strange, failed plea negotiation. He claimed they would incriminate Arkansas gun dealer Roger Moore in the bomb plot. I had followed this curious twist in the story with amazement over its surprise *America's Most Wanted* angle.

The prisoner two cells away from Nichols, who had learned of the location of the explosives from Nichols's notes, was none other than New York City mobster Gregory Scarpa Jr. We had profiled Scarpa as a fugitive in the first season of *America's Most Wanted*. Our viewers led deputy US marshals to him six months later, hiding in a New Jersey motel. The capture eventually landed

Scarpa on the same cellblock with Nichols to play his odd part in searching for the truth about the Oklahoma City bombing.

At moments like this, of which Jesse and I have shared more than a few, he's likely to quote his hillbilly granny in her Highland South dialect: "Tain't no setch a thang as a coincidence."

A tip-off from Scarpa led the FBI to search for the explosives Nichols claimed he buried in Kansas. Because it was the tenth anniversary of the bombing, the moment was full of portent. It was April. Rumors swirled that another bombing might be planned and that someone might use these very explosives in a fresh attack.

When agents searched underneath Nichols's porch, sure enough, they found cardboard cartons containing glass tubes of the liquid explosive component nitromethane and blasting caps. In a preliminary report in June 2005, the FBI's crime lab disclosed that it found no useful fingerprints on the cardboard boxes. However, sixteen of the sixty-eight glass tubes of nitromethane did have fingerprints on them, which the lab was photographing "before analysis for useful prints." Almost three years later, in a reporting delay that raised doubt in some quarters, the FBI lab concluded that those fingerprints were not recoverable.

Roger Charles knew there was more to the story. He went public with it in 2012, telling radio host Scott Horton that his friend, journalist John Solomon, was told by a senior FBI agent that there were four sets of fingerprints recovered, belonging to McVeigh, Nichols, Moore, and Richard Guthrie.[204] Perplexingly, no record exists of further examination by the FBI. Solomon's hot lead faded into a footnote, never mentioned in media coverage of the case after Roger's radio interview.

Our interview with Terry Nichols came a year and a half after the Herington explosives caper, but the episode still reverberated. It had embarrassed the FBI for missing such a vital piece of evidence in the first place back in 1995. It had also propelled Representative Rohrabacher to seek face-to-face interviews with a criminal he was sure knew more than he had ever told about the bombing.

For us, anticipation turned to suspense in the weeks before our January 2007 interview in Colorado. Jesse and Nichols exchanged a dozen letters, attempting to foresee if and how the prison might try to block our visit. Nichols fretted about securing a private cache of documents he wanted to share with Jesse. He was afraid to let them out of his sight by mailing them or allowing prison staff to copy them.

By mid-December, however, we were all beginning to believe the visit would happen. "And I believe that the only avenue left is to go thru you to get this out to the public and expose the government's cover-up," Nichols wrote to Jesse. Because of Nichols's caution over the prospect of a shutdown, we got only a scant preview of what he would tell us. On January 18, 2007, we were still in suspense when a prison escort at ADX Florence delivered us to the facility's brightly lit communal interview room, divided by glass panels into a honeycomb of cubicles that could accommodate multiple simultaneous meetings of prisoners, their lawyers, and others.

⅄

I first saw Terry Nichols from a dozen feet away in the cavernous interview room. Guards had seated Jesse and me in the wrong cubicle, so we were kitty-cornered from Nichols, one cubicle over, instead of facing him. While we waited for someone to sort out the mistake, Nichols gazed across our diagonal sight line with a wry look. Slowly and theatrically, he mouthed words that were the day's headline for him and ridiculously easy to lip-read. "They have a lot of power," he said.

At fifty-two years old, Terry Nichols was smaller than I expected and frail. He was dressed in what looked like a padded white-denim jumpsuit, his face anonymous except for eyes that seemed to search for the effect his words produced on us. He mostly spoke softly, in a somber, flatline tone, only occasionally broken by his joshing aw-shucks humor. Late in the day, though, my question about his marriage would dissolve him into tears of hopelessness.

"Crucial parts of this terrorist act remain hidden from the American people—especially the identities of the 'others unknown' who collaborated with McVeigh in the bombing," Nichols told us. "There are others who assisted McVeigh whose identities are unknown to me, but there are two individuals who I believe to have been coconspirators and will name as such." From this crux of Nichols's account to us that day and other key statements he went on to make, Jesse would file an affidavit in his FOIA case.

A few months earlier, Nichols had previewed his roster of bomb plot conspirators this way in a letter to Kathy Sanders, which he gave us during our interview. "Timothy McVeigh was the manipulated foot soldier, Roger Moore the middleman who supplied Tim with encouragement, instructions, and some explosives. And the top dog, the director, who orchestrated it all, is a rogue FBI agent...who has the power to cover things up, to protect Roger Moore, and to guide and control the outcome of an investigation."

We were counting on Nichols to flesh out this incredible sounding scenario—and to name the "top dog" to us. But first, this outwardly meek and mild man on the other side of the glass delivered an informational jolt in what would become a day of whiplashes for me as a journalist. According to Terry Nichols, Timothy McVeigh was not a terrorist mastermind. He was an undercover federal government operative. Secret Agent Timothy McVeigh? It was no use pressing for details. Nichols had only a few to offer.

He told us that McVeigh's first and practically only mention of his secret government identity came on a visit Nichols made to McVeigh in Lockport, New York, in December 1992. As the former Army buddies talked, McVeigh revealed that while he was still serving in the US Army earlier that year, he had been "recruited to carry out undercover missions" of an unspecified nature.[205]

"I really didn't put much stock into what he was saying at the time," Nichols recalled in writings that he gave Jesse and me that day. "He even produced a picture of an older man, possibly late fifties or sixties, dressed in an all-white business suit, including a white hat," Nichols wrote. "I reached out to take it, but McV insisted that I not touch it," Nichols added, shortening "McVeigh" to "McV," as he often did in his writings. "This guy was either someone who recruited Tim or was to be his contact. I don't recall which."[206]

However fragmentary, Nichols's information certainly put a novel spin on the bombing conspiracy: Timothy McVeigh, according to Nichols, had been a military-connected sleeper agent who said during their New York visit that he would "soon be making his first contact down South."[207] And so McVeigh did make contact, when he traveled to Florida the following month, in January

1993. There he met "the middleman" in Nichols's bomb plot scenario at a Fort Lauderdale gun show, apparently by happenstance but also precisely according to the plan McVeigh said was given to him by his recruiter.

Enter Arkansas gun dealer Roger Moore, the middleman in Nichols's scenario. Among researchers drilling down into the bombing case, Moore has long sparked curiosity about his possible CIA ties. Of particular interest: his Florida boat-building business in the 1970s and '80s, his movements in the Cold War orbit of Oliver North and the Iran Contra activists, and a series of law enforcement investigations targeting Moore. As author Wendy Painting has pointed out, those investigations included "plans to mail hundreds of pounds of C-4 explosives through the mail; sale of government property stolen from military installations (including ammunition); intent to sell explosives and bootlegged porn (origins of which are unknown); and the sale of ammunition, grenades, and flares, that he, again, shipped through the mail."[208]

Yet when Moore faced investigation, fortune always seemed to smile on him, and he escaped untouched more than once when an investigator closed a case in process, letting Moore off the hook. His luck seemed to hold in the bombing case. Government prosecutors presented Moore as the innocent victim of McVeigh and Nichols's 1994 robbery of $60,000 worth of guns, jewelry, and cash from his home. They never investigated Moore even when evidence surfaced that the robbery might have been staged. Nichols intended to set matters straight about that robbery in our interview. He told us it *was* staged. He knew this because Timothy McVeigh admitted it to him.

⅄

Nichols told us that in November 1994, right before his last trip to the Philippines, McVeigh coerced him into doing one more thing for his bomb plot: the Moore robbery. Until then, Nichols saw the gun dealer as a prospective financial backer of his and McVeigh's Army surplus business. When McVeigh insisted that he commit the robbery, Nichols didn't know what to think. He reluctantly followed orders.

On the morning of Saturday, November 5, 1994, following McVeigh's detailed instructions, Nichols waited outside Moore's farmhouse near Royal, Arkansas, at 9:00. When Moore came out to feed his animals, Nichols forced him back inside, tied him up, then loaded guns, jewelry, and cash into Moore's camper van, and drove off, transferring it all to his vehicle that was parked nearby.

Before leaving the house, however, Nichols picked up two large boxes next to the door, where they had been delivered unopened. "And the second box was that case of little tubes of nitromethane—the very same case that the FBI later recovered from my former KS home in April 2005!" Nichols wrote in a thick dossier of personal writings and supporting documents that he turned over to Jesse and me at ADX Florence.[209] "This is the liquid portion of the explosive known as 'Kinestik' and of which Moore claims to know nothing about. Now this case of nitromethane was an item that I was not supposed to take, but mistakes happen."

Two months after the robbery, in January 1995, when Nichols returned from his Philippines trip, the already strained relationship between the partners reached a breaking point. When they met up again in Junction City, Kansas, McVeigh was in a state of high anxiety. His plans were unraveling. He was using methamphetamine.

"I saw a side of McV that I had never seen before—an evil madman bent on achieving his goals and willing to eliminate anyone who might stand in his way,"[210] Nichols wrote in his dossier. "I didn't know how to deal with someone high on drugs and toting a weapon all the time and not knowing what might trigger him in going off into a wild rage. My mind was confused and numb."

Nichols's response to McVeigh's transformation was to play cat and mouse in search of information he might one day be able to use as leverage to get out of the relationship. As they talked, McVeigh shocked Nichols by revealing a secret about the robbery. McVeigh said he and Roger Moore had concocted it to give Moore cover as a victim in case McVeigh's plot failed. Now Nichols knew that McVeigh and Moore were also partners and that they had used him.

"McV told me that when he became activated [as an undercover operative] he told Roger that to do his mission he needed a large amount of funds quickly so that he could buy his recruits' trust & loyalty or if that didn't work then bribe those he wanted to recruit to help him complete his mission,"[211] Nichols wrote.

However, Roger Moore "didn't want to just hand over a large sum of cash, Tim said, and since Moore was concerned about being tied to McV's mission if things went wrong, the two of them came up with doing a 'staged' robbery, which would resolve the funding issue—which McV would use to buy, bribe or 'persuade' those he needed," Nichols wrote. "So if any investigation tracked back to Moore he could claim being a victim of a home robbery rather than a supplier of funds & explosives."

In the heat of the moment, Nichols may have been more stung by McVeigh's betrayal than curious about the bigger picture of the bombing conspiracy McVeigh had revealed. To protect Moore, McVeigh had deceived Nichols and, in the process, acquired more control over him, which soon would destroy him. Two months hence, when McVeigh ordered Nichols to help build the bomb, he would have to obey.

Still, folded inside Terry Nichols's seething resentment, the seed of a remarkable investigation into Roger Moore's possible role in the Oklahoma City bombing had been planted. It sprouted in the strange and failed off-the-books plea negotiation in the run-up to Nichols's state trial, when the lawyer emissary, allegedly from the Justice Department in Washington, said that Moore was "untouchable." The seed grew into Nichols's letter to the attorney general, accusing the government of involvement with Moore in the bombing conspiracy. Finally, in ADX Florence, it evolved into some 300 pages of handwritten personal analysis, letters, affidavits, FBI and other investigative records, and newspaper clippings that filled his dossier, much of it devoted to Roger Moore.

According to Nichols, Moore, like McVeigh, had blood on his hands in the Oklahoma City bombing because he made multiple sales to McVeigh of the binary explosive known as Kinestik: one part liquid nitromethane in a glass tube and the other part granular ammonium nitrate. When combined in a cardboard tube, the explosive resembled a dynamite stick. According to Nichols, McVeigh used the Kinestiks from Moore to detonate his bomb, thus making the gun dealer an accomplice in mass murder.

To support this claim, Nichols gave us a memorandum, prepared by a McVeigh defense investigator in December 1995 after interviewing McVeigh in the federal prison in El Reno. The memo reported on McVeigh's telling reaction to the possibility that Moore might testify against him. "The expression on Mr. McVeigh's face was that of anger," the investigator recounted. "Mr. McVeigh stated that if Moore ever decided to testify against him, that there was enough evidence available to sink Roger Moore."

According to the memo, "Mr. McVeigh stated that he bought nine Kinestiks from Moore for ten dollars each during August and September 1994." McVeigh told the investigator that Moore was "very much anti-government" and that Moore even commented to him that "he didn't mind selling him the 'Kinestiks' because he knew that he (McVeigh) would put them to good use."[212]

Nichols also gave us an FBI interview report stating that Michael Fortier turned over Kinestik explosives in his possession to FBI investigators when he made his plea deal.[213] "Fortier KNOWS where Tim got his Kinestik from,"[214] Nichols wrote in the dossier, adding: "McV had divulged to me as early as the summer of 1993 where he was getting his Kinestik from, and he certainly divulged the same to Mike, for Tim was closer to Mike than to me."

McVeigh's 2001 authorized biography, *American Terrorist,* by journalists Lou Michel and Dan Herbeck, published the month before his execution, never mentioned Kinestik in McVeigh's first and only detailed description of the bomb. According to Nichols, the carefully worded description there deliberately misled readers into believing Tovex was the bomb's explosive component.

"No!" Nichols wrote in his dossier. "The authors have NOT made a simple error in describing nor confusing the Kinestik with other explosives, but rather there is a deliberate & concerted effort to hide the truth regarding the use of Kinestik and where it came from."[215]

For Nichols, the smoking gun against Roger Moore lived on in his own memory of helping McVeigh build the bomb at Geary Lake State Park, near Junction City, Kansas, the day before the Oklahoma City blast. The bomb's contents were simple: some ninety bags of ammonium nitrate fertilizer packed into barrels, topped off with two kinds of explosive sticks and secured to the floor of the bomb truck with wooden poles. Nichols told us he watched Timothy McVeigh put the finishing touches on each barrel by adding one stick of Tovex explosive, which they had stolen from a quarry in Marion, Kansas, and one stick of Kinestik explosive, sold to McVeigh by Roger Moore.

"The bomb that McV built was simply an extremely supersized Kinestik,"[216] Nichols wrote in his dossier. "Both contain the same exact two ingredients. And where did McV get his Kinestik from?!" To Nichols, that question needed no answer.

From his prison cell, without a telephone or free access to the US mail, Terry Nichols had managed to reinvestigate the bomb plot with devastating results. Regardless of Nichols's credibility issues, in light of his dossier, it was hard to imagine the government presenting Roger Moore as an innocent victim in the bombing case without investigating further.

Or was it possible, as Nichols believed, that Moore was an undercover government operative, a "provocateur" who crossed the line into criminality in his collaboration with Timothy McVeigh?

In fact, as Nichols began to pore over hidden corners of Moore's life from his solitary confinement cell at ADX Florence, it hadn't taken professional-level detective skills to dig up plenty of evidence of Moore's covert government connections. His eccentric behavior following a 1993 road rage incident in Oklahoma and following the 1994 Nichols robbery had raised red flags with authorities and the media. Both incidents surfaced strong hints of Moore's possible government informant status.

The road rage arrest in Oklahoma eventually led to Moore's 1995 falling-out with his attorney there. Before throwing Moore out of his office, the angry lawyer, apparently privy to some of Moore's recent Oklahoma backstory, reportedly said he hoped Moore would face trial in the bombing case. To which Moore retorted that he was "protected" from prosecution.[217]

Following the robbery carried out by Nichols, police released Moore's name as the victim, causing him to complain to a reporter: "Whatever I was doing for the FBI is all f---ed up. They blew my cover." The *Arkansas Democrat* ran the story on page one.[218]

What *was* Roger Moore doing for the FBI in late 1994? The clues to Moore's possible ties to the Oklahoma City bombing were so manifest, they raised the question Nichols posed in his dossier: "Why is Roger Moore being protected and the truth kept hidden from the American people?"[219]

To Terry Nichols, the answer was clear. "The truth is Roger Moore is being protected because by revealing the truth [it] will implicate the federal government (our own gov't) in the OKC bombing!!"[220] Nichols wrote in the dossier.

⅄

Our interview was nearing its end. It was now or never. Would Terry Nichols reveal the name of the rogue FBI official he has called variously "the recruiter," "the top dog," and "the devil" in his writings? Here is how Nichols summed up "the top dog" in his dossier:

> This is a person in our federal government who had access to important & classified information along with other resources to be able to find the "right" recruit. And he found such in McV—someone who had initiative and the ability to be resourceful and to see the mission thru, but who was also susceptible to being manipulated, and this was "McV."
>
> The truth is Tim was playing out of his league, and he didn't know it. McV was dealing with professionals who understood the art of manipulation and who had many years of experience under their belt.[221]

Nichols told us that he learned the "top dog's" identity after his return from the Philippines, during the time he and McVeigh spent together in Junction City, where Nichols found McVeigh in such an alarming state of anxiety and where McVeigh revealed the truth about the staged Moore robbery. Recalling that strange time, Nichols told us that he never could figure out how McVeigh always seemed to know exactly where he was, as if someone had him under surveillance. Hours after his unscheduled return from the Philippines, McVeigh had called Nichols at his ex-wife's home in Las Vegas. Nichols told us that no one outside his family knew he was back in the US.

It wasn't the first time this had happened either. The previous fall, after McVeigh and Nichols argued in Arizona and split up, driving separate cars, McVeigh had appeared at Geary Lake State Park in Kansas. Nichols had made an impromptu stop to camp overnight when McVeigh appeared out of nowhere. It spooked Nichols, as did much of their journey together.

According to Nichols, that winter of 1995, in Junction City, McVeigh accidentally let slip his FBI handler's name. "McVeigh was extremely upset and angry," Nichols told us. "There, in what I believe was an accidental slip of the tongue, McVeigh revealed the identity of a high-ranking FBI official who was apparently directing McVeigh in the bomb plot."

I was mesmerized. Now, as Jesse and I sat watching our source through the glass divider, came a stunningly surreal moment. With a hesitating hand, Terry Nichols used his prison-issued pen to slowly fill in a name in a blank space on an affidavit that Jesse had provided him in advance.

"The name McVeigh let slip was Larry Potts—lead FBI agent at Ruby Ridge," Nichols told us, which Jesse included in the affidavit for the FOIA case. "McVeigh said he believed Potts was manipulating him and forcing him to go off script, which I understood meant to change the target of the bombing," Nichols said. "That was the only time I ever heard McVeigh refer to Larry Potts in that context."

Larry Potts, the demoted former FBI deputy director, would surely have outraged McVeigh for his prominent roles in the FBI sieges at Ruby Ridge and Waco. Potts had set the rules of engagement that led to the horrendous sniper killing of Vicki Weaver on her cabin porch in Ruby Ridge, Idaho, as she held her newborn baby in her arms. Then at Waco, Potts had toured the scene late in the FBI's long siege and recommended the attorney general approve the deadly tear gas raid that ended the Texas standoff with scores of deaths.

In McVeigh's mind, Potts would have personified militarized government overreach. But what was the rest of Nichols's cryptic recitation about? What manipulation had triggered McVeigh's fury as Nichols described it?

"I understood from McVeigh's comments that no bombing had taken place during my absence in the Philippines because the target had been changed, that Potts had had something to do with the change in targets, and that Michael Fortier had backed out of the bombing plot," Nichols told us. "McVeigh said that he would get even by using the first blow as a diversion for his second," Nichols said, signaling McVeigh's apparent intention to carry out a second bombing. "McVeigh did not, however, reveal to me either of his targets," Nichols said.[222]

I was beyond skeptical of Nichols's reveal of Larry Potts as Timothy McVeigh's handler in an FBI spy operation. If you were to script this scene for a Hollywood thriller, Potts would deliver a satisfying payoff as the villain behind the curtain, personifying a prime target of Timothy McVeigh's political vendetta. However, in the real world, wasn't this storyline too neat? Roger's coauthor, Andrew Gumbel, probably got it right in saying the name "Potts" was a symbolic choice by McVeigh, not a literal one.

Still, sitting there in that fortress, under the absolute control of his federal government keepers, would Nichols risk falsely accusing one of the FBI's own? Was it possible that the name "Potts" was a placeholder for someone down the line from Larry Potts in the FBI chain of command? Could McVeigh have been telling part of the truth, about having an undercover role, but not all of it, which would have required him to out his handler using an actual name?

Ever since his trials, Terry Nichols had attempted to engage the ear of someone he could safely tell the rest of the bombing story. So far, we were the only takers. Once again, after several hours spent at ADX Florence, I wondered: Who is this guy? Can he be for real? I was inside his supermax prison, but also inside an episode of *The X-Files*. Breathe.

⅄

It might have been possible to dismiss what I heard at ADX Florence as an unhinged conspiracy theory from Terry Nichols. In his letter to Jesse the previous fall, Nichols had led us to believe he could connect McVeigh to the Aryan Republican Army. In an August 2006 affidavit for Kathy Sanders, Nichols had gone further, stating:

> You see, Tim supplied Roger with blasting caps, and Roger supplied Tim with additional Kinestik which he used in the bombing.[223] Now Roger in turn supplied The Midwest Bank Robbers with blasting caps, and probably other explosive components as well.— You may want to ask Peter Langan about this.—And this is why the ATF destroyed those blasting caps, so they couldn't be traced back to Roger Moore, back to McVeigh, and back to the Marion Quarry. Because this would open up a whole can of worms for the government.

Nichols was mistaken here about the ATF destroying the blasting caps from the ARA's Columbus, Ohio, safe house. The FBI had been responsible for that mistake. Nichols's hint that he would connect McVeigh to the ARA had not panned out for us either, though the details of the scenario he gave Sanders were fascinating. We never found out how Nichols formulated that scenario or if he was guessing. Even when Jesse posed a series of questions about the ARA, Guthrie, the bank robberies, McVeigh,

Elohim City, and the bomb in a letter to Nichols in October 2006, he repeatedly said he didn't know.[224]

Instead of the ARA, Nichols had given us his nemesis Roger Moore, along with McVeigh, in a wild undercover scenario and hardcore conspiracy theory excoriating the evils of the federal government. One such passage in Nichols's dossier opened with the question: Who benefited from the Oklahoma City bombing? Nichols's answer: It wasn't McVeigh. He got executed. And it wasn't Nichols. He got life in a supermax prison.

Instead, as Nichols saw it, the beneficiary of the bombing was FBI Director Louis Freeh, whose budget Nichols claimed soared by 58 percent afterward.[225] In another passage of the dossier, Nichols called out the Justice Department's use of undercover operatives as the mechanism powering a vast government conspiracy:

> In summary, the truth is some powerful people within our very own gov't have an agenda to strip away all the people's freedoms & liberties which our Constitution provides each of us, and they've found a way to do it thru our Justice Dept. & its subsidiaries. They enlist agents, informants & provocateurs to infiltrate, supply, support and/or encourage & manipulate individuals and or groups, who usually have issues with our gov't and are easily manipulated, or coerced, or threatened, to carry out criminal act(s). And they have the power to cover up their people and involvement.[226]

Whatever extreme political fringe Terry Nichols occupied, I couldn't write off his *X-Files* scenario for the bomb plot. He had too much evidence backing up some of his claims. After our interview, I spent most of the night reading Nichols's dossier, especially the supporting documents. While his claim about the FBI's Larry Potts hung by the slenderest thread, Nichols's case against Roger Moore as an undercover FBI operative was credible. Whether it was provable was another question.

So far, Nichols's effort to tie Moore to McVeigh's explosives had fallen short. When Nichols led the FBI to the nitromethane buried under the porch in Herington, Roger Moore had managed to elude investigation once again. Whether because the box sat buried too long, or the FBI waited too long to test it for fingerprints, or Moore's prints were never there, or because Roger Moore died in 2018, the box of nitromethane on which Nichols had pinned such high hopes proved to be a mirage.

Was Moore an undercover operative who crossed the line into criminality or betrayed his federal government handlers? Whatever had happened when Timothy McVeigh stepped into Roger Moore's world of gun shows, explosives, and robbery had seemingly spawned a vast cover-up. The bombing trials had skirted those questions by allowing Moore to fly under the radar until Terry Nichols stalked him from his supermax prison cell.

For Jesse's circle, however, Nichols's digging had yielded a solid lead. Roger Moore would now join Andreas Strassmeir and Dennis Mahon as a person of high interest in our continuing investigation. Jesse would use the Nichols dossier for another FOIA lawsuit seeking secret FBI files on Moore, with an astonishing result. The FBI confirmed that it possessed 32,580 secret records on Roger Moore, but by 2024, it had only released a few of them to Jesse.[227] Asked what that volume of intel might signify, a retired FBI agent told Jesse without hesitation: "If we have 32,580 pages on him and he wasn't indicted, he was working for us. There's no way in hell he's not one of ours."[228]

Something else Nichols told us, almost as an aside, began to obsess me as another potential clue. With all the time in the world to relive the past in his prison cell, Terry Nichols must have reviewed building the bomb countless times. Imagine his surprise, then, when McVeigh's biography came out in 2001, and the bomb McVeigh described wasn't the same bomb Nichols remembered!

According to Nichols, the actual bomb "was in a 'V' shape, not a backward 'J' shape, and it took up only about half the truck, not almost the entire truck as McVeigh's design would require as described in *American Terrorist*."[229] Nichols told us that the much larger bomb McVeigh described would have required more materials than they had in their Herington storage locker. There was one more telltale: "The bomb McVeigh described also displayed a level of expertise and sophistication which neither McVeigh nor I had in building a bomb," Nichols told us. It was that simple, according to him: They didn't build the bomb McVeigh described because they didn't know how.

When he looked back on that fateful day at Geary Lake State Park, what stuck in Nichols's memory was how the stored bags of fertilizer had gotten wet and solidified, requiring McVeigh to break the fertilizer apart and force the pieces into the plastic barrels. Before our interview, Jesse had consulted some experts who told him that solidified fertilizer wouldn't explode. Nichols agreed.

In his dossier, Nichols recounted that when they were done building the bomb, their hurried creation looked to him like a dud, even making him wonder if McVeigh might have built another bomb somewhere else. What an alarming thought. If McVeigh and Nichols didn't build the bomb that destroyed the Murrah Building, who did?

⅄

As Jesse and I drove away from ADX Florence, I realized that I had a shot at answers to that baffling question on the second stop of my maximum-security prison road trip that spring of 2007. I was headed to federal death row next for a face-to-face interview with David Hammer. He had spent twenty-three months interviewing Timothy McVeigh on death row for a book about the bombing that was nothing like the story told in *American Terrorist*. Had Terry Nichols just given credence to McVeigh's subversive death row declaration about who helped him deliver the bomb, as told to the outlaw journalist Hammer?

What was that road sign coming up? Caution: Curves Ahead.

CHAPTER 13

DEATH ROW SECRETS

HEADING FOR DEATH ROW two months after the Nichols interview, I drove a rental car from the Indianapolis airport to Terre Haute, probably following the same route as the US Marshals Service vans that transported Timothy McVeigh and David Hammer eight years earlier. Operation Golden Eagle had landed in the blazing Indiana heat of July 1999, with Hammer and McVeigh among the first group of twenty condemned prisoners to occupy the nation's newly designated federal death row.

Hammer's 2004 prison memoir, *Secrets Worth Dying For*, described their arrival. On day two, an inmate in the prison's general population died of heat stroke as the temperature spiked to 105 degrees. Still, the newcomers had to stay in their cells without shower privileges for several days until they received the green light for a recreation period.

But first, the prisoners underwent a rite of passage, stripping down and packaging their rank underclothes in ziplock bags, along with a clean washcloth they used to swab their armpits and genitals, for storage in a prison freezer. Guards told them that in case they ever escaped, they were creating a scent pool for bloodhounds to track them down. This news prompted McVeigh to wonder aloud how much his dirty underwear would be worth after his execution.

The new inmates' red jumpsuits bled onto everything else in the prison wash, turning it pink and transforming their daily recreation period into a comedy hour. To work out in the prison recreation yard, the worst of America's most notorious criminals had to strip down to boxer shorts and T-shirts of a hue that McVeigh called "fairy pink."

As the only white inmates on death row, Hammer, McVeigh, and Jeffery Paul, Hammer's coauthor, gravitated as a threesome to one of the cages in the yard. McVeigh and Paul would lift weights while Hammer ran their wide-ranging conversations about the bombing case. Timothy McVeigh speaks from beyond the grave in *Secrets Worth Dying For*. The book contains McVeigh's outlier account of the bombing conspiracy as told to Hammer and Paul during their daily recreation periods over the twenty-three months leading up to McVeigh's execution in June 2001.

"I needed the truth from Timothy McVeigh for a book I wanted to write about the Oklahoma City bombing: a book that would go beyond the unconvincing lone-wolf scenario McVeigh and the US government were so carefully constructing," Hammer wrote in *Deadly Secrets*, his 2010 sequel to *Secrets Worth Dying For*. The bombing was personal for Hammer, who was born and raised in Oklahoma.

I learned of *Secrets Worth Dying For* on my trip to Oklahoma City to meet Jannie Coverdale. The book had been a hot topic of conversation around Jannie's dining-room table. Driving to Terre Haute a year later, I could still hear the bewildering buzz of unfamiliar names flying around the room: Hammer, Trentadue, and the mysterious Poindexter. I ordered the book on Amazon and devoured it in one sitting.

Soon after meeting Jesse, I was on the phone regularly with Hammer, in secure calls to death row that would have been impossible if Jesse hadn't organized them as Hammer's attorney. A floodgate of confidential information about Hammer's McVeigh interviews opened, leading to my first face-to-face interview with Hammer over two days in 2006 and the coming visit in March 2007. Still later, I would edit Hammer's sequel, *Deadly Secrets*, containing additional exclusive information he shared with me from 2006–10 about McVeigh and the bombing.

"I spent hundreds of hours talking with McVeigh about his time prior to the bombing of the Alfred P. Murrah Federal Building," Hammer would state in his 2007 affidavit for Jesse's FOIA case, based on my death row interviews. "He [McVeigh] provided me with specific information, documentation from his trial, hearings, and FBI 302 [interview] statements. Most of the information provided by McVeigh has since been verified by independent sources."

When I confided to Hammer that I wished I could have been a fly on the wall for those brainstorms in the recreation yard, he said he was confident the prison secretly taped every session and equally as sure we would never hear those tapes. But moments into our first face-to-face interview, Hammer told me how the book project originated.

A guard had escorted me that day on an elevator ride up to "Dog Unit," as Hammer sometimes called death row, and then released me. Down a long, wide institutional hallway, I took a breath and let myself into the interview room. There stood Hammer, a large, brooding man with a predator's patient demeanor. Imagine Nicolas Cage in handcuffs and heavy leg irons.

While I sat at a wide table separating us, Hammer paced the floor on his side of the small room. I could see a guard sitting outside in the hallway through a window in the door behind Hammer. When Hammer moved closer to the table, the guard would bob up like a jack-in-the-box, a comical pantomime, until I realized this was for my protection.

Hammer was Hammer's real last name. Always a genial and amusing conversationalist, he had killed a cellmate without warning and, a few years down the road, would kill another. In this prison interview room, I was Hammer's cellmate for several hours, but I hardly ever felt threatened. The monster within Hammer only made one fleeting appearance. It came at the start of that first interview when I learned the origin of his book deal with McVeigh.

"What can you tell me about Timothy McVeigh?" I asked.

"I can tell you he was raped in prison," Hammer replied, obligingly. A reptilian smirk crossed his face.

According to Hammer, by September 1999, two months after their move to death row, it was a foregone conclusion that trouble was coming for Timothy McVeigh. "[His] mouth was his worst enemy," Hammer said.[230] McVeigh insulted Hispanic inmates by calling them "wetbacks," referred to Buffalo's African American community as "porch monkeys," and called fellow inmates "punks" without realizing that in prison, a punk was a sexually submissive victim.

McVeigh lived in fear of his cellblock mates, including Hammer. McVeigh had read a legal opinion describing Hammer as a "clever, manipulative, dangerous, violent criminal," known to have taken a prison psychologist hostage using a weapon. "All it would take is a drop of my blood on their hands to get on the cover of *Time*, and they know it," McVeigh reportedly whispered to Jeffery Paul about the other condemned prisoners. But according to Hammer, the rape happened differently. Hammer said that guards who despised McVeigh left the door of his cell open to prisoners in an adjoining unit housing Cuban detainees in the custody of the Immigration and Naturalization Service.

"He was rocked to his very soul," Hammer wrote in *Deadly Secrets*. "His biggest fear had become a reality. He asked [Jeffery] Paul to make him a shank so that if the Cubans ever came back, he would be able to defend himself. He swore us to secrecy but knew that others on the tier had seen and heard what happened to him."

The assault set the stage for a death-row bargain, a protection contract. Hammer showed McVeigh a *National Enquirer* story offering $10,000 for information on the infamous Oklahoma City bomber. Hammer told McVeigh: "I think the public might be interested in knowing that you have been turned into a prison sex slave and how the guards turn a blind eye to your plight."

So it was that a highly unusual literary collaboration was formed. The older, wiser inmate Hammer, who had spent most of his life behind bars, would protect the notorious newcomer to prison life from other inmates, guards, and, above all, publicity about what had just happened. In exchange, McVeigh would open up to Hammer about his actual role in the Oklahoma City bombing.

McVeigh, Hammer, and Paul agreed to cooperate, leading to the publication of *Secrets Worth Dying For*. "A deal with the devil beats the unknown and uncontrolled," Hammer quoted McVeigh telling Paul about their bargain.[231]

⅄

The strange tales of Timothy McVeigh told by David Hammer and Terry Nichols flooded my mind on the drive to Terre Haute. For me, the Nichols interview had been a game-changer. On two crucial points, he had echoed Hammer's account in *Secrets Worth Dying For,* telling Jesse and me that Timothy McVeigh was an admitted government agent and that the bomb built in Kansas was amateurish, almost certainly a dud that couldn't have destroyed the Murrah Building. After hearing these outlandish claims twice, I had to reconsider them.

Later, I discovered two other stray pieces of evidence from more credible sources supporting the claim that Timothy McVeigh was an undercover government operative. In October 1993, McVeigh wrote a letter to his sister describing his Special Forces training at Fort Bragg. *The New York Times* printed the letter in 1998. In it, McVeigh claimed that he and nine others had been handpicked as fitting an "ultimate warrior" type to serve in a unique military unit that would carry out domestic and foreign "covert operations."[232]

According to Army records, McVeigh soon washed out of the Special Forces tryout when severe foot blisters made meeting rigorous physical requirements impossible. Or was that a cover story?

While researching her 2016 book, *Aberration in the Heartland of the Real,* author Wendy Painting discovered a record in the University of Texas archive of materials from McVeigh's defense attorney, Stephen Jones. It revealed that McVeigh told his first attorneys from the public defender's office almost the same thing he told his sister: that while in the Army, he was assigned to work undercover in a Department of Defense domestic security operation.

To his lawyers, McVeigh went further, telling them his mission was to infiltrate neo-Nazis, among other domestic terror threats. Reporting on the document, Painting wrote: "McVeigh then said that after having discovered the bombing plot, he reported it to his handlers but was instructed to continue in his role, remain embedded within the conspiracy and even go so far as to participate in the bombing; but ensure that only a couple of windows were blown out of the Murrah building."[233]

Lending some credence to Terry Nichols's claim about the bomb, McVeigh also told his first lawyers that the shocking scope of damage he witnessed made him wonder "if someone had switched the truck at the last minute," according to Painting's reporting on the document in the Jones collection.

In *Others Unknown*, his memoir about the case, Jones added another thought-provoking note about this moment in the McVeigh prosecution. Jones recalled that when public defender Susan Otto handed McVeigh over to Jones, she said: "When you know everything I know, and you will soon enough, you will never think of the United States of America in the same way."[234]

Heading to my 2007 interview with Hammer, I didn't know about these pieces of evidence. Still, Nichols and Hammer might be on to something. Compared with Hammer's book-length rendering of McVeigh in *Secrets Worth Dying For*, the Nichols interview was merely a stick figure sketch. Still, the crux of McVeigh's admissions to both men was almost identical. My Hammer interview would offer an advantage no other journalist would have: a chance to probe the eerie commonality of the bomb plot stories told by criminals who knew McVeigh personally.

In Hammer's death row interviews over nearly two years, McVeigh claimed that he was an undercover operative, not for the FBI as in the Nichols account, but for an unspecified Department of Defense unit, as McVeigh told his sister and his initial lawyers. To Hammer, McVeigh described how a shadowy military officer he called "the Major" had plucked him from Special Forces training to join a secret Defense Department unit. A year later, amid blowback from the siege at Ruby Ridge, the Major instructed his sleeper agent McVeigh to prepare for his mission, telling him: "The survivalist and militia malcontents can destroy this country. It is up to you to prevent that from happening."[235]

After cash infusions from the Major totaling $60,000 in used bills, McVeigh headed south from New York state to Florida. There, Hammer and Nichols agreed, McVeigh met Roger Moore in January 1993 at a Fort Lauderdale gun show.

From there, both accounts tracked McVeigh's path to Oklahoma City over the next two years and several months, both noting McVeigh's meetup with Andreas Strassmeir at a 1993 Tulsa gun show, multiple visits to Roger Moore's Arkansas ranch, and Moore's November 1994 robbery there. Then, back to Kingman, where McVeigh tried to enlist Michael Fortier in the bomb plot.

In one notable discrepancy, Hammer quoted McVeigh claiming that the ARA's Richard Guthrie and Michael Brescia committed the Moore robbery, not Terry Nichols, who told Jesse and me that he robbed Moore.

As for McVeigh's association with Stephen Colbern, McVeigh told Hammer they became good friends in the Arizona desert near Kingman, pursuing their shared interest in survivalism while camping in the desert caves.[236] In 1994, Colbern, a university-trained biochemist and fugitive from federal weapons charges, was hiding out in Arizona, sometimes picking up mail for McVeigh in Kingman.

The bombing investigation established that Karen Anderson, Roger Moore's girlfriend and partner in a mail-order ammunition business, had taken steps to introduce McVeigh and Colbern. Moore told the FBI that he doubted McVeigh and Colbern ever met, and the FBI appeared to have taken his word for this. However, McVeigh told a different story to Hammer. According to McVeigh, when he departed Arizona to commit the bombing, he said his goodbyes to Colbern, "but only after obtaining specific information he needed for building a bomb," Hammer wrote in *Deadly Secrets*. "McVeigh now had in his pocket a complete list of components needed for his bombing mission."[237]

Most sensationally, Hammer's two books dished out potentially incriminating revelations about the Aryan Republican Army. McVeigh admitted to Hammer that he robbed banks with the ARA and planned the bombing with them and others in meetings at Elohim City.[238] McVeigh named the ARA as his support team in Kansas and on the Oklahoma City bombing run. If he was telling Hammer the truth, the *Secrets* books closed the case on the "others unknown." According to Timothy McVeigh, the "others" were the Aryan Republican Army.

Alongside McVeigh, according to his interviews with Hammer, the enigmatic Andreas Strassmeir also played an undercover role in the bombing conspiracy. In McVeigh's telling, Strassmeir was a second Pentagon undercover operative inside the bomb plot, reporting to the same Department of Defense unit as McVeigh but to a different handler.[239] "McVeigh and Strassmeir worked together to obtain information and to plan and then bomb the

Federal Building in Oklahoma City," Hammer said in his affidavit for Jesse's FOIA case.[240]

Deadly Secrets covers an array of bombing mysteries that have gathered a cult following over time. In their interviews, McVeigh told Hammer that it was Michael Brescia who picked him up at the McDonald's in Junction City on April 17, 1995, two days before the bombing, and drove him to Elliott's Body Shop to rent the bomb truck. In McVeigh's telling, Brescia launched the legend of John Doe 2 as he stood in the doorway of Elliott's smoking a cigarette. That night at the Dreamland motel, according to McVeigh, the ARA's Scott Stedeford, not McVeigh, took delivery of moo goo gai pan in room 25, where McVeigh was staying.[241]

According to *Deadly Secrets*, followers of the bombing case who insisted that two Ryder trucks were involved in the crime were correct. But McVeigh constructing the bomb with Nichols at Geary Lake State Park on Tuesday, April 18, 1995, never happened. Instead, on that day, members of the Aryan Republican Army pitched in to retrieve bomb components from a storage locker in nearby Herington, Kansas.

As Hammer admitted in *Deadly Secrets* and to me in interviews, McVeigh sometimes changed his story without explanation. On one occasion, he told Hammer that he and Nichols constructed a "half-assed" bomb but that it was not the bomb that destroyed the Murrah Building.[242] McVeigh later told Hammer that "a professional" built the bomb, not in Kansas but in Oklahoma City.

In any case, according to Hammer's interviews, on Tuesday, April 18, the day before the bombing, McVeigh led a convoy from Kansas to a warehouse in Oklahoma City. The convoy included two Ryder trucks and assorted vehicles carrying materials, the ARA crew, and the man called "Poindexter," the Major's chosen bombmaker. Members of the ARA making the trip with McVeigh were Richard Guthrie, Peter Langan, Michael Brescia, Kevin McCarthy, and Scott Stedeford. According to McVeigh, he drove one Ryder truck while Guthrie drove the other one to Oklahoma City.

Based on his interviews with McVeigh and a handwritten note in the Mercury Marquis getaway car after McVeigh's arrest, Hammer believed the warehouse was Emrick's Allied Storage on Northwest Third Street in Oklahoma City.[243] Drilling into this clue, Hammer said he located an FBI interview report stating that Tinker Air Force Base military personnel used Emrick's for long-term storage of military material and equipment.[244] "Why was the FBI agent in the bombing case focusing on the military aspect of Emrick's?" Hammer wondered in *Deadly Secrets*.[245] Could it be because McVeigh was, as he told Hammer, acting as a government agent in an undercover military mission?

At the warehouse on the night of April 18, 1995, according to McVeigh, he and the ARA's Richard Guthrie helped Poindexter build a massive 7,000-pound bomb, lacing it with military-grade explosives. After the Major inspected their work, with handshakes all around, and while Poindexter stood admiring his creation, McVeigh told Hammer that an operative of the Major's stepped behind Poindexter and slit his throat from ear to ear.

"Soldier, he was just hired help, not one of us," the Major told a startled McVeigh with a hand on his shoulder.[246] McVeigh and the assassin loaded Poindexter's body into the bomb truck, thus depositing a haunting clue. Did the severed mystery leg buried in Oklahoma City's memorial grove for victims belong to the bombmaker?

McVeigh told Hammer he learned from conversation with the Major at the warehouse that his team had installed C-4 explosives inside the Murrah Building to ensure maximum damage. McVeigh carried a handheld transmitter to detonate the explosives in the truck and the building.

On Wednesday morning, April 19, 1995, McVeigh told Hammer that he, Richard Guthrie, and Michael Brescia returned to the warehouse, equipped themselves with headsets and mouthpieces, and set forth on the catastrophic bombing run. After dropping them off, according to McVeigh, Peter Langan returned to their hotel to assemble the rest of the ARA crew as lookouts near the Murrah Building.

Hammer's accounts of the bomb delivery in the two books contain discrepancies of his making, a reminder that McVeigh's credibility isn't the only one at issue in evaluating the books as testimony. In *Secrets Worth Dying For*, McVeigh said that Brescia rode with him in the bomb truck while Guthrie tailed them in another vehicle. In the sequel *Deadly Secrets*, however, McVeigh said Brescia and Guthrie both rode with him in the bomb truck, with Brescia exiting a half block from their target and trailing on foot. Then, while McVeigh parked the yellow Ryder, Guthrie stepped out, conveniently placing Guthrie and Brescia standing together by the bomb truck. This deft and dubious formulation by Hammer left the mystery of John Doe 2 unresolvable. Was it Brescia? Or Guthrie?

Hammer and I, author and editor, went around and around on this point and others during the writing of *Deadly Secrets*, leading Hammer to tell me I was the most stubborn person he had ever dealt with. Coming from a criminal on death row, I took that as grudging respect. As I reread *Deadly Secrets* today, I now believe that Hammer, in 2010, wove Guthrie into McVeigh's account of the passengers in the bomb truck. Hammer may have done this to align the John Doe 2 story with McVeigh's pivotal 2001 lead to Jesse, disclosing that Guthrie was John Doe 2. Hammer's credibility on the facts was usually impeccable, but this time was different. The scenario of Brescia riding next to McVeigh, as told in the earlier book, is more believable.

After the bomb went off, Guthrie and Brescia were supposed to pick up McVeigh in an SUV belonging to him for their escape from Oklahoma City. For reasons unknown to McVeigh, however, they never showed up, forcing him to turn to plan B, his escape alone in the yellow Mercury without a license plate, which led to his arrest ninety minutes later.

Somewhere on Interstate 70, a lightbulb went on about this interview as I drove toward Terre Haute and death row. Hammer's oddly affecting inscription in my copy of *Secrets Worth Dying For* sparked a realization. "To my Friend, Margaret," Hammer wrote. "I hope that together we can spread the truth and find answers to OKC. Maybe in some small way, we can help ease the hurt and heartache of some who suffered at the hands of McVeigh and others."

Suddenly, there it was, my angle for this interview. As Jesse's granny might have said, "If it was a snake, it would have bit you."

Today would be about the big picture of the bombing case, not the details. Weren't the others unknown right there in Hammer's neatly penned inscription? The bombing was no longer a mystery to him. It was a case the FBI didn't want to close. Hammer had published Timothy McVeigh's subversive story chapter and verse.

He had named names. The crucial question that remained was: Did McVeigh tell Hammer the truth? Or, at least, did Hammer believe McVeigh? That was my angle. I would press Hammer as hard as I dared. It would be my last interview and my last chance.

I was ready now, which was good because I had arrived in the prison's reception area in Terre Haute, with its wall of lockers where you parked all your worldly belongings except pen and paper. My silent escort led the way through familiar hallways, around corners, and through heavy swinging doors to the elevator. An enormous ring of keys swung on his belt, and a bottle of hand sanitizer poked out of the pocket of his uniform trousers.

Upstairs, I headed for the familiar interview room where I would find Hammer. We had a good run together in this room that I thought of as Hammer's private death row think tank. I knew what Hammer believed were the pressure points that still might crack the case open. One was a thousand fingerprints on McVeigh's car, motel room, and the countertop from Elliott's Body Shop that the FBI never ran against its fingerprint databases. Another was the DNA from the severed leg that might belong to Poindexter, but which, again, the FBI never tested against genetic databases. Another, of course, was the audiotapes Hammer was sure the prison made of the McVeigh interviews.

Then there were the Kehoe brothers, on Hammer's short list of hot leads to crack the bombing case for reasons he never shared. Imagine my surprise when I arrived in the interview room on the second day of my previous visit to find not Hammer but a total stranger. He was young and good-looking except for a milky blind eye that earned him his prison nickname, Cyclops.

"I zigged when I should have zagged," said Daniel Lee, convicted along with Chevie Kehoe in the Mueller family murders.

I took my seat as casually as I could manage. The encounter was vintage Hammer. He had somehow pulled strings to arrange an off-the-books meeting for Lee to plead his case with a visiting journalist, saying he was innocent.

I couldn't help Daniel Lee, though his story was another doozy. A judge reviewing the case characterized Chevie Kehoe as the "ringleader" in the crime and Lee as the "faithful dog." Testifying against her son, Gloria Kehoe said that Lee lacked the "stomach," to kill the little girl, so Chevie Kehoe did it. Still, Kehoe's jury spared his life, while Daniel Lee, described by prosecutors as a "locked, loaded gun," and with his dead eye and an ugly Nazi tattoo on his neck, received the ultimate punishment.

Despite Hammer's advocacy efforts, he couldn't help either. Daniel Lee was put to death in 2020 after a long legal hiatus in federal executions. By then, the family of his victim, Nancy Mueller, and one of the prosecutors in the case had mounted a passionate effort to save Lee's life. The battle went to the United States Supreme Court before failing on a 5–4 vote.

My takeaway from my glimpse into the Daniel Lee case was that Hammer knew more about Chevie Kehoe and his brother Cheyne than he ever shared. In *Deadly Secrets*, McVeigh claimed that Cheyne, who McVeigh said owed him money, drove the second Ryder truck used in the bombing from Arizona to Kansas. Whatever had put the Kehoe brothers on Hammer's hotlist, I wouldn't bet against him.

A news story in the Seattle *Spokesman-Review* on January 16, 1998, might contain a clue. The former manager of a Seattle motel where Chevie Kehoe was staying in April 1995 told the paper that days before the bombing, Kehoe predicted something was going to happen that would "wake people up." On the morning of the bombing, the manager said Kehoe showed up in his living quarters forty-five minutes before the bombing asking to watch CNN. When a bulletin reported the blast, Kehoe was "ecstatic," the manager recalled.

As always, Hammer and I batted these riddles from the bombing case back and forth, but an unfamiliar solemnity infused our talk on this day. Our time together was almost up, and, strange as this would sound, I realized that Hammer and I were nearly friends. I am famously bad at goodbyes anyway, but this one, considering Hammer's condemned status, was so awkward that I ducked it and got on with my mission.

Face-to-face, I asked David Hammer what he believed, what his gut told him, about the truthfulness of Timothy McVeigh's story. What about McVeigh's claim that he was a government agent? What about his claim that members of the Aryan Republican Army gang were his accomplices? Did Hammer believe McVeigh? Why or why not?

In response, my fellow traveler, through the labyrinth of the bombing mystery, was as coy as ever or as honest. As I recall, Hammer sat there as silent as the Great Sphinx. Or was he the Wizard of Oz? He told me what he always told me when pressed on these points. It was up to me to decide what I believed. He was only the messenger.

Perhaps sensing a looming goodbye as awkward for him as for me, Hammer steered the conversation back into the comfort zone of crime-solving. He reminded me that he had gifted me with an exclusive lead from McVeigh that someone urgently needed to pursue. I'm sharing it publicly for the first time in honor of that moment. Here is that clue, straight from Timothy McVeigh. He claimed that the FBI could identify the severed leg—and likely the McVeigh accomplice the leg belonged to—in short order. All the FBI needed to do was run the leg's DNA against samples collected by the Army from every soldier in McVeigh's Desert Storm company. Hammer was right. It *was* a hot lead, fitting for our last words together face-to-face.

When Hammer died in prison in 2018, not by execution but in a prison medical facility from chronic disease, Jesse wrote this to me in an email: "Brilliant, cunning and always scheming, especially against anyone foolish enough to believe that he was a friend. I have known David Paul Hammer since 1995. He was a lot of help to me, and I liked him. But I never forgot that to Hammer friends were potential victims. Will see him again in hell someday."

On the road again, heading away from Terre Haute with death row in the rearview mirror, I thought I understood why Hammer chose the Oscar Wilde epigram that opens *Secrets Worth Dying For*: "The Truth Is Rarely Pure and Never Simple." Those words inspired me as I headed for my prison road trip's third and final stop that spring of 2007. If Timothy McVeigh told Hammer the truth, the inmate I was going to meet next was one of the architects of the Oklahoma City bombing, one who was there with McVeigh on the bombing run on April 19, 1995. Next on my Wilde ride: the Aryan Republican Army's coleader Peter Langan.

CHAPTER 14

BLOOD OF OKLAHOMA

THE ARYAN REPUBLICAN ARMY recruiting tape had been my first solid lead. That clue, which Jesse handed me in Salt Lake City, was developing in a most intriguing way. I knew the backstory. The flood of evidence that the ARA was involved in the bombing had crested with Roger Charles's discovery of the FBI director's teletypes and John Solomon's reporting for the Associated Press.[247]Then the story stalled.

"John Solomon had it all sewed up back in 2003, but then nothing happened," recalled Michael Hubbard, the former Senate investigator. Jesse's FOIA lawsuit in 2004 was the latest contender to uncover the hidden story. Jesse knew that Timothy McVeigh's sensational death-row disclosures about the neo-Nazi terror group would not be credible alone. But he had another angle to play with Peter Langan, the Aryan Republican Army's imprisoned coleader.

Except for Richard Guthrie, who died mysteriously in his jail cell in 1996, the members of the ARA gang went to prison for their bank robberies but never faced an investigation into the bombing. Most of them scored lenient plea deals and short prison sentences. Except for Langan, they all served their time and regained their freedom.

Langan's plea negotiations fell through. He received a sentence of life without the possibility of parole plus thirty-five years. Peter Langan would never taste freedom again without a miracle. Maybe that was motivation enough for him to spill secrets about the Oklahoma City bombing. That was Jesse's gamble when he arranged for me to interview the surviving head of the ARA for his FOIA lawsuit.

Who was Peter Langan? Mark Hamm's book *In Bad Company* introduced me to Langan's incredible life story. He once told a reporter that as a child living abroad during the 1960s, he had fantasized about his father going on secret missions. That was before he knew his father was a high-ranking CIA officer in Saigon amid a calamitous geopolitical collapse for America.[248] When I interviewed Peter Langan in prison, he was forty-seven years old, looking back on his own secret mission as a government informant, which had crashed and burned with his capture by the FBI-led SWAT team in Ohio in 1996.

In a life of escalating crime and secrets, Langan had eventually bonded with the legend of white supremacist outlaw hero Robert Jay Mathews, founder of The Order. When trapped and facing prison in 1993 for the robbery he had committed with Richard Guthrie, his politically radical partner in crime, Langan saved himself by using his wits. That was when he made his highly unusual informant deal with the Secret Service: his freedom for Guthrie's. Instead, Langan reunited with Guthrie and helped form the ARA.

In 2007, after J.D. Cash developed Langan as a source and after Langan connected with Jesse from prison, he was once again looking for a deal with federal authorities. However, his avenues to appeal his life sentence had virtually all closed. It was a long shot, but Jesse's FOIA lawsuit might create leverage for Langan with federal authorities.

With their agreement for Langan to submit an affidavit in the lawsuit, a deep game of mutual interest was underway. Or so it seemed to me. If anyone else knew the secrets Richard Guthrie took to the grave about the Aryan Republican Army and its possible connection to the bombing, it was Peter Langan. On the other hand, if anyone had the platform to make something happen with those secrets using the authority of the FOIA, it was Jesse. For both of them, the crucial calculus was this: How explosive would the information need to be?

By nature, I thrive on the kind of wildcat effort that David Hammer and I had pursued for the past year, brainstorming, chasing down leads, and savoring the rush of fresh insight and the possibility of a new chase. Jesse and Langan played a different game: methodical, patient, and inexorable. In my interview, I wouldn't be pushing buttons in the hope that the ARA's imprisoned coleader might spill a clue about the terror organization's role in the bombing. Instead, I would be dutifully recording what Peter Langan wanted the world to hear, opening doors of questioning that Jesse hoped Langan would walk through in his high-risk effort to open a path to an appeal of his life sentence for the bank robberies.

How significant a risk would Peter Langan take?

⅄

Mark Hamm's book *In Bad Company,* profiling the Aryan Republican Army, is a touchstone of my investigation along with Ambrose Evans-Pritchard's *The Secret Life of Bill Clinton,* David Hoffman's *The Oklahoma City Bombing and the Politics of Terror,* and Stephen Jones's *Others Unknown*. Later came Roger Charles's *Oklahoma City,* coauthored with Andrew Gumbel, and Wendy Painting's *Aberration in the Heartland of the Real*. Each of these books is one of a kind, but *In Bad Company* may be the most unique.

Since I was in Indiana that spring of 2007, headed for the Peter Langan interview, I reached out to Mark Hamm in Bloomington, where he taught sociology at Indiana State University. He graciously agreed to meet me for beers at Nick's, an iconic college town pub with framed photos and autographs on wood-paneled walls, a polished bar, and booths for swapping secrets.

What amazed me about Hamm's book was that, as an author, he devised a strategy to tell a story virtually off-limits to mainstream journalism. Two bombing trials had set the official account in stone. How could a journalist report on evidence pointing to the Aryan Republican Army's possible role, not just in the bank robberies, but in the bombing? Hadn't the trials proven the crime was an act of lone-wolf terror by Timothy McVeigh?

Hamm smiled knowingly. He'd heard this dilemma before from mainstream news journalists whose bosses had tied their hands from reporting on the ARA. Hamm's storytelling strategy was as simple as it was brilliant: presenting his book not as journalism but as sociology. He cloaked his chronicle of the ARA's alleged role as Timothy McVeigh's strike force not as a verifiable fact but as a sociological theory.

The resulting book, published in 2002, was a journalistic Trojan horse, drawing on unnamed sources inside the ARA to explore credible evidence that they were McVeigh's accomplices.

Time passed, and more evidence, primarily from J.D. Cash and Roger Charles, piled up, pointing to the ARA. *In Bad Company* took on a sharper cutting edge. However, through a stroke of bad luck, the book remained something of a sleeper. Hamm was set for a round of national TV appearances when planes struck their targets on September 11, 2001, burying the Oklahoma City investigation under the events of the day.

While preparing for my interview, I replayed the ARA recruiting video Jesse gave me. As a video production, *The Aryan Republican Army Presents: The Armed Struggle Underground* was a hot mess to watch. Guthrie and Langan bombastically held forth about their revolutionary mission. They dressed in Halloween-like costumes, brandishing weapons from their terrorist arsenal and packing mason jars with fake cash representing the gang's bank robbery loot.

This over-the-top propaganda tape, produced in February 1995, ran for almost two hours, including parody commercials for "Blammo Ammo" and other terrorist must-haves. In its closing moments, Guthrie appeared to realize the video's tone was a train wreck and seemed to struggle to find a way to end it.

Still, Mark Hamm cautioned against underestimating the ARA leaders' seriousness. Their menace was real. Their message was poisonous and chilling. Guthrie's shorthand, "go to work," advocated for would-be revolutionaries to commit widespread robbery and murder and to eradicate non-Aryan citizens from the face of America.

I'm speculating now, but it seems likely that after more than a year of robbing banks and lavishing money on white power causes, Richard Guthrie and Peter Langan's Aryan Republican Army had achieved a cult following in the white power underground. In early 1995, the ARA's founders were creating a bigger tent. As Langan boasted on camera, they never got caught in their many robberies, presenting themselves as proven professionals knocking on the door of outlaw glory.

Compare that record to McVeigh and Nichols, and Hamm's caution becomes more compelling. Revolutionaries Langan and Guthrie could count on stoking the passions of youths in search of a cause.

Next, the gang was about to set out for the Arizona desert near Kingman and McVeigh, where some believe they practiced bomb-making skills together. When the FBI raided the ARA's Columbus, Ohio, safe house after capturing Langan in January 1996, agents found the recruitment videocassettes. One was addressed to Louis Beam in a possible tribute to the godfather of leaderless resistance, which the ARA video espoused in its offbeat way.

A year had passed, but the cassettes were still in the safe house, unmailed and unscreened. Why? Could it be because the video included Guthrie and Langan discussing a coming massacre and even using the infamous McVeigh phrase "collateral damage" before he did? Two months after Langan and Guthrie shot the video, the bomb exploded in Oklahoma City. The massacre prophecy came true, though at a federal building, not a courthouse, as they predicted. Did seeming hints about the bombing render the tapes too hot to distribute?

The question never occurred to FBI investigators who cleared the ARA safe house after Langan's capture. Somehow, the videos, along with blasting caps wrapped as Christmas presents, like the ones Lori Fortier helped McVeigh prepare, and the fake Roger Moore driver's license among Guthrie's possessions failed to arouse the FBI's suspicions. Could the bureau have closed in on the "others unknown"? Or was the FBI looking the other way?

Sitting in the booth at Nick's, Mark Hamm summarized the Oklahoma City bombing as the "mother of all great American crime stories," pointing to its mountain of riddles. As for me, I was heading to meet the man with some of the answers: Peter Langan, also known as Commander Pedro of the Aryan Republican Army.

⅄

Most descriptions of Peter Langan portray him as small and slender, with physical traits that might seem to prefigure his journey toward a sex change that would come later in federal prison. After his violent arrest by the FBI, doctors tending Langan's gunshot wounds were shocked. They discovered that the macho neo-Nazi bank robber had shaved his body hair and had traces of pink polish on his toenails. In his secret life away from the ARA, Langan enjoyed dressing in women's clothes and calling himself Donna.

The waif-like Langan had saved himself in the SWAT assault by squirreling away inside a wooden toolbox in his truck. His profile hardly seemed to fit with the macho Commander Pedro in the recruiting video, who snarled: "Are you a bunch of sniveling cowards, or are you going to pick up the sword? And I tell you, my patience runs thin sometimes for some of you people. The quality of my mercy is strained."

Neither one of these Peter Langans squared with the man I met that spring of 2007 in the federal prison at Marion, Illinois, another formidable maximum-security penitentiary. After a decade of imprisonment, Langan appeared ruggedly handsome with a full head of brown hair, a solid athletic build, and the restless, intense demeanor of a giant cat caged in a zoo. We sat together in the back of an auditorium-like room with one prison official stationed in the front. The scene was unlike anything in *The Silence of the Lambs*. It felt like Langan and I were the last two students in a college classroom, poring over a final exam.

I knew that Langan had backed away from implicating fellow gang members in the bombing when Congressman Dana Rohrabacher recently encountered him. But this was a new day, and Langan faced an exquisite dilemma. If he didn't go far enough signaling that he possessed information tying the ARA to the bombing, there would be no takers for an appeal bid. If he went too far, he might face a mass-murder investigation.

Peter Langan chose to roll the dice. He put on record sweeping allegations of the federal government's role in the ARA's origin, his claim of firsthand knowledge of gang member Kevin McCarthy's role as one of Timothy McVeigh's accomplices, and the government's systematic campaign to cover the ARA's tracks.

An edited version of the affidavit that Jesse Trentadue prepared for the FOIA case follows, based on my interview in March 2007. Here is what the Aryan Republican Army's coleader Peter Langan said:

> In April 1995, at the time of the Oklahoma City Bombing, I was living at 1103 Elm Street, Pittsburg, Kansas, in a house I shared with Richard Lee Guthrie. How we came to be together was a highly unusual circumstance.
>
> In 1993, while I was in jail in Georgia awaiting trial on armed robbery charges, the United States Secret Service offered me a deal: If I would find Guthrie, infiltrate those working with Guthrie, and testify against him, the Secret Service would arrange immunity for me. I accepted the

offer—under duress—after ten months in jail, six months in Ohio, and four months in Georgia.

September 1993: I was released from custody and became a Secret Service informant. Sometime around October 1993, I connected with Richard Guthrie.

By the time of the Oklahoma City Bombing, Richard Guthrie and I had lived in that house in Pittsburg, Kansas, for about a year. I first heard about the bombing sometime on the morning of April 19, 1995, when returning to the house in Pittsburg from Joplin, Missouri.

At that time, Kevin McCarthy and Scott Stedeford—associates of Guthrie's and mine—were overdue to arrive at the house in Pittsburg. Around April 1, 1995, McCarthy and Stedeford had driven to Oklahoma. They went to the Christian Identity compound of Elohim City, near Muldrow, Oklahoma. At Elohim City, McCarthy and Stedeford were staying at the residence of Andreas Strassmeir, where they had sometimes stayed in the past.

I watched TV coverage of the bombing and its aftermath on the day and night of April 19, 1995. As I watched the bombing coverage, I wondered as to the whereabouts of McCarthy and Stedeford and if they or their associates at Elohim City were involved in the bombing. I was concerned about their involvement in the bombing because it could jeopardize my security.

In the early morning hours of April 20, 1995—between 1:00 AM and 2:00 AM—McCarthy and Stedeford arrived at the house in Pittsburg. They were driving a 1983 white Chevrolet Suburban, a vehicle I had never seen before.

McCarthy and Stedeford said they had purchased it in Fort Smith, Arkansas, on April 17, 1995. I would later learn that Andreas Strassmeir bought Stedeford's old 1976 maroon Suburban, which Stedeford and McCarthy had driven to Elohim City. The white Suburban they were driving had no license plates when they arrived in Pittsburg, Kansas.

I questioned McCarthy and Stedeford about the bombing. They said they were not involved. McCarthy and Stedeford said that they were not even aware of the bombing, even though they had been on the road, driving through Oklahoma, amid intense media coverage of the bombing, for at least six hours or more on April 19 and 20. They said they had not been listening to the radio on their drive but had listened to CDs and cassettes in the Suburban the whole time. My impression was that they were lying. McCarthy and Stedeford also volunteered that Strassmeir and the others at Elohim City were not involved in the bombing.

We discussed the problem caused by the lack of license plates on the Suburban, which could easily draw the attention of law enforcement on us. We decided that McCarthy and Stedeford would travel immediately to Iowa to obtain tags for the new vehicle. They left Kansas, driving a blue Ford van that belonged to Guthrie and me, on the morning of April 20, 1995, at about 10:00 AM.

McCarthy and Stedeford returned to Pittsburg sometime on April 22, 1995, with new Iowa tags for the Suburban. Guthrie, McCarthy, Stedeford, and I then watched continuing TV news coverage of the bombing, including early media speculation that bank robbers may have helped to fund that attack.

Several months later, in July 1995, Richard Guthrie traveled to Pennsylvania to visit McCarthy, Stedeford, and another associate of ours, Mark Thomas, at Thomas's Pennsylvania home. Guthrie's visit lasted several weeks.

On that visit, Guthrie reportedly told Thomas that John Doe 2—the unidentified Oklahoma City bombing suspect who was never apprehended—was really Kevin McCarthy. Referring to McCarthy, Guthrie allegedly said: "Your young Mr. Wizard took out the Murrah Building."

Sometime in the months that followed, Guthrie, McCarthy, and Stedeford had a falling out and no longer wanted to work together. McCarthy and Stedeford returned to Pennsylvania.

As a result of this falling out, Guthrie said to me that McCarthy and Stedeford were a danger to us because of their possible involvement in the Oklahoma City bombing. Guthrie said he knew this because of discussions he had with Mark Thomas, McCarthy, and Stedeford on his trip to Pennsylvania.

In December 1995, I had one last conversation with Kevin McCarthy in Columbus, Ohio. I told McCarthy that I was considering no longer having any dealings with him due to Guthrie's attitude and the allegations regarding him and Stedeford. I told McCarthy that the situation was causing too many problems for me.

McCarthy responded by saying that he understood my difficulty but that he had overriding concerns. I asked him to elaborate. He told me that, contrary to his past statements, he and others unspecified did have legal "liabilities" concerning the Oklahoma City bombing. I remember thinking: "Liabilities" is a big word. But sometimes McCarthy talked like that. I asked him to be more specific concerning who, what, and when, but he declined to give me any details. He asked me not to mention this conversation to Stedeford or anyone else.

McCarthy stated that he was only telling me this because he wanted me to know how badly he might need help in going underground if the Oklahoma City bombing connection became a problem for him. I realized, too, that it might be a problem for me due to our association and past travels.

On January 18, 1996, I was arrested in Columbus, Ohio, while leaving Guthrie's house. During my arrest, I never fired or even pointed a weapon at anyone. Nevertheless, despite being an informant for the Secret Service, a SWAT Team comprised of FBI agents, Deputy United States Marshals, and other law enforcement personnel fired 48 rounds at me that day. They never offered me an opportunity to surrender prior to shooting me.

After being stomped and kicked by arresting officers and undergoing surgery for gunshot wounds in a hospital emergency room, I was chained to a wall in a police station and questioned by FBI Special Agent Ed Woods. I did not want this interrogation. I wanted a lawyer, and

I asked for one repeatedly. My requests for an attorney, however, were refused.

Instead of obtaining an attorney for me, Agent Woods insisted on playing phone messages from Guthrie's answering machine on a tape recorder. When Agent Woods taunted me with the inference that my associates had betrayed me and would testify against me, I had had enough. I told him: "You're going to have problems with your witnesses because they have the blood of Oklahoma City on their hands." Agent Woods definitely took note. "You certainly have my attention now," he said. This turn of events put an end to the interrogation soon thereafter.

Subsequently, my attorney, Kevin Durkin, informed me that the government wanted to talk to me about the Oklahoma City bombing. My attorney referred to this as a "proffer" or "prelude" to a plea agreement. I was amicable to such a discussion, but I wanted ironclad assurances of the terms or details of any type of deal. My attorney later told me the offer had been withdrawn.

The others eventually charged along with me in cases stemming from the FBI's mid-west bank robbery investigation known as "BOMBROB" were Richard Guthrie, Kevin McCarthy, Scott Stedeford, Mark Thomas, and Michael Brescia. Although involved in the robberies, Shawn Kenny was not prosecuted. I later learned that he, too, was an FBI informant.

Through the pretrial discovery process in *United States of America v. Peter Kevin Langan* and through case-related media reports, I learned more information confirming my suspicions regarding Kevin McCarthy's involvement in the Oklahoma City bombing.

One such disclosure was that on April 5, Timothy McVeigh telephoned Elohim City and asked to speak to Andreas Strassmeir. At the time, Kevin McCarthy was staying with Strassmeir.

I also learned of an FBI 302 [interview report] in which McCarthy stated that he was with me in Pittsburg, Kansas, on April 19, 1995. However, McCarthy was not with me in Pittsburg, Kansas, on April 19, 1995, nor anywhere else that day other than in the State of Oklahoma.

Also, during the discovery process in *US v. Langan*, I became aware of a pattern and practice on the part of the government of destroying evidence and presenting false or biased testimony—especially in regards to anything related to the Oklahoma City bombing. This included the destruction of blasting caps the government seized from Richard Guthrie's residence—blasting caps that were given to us by Kevin McCarthy.

In July 1996, I was informed that Richard Guthrie had killed himself, reportedly after threatening to reveal new facts about events outside our case, including the Oklahoma City bombing. At the time of his suspicious hanging in his jail cell, Guthrie was under subpoena by my attorney to testify at a hearing in my case just days later.

In 1997, I was convicted of five bank robbery-related charges in federal district court in Columbus, Ohio. I was sentenced to life without the possibility of parole plus 35 years.

Kevin McCarthy was facing a mandatory minimum sentence of 105 years on bank robbery-related charges unless he made a deal with federal prosecutors to testify against me and others. McCarthy made that deal. In exchange, McCarthy received a sentence of five years in prison.

From 2002 to the present—I have received still more relevant material/evidence from various sources about the Oklahoma City bombing case. Most of this material is in the form of official government documents from the FBI, including teletypes, electronic communications, FD 302s, etc. These documents detail a systematic attempt by the government to link my case (FBI case designation: BOMBROB) to the Oklahoma City bombing (FBI case designation: OKBOMB). This is in direct contradiction to the government's stated position denying this investigation—and this linkage.

In 2003, I was contacted by an attorney representing Terry Nichols in his state murder case. Nichols's attorney, Mr. Mark Ernest, and I discussed the linkage between the Oklahoma City bombing investigation and the Midwest Bank Robbery investigation. Through these discussions, I learned of still more suppressed evidence: an FD 302 containing a second and contradictory statement by Kevin McCarthy concerning his whereabouts on April 19, 1995, when he first heard about the bombing.

In this later statement, McCarthy says that he was in Iowa—not Pittsburg, Kansas, with me—when he first heard about the bombing. He also changed the date from April 20, 1995, to a day later, April 21, 1995. This contradictory 302 was never turned over to my defense attorney. McCarthy's alleged presence in Iowa when he first learned of the bombing was also the subject of testimony in the Nichols case.

During the time I was meeting with Nichols's attorney, I likewise learned about statements made by Mark Thomas, another defendant in the BOMBROB case, to his girlfriend, prior to April 19, 1995, implicating himself in a future attack on the government.

Due to my being named as a potential defense witness in Nichols's state trial, the State of Oklahoma requested a hearing to air its objection. At this hearing, FBI Special Agent Jon Hersley, the Oklahoma City bombing case agent, stated under oath that McCarthy was in Iowa when he first heard about the bombing. Hersley vouched for McCarthy's Iowa alibi statement even though it conflicted with what McCarthy said earlier, and even though it conflicted with the customary same-day time frame for tagging vehicles in Iowa.

Still, the government succeeded in its goal of putting Agent Hersley on the stand. The judge accepted Agent Hersley's support for McCarthy's alibi and rejected me from testifying at Nichols's trial.

In effect, the government's move buried the truth by barring Nichols's attorneys from exploring evidence from me of Kevin McCarthy's involvement in the bombing.

My experience in trying to defend my case clearly shows that there is more evidence out there that is being withheld or suppressed in my case—and also in the Oklahoma City bombing case.

Most or all of the defendants in the BOMBROB case had knowledge of aspects of the Oklahoma City bombing. But as my case demonstrates, the federal government has gone to extreme lengths to keep those fragments of the truth from coming out and coming together into a coherent story.

Despite compelling evidence linking Kevin McCarthy to the bombing, no known record exists of the government investigating or even questioning McCarthy about that crime.

Another BOMBROB defendant, Mark Thomas, was also silenced by the federal government. During my trial, Thomas agreed to testify in my defense as to what he knew about Kevin McCarthy's connection to the bombing. But at the 11th hour, the government indicted Thomas, effectively canceling his appearance at my trial. Thomas's indictment also set the stage for him to become an FBI informant and protected federal witness.

Richard Guthrie's mysterious death by hanging while he was in jail cooperating with federal prosecutors also helped the government bury the truth about the Oklahoma City bombing. Despite Guthrie's claim that he would soon reveal information about the bombing, I know of no other record related to the government investigating Guthrie's possible link to the bombing or even questioning him about that matter.

⅄

Kevin McCarthy, the ARA's youngest member, eighteen years old at the time of the bombing, made a lenient plea deal after his arrest for the gang's bank robbery spree. He then became the star witness against Peter Langan in his trial for those crimes. On one level, revenge might explain Langan's motivation to incriminate McCarthy. However, Langan offered credible factual evidence impeaching McCarthy, including his conflicting accounts of his whereabouts following the bombing and evidence for tagging vehicles in Iowa.

Langan's striking claim that the blasting caps recovered from the ARA's Ohio safe house "were given to us by Kevin McCarthy" would undoubtedly catch the attention of federal authorities Langan hoped to interest in his pursuit of an appeal. Recovered from the safe house, those blasting caps appeared to match the ones McVeigh had wrapped as Christmas packages, which somehow wound up with Guthrie and Langan. If Langan could back up his claim, did the blasting caps tie McCarthy to McVeigh?

Langan's claim of the government's systematic effort to keep the truth from "coming together into a coherent story" might also be eye-catching in a review of the plea deals for McCarthy and the ARA's Mark Thomas, which had seemingly derailed them from testifying in Langan's defense about their knowledge of the bombing.

In prison interviews following his conviction, Langan told Mark Hamm that the ARA's Guthrie and McCarthy were involved in the bombing but that prosecutors chose to overlook their roles to secure them as witnesses against him.[249] Above all, Langan said, he represented a grave potential embarrassment to the government because of his informant status. If the Secret Service hadn't freed Langan from jail in 1993 to become its informant, there might never have been an ARA to play a role in the Oklahoma City bombing.[250]

Curiously, even after going rogue and joining Guthrie's terror mission, when captured in 1996, Langan still considered himself to be a federal undercover informant. That seemingly led to his complaint in the affidavit that the SWAT team unloaded forty-eight rounds on him "despite being an informant for the Secret Service."

How many undercover informants were there in the bombing conspiracy anyway? So far, Jesse's investigation had confirmed three. All of them were gathering intelligence for federal handlers prior to the bombing and passing on information relating to the bomb plot or the ARA, which mounting evidence suggested was connected to the plot.

The first was Langan, sprung from jail by the Secret Service in 1993 to find Guthrie after a witness overheard him threatening the life of President George H.W. Bush. Next was Carol Howe, spying on the neo-Nazis in Elohim City from August 1994 to March 1995. The third was the unnamed Southern Poverty Law Center informant inside Elohim City who reported on Timothy McVeigh's April 17 phone call in search of Andreas Strassmeir.

J.D. Cash and Roger Charles had looked hard at several other candidates whose informant status could not be verified 100 percent or who denied any such role despite compelling evidence. Then there was the riddle of Timothy McVeigh himself, reputedly confessing his undercover role to Terry Nichols and to David Hammer in their death row interviews.

Still, as of 2007, the federal government claimed it had received no advance warning about the Oklahoma City bombing. With his prison interview, Peter Langan followed the dangerous lead of Carol Howe a decade earlier. Breaking the code of silence that usually applies to undercover agents, operatives, and informants, Langan was going public with a challenge to government insiders who were still holding fast to a guilty secret. All Langan needed to succeed in his daring move against a cover-up in its twelfth year was the public notice he and Jesse Trentadue were counting on to result from my maximum-security road trip.

Armed with the prison interviews of Terry Nichols, David Hammer, and Peter Langan, Jesse's investigation was loaded for bear, as he might say. His next move was unprecedented in a FOIA case. Jesse asked Judge Kimball to allow him to videotape depositions of Terry Nichols and David Hammer as evidence of what additional files the FBI might be hiding about its undercover operation relating to the Oklahoma City bombing.

As Jesse awaited the judge's decision, he was counting on a dynamic he believed was in play behind the scenes. Judge Kimball had now read the contested documents in Jesse's FOIA lawsuit that he had ordered the FBI to turn over to him in their unredacted states. After his in-camera review, this judge, alone outside the FBI, knew some of the rest of the story of the failed sting operation Jesse was working to expose.

To the outer limits of his discretion, Jesse needed Judge Kimball to support his quest. The judge did just that. In September 2008, he approved Jesse's motion to depose the two prisoners on videotape, handing Jesse a rare moment of pure victory. The ruling meant that Judge Kimball wanted to see and hear who was telling the truth about the bomb plot—the government or the criminals.

In his order, Judge Kimball nodded to the wrongdoing Jesse's FOIA suit alleged. The judge cited the lawsuit's murder-by-mistaken-identity theory of Kenneth's death, mentioning the ARA's Richard Guthrie by name and noting that "while officials ruled the death a suicide, Plaintiff unearthed significant evidence of foul play."

The FBI's lawyers objected to the videotaped depositions on the ground that questioning Nichols and Hammer would involve "the Oklahoma City Bombing." In a reply brief, Jesse shot back: "It undoubtedly will, but that is not inconsistent with the purposes of FOIA. Under FOIA, the public's interest in ensuring the integrity and reliability of the government through disclosure is greatest when there is evidence of wrongdoing on the part of government."

By this time, the FOIA lawsuit had evolved into a bitter feud, even in the footnotes of its pleadings. "FBI Defendants' enmity towards Plaintiff stems from fear of being exposed as a participant in the greatest act of domestic terrorism in the 20th Century," Jesse wrote in one such footnote. "From Plaintiff's perspective, this enmity is certainly understandable given the murder of his brother and FBI Defendants' attempts to indict Plaintiff using perjured statements from FBI operatives. FOIA does not say that only people who like and respect an Agency are entitled to its records."

Personal animosity aside, a stunning reality had emerged on Jesse's side of the debate over whether he was on a fishing expedition. The evidence Jesse's investigation was uncovering, some of it from government files, supported the criminals' version of the bombing over the government's. Contrary to the official story of lone-wolf terror, the criminals we interviewed and factual evidence supporting their testimony pointed to a wide-ranging neo-Nazi conspiracy crowded with undercover federal operatives.

When the judge denied the FBI's request to vacate his order, Jesse marked the victory by sending the three prisoner affidavits to his nemesis, FBI Director Robert Mueller. Jesse included a taunting note signed "Semper fi" and predicted: "After you read these materials, I bet your sphincter will be tight enough to suck buttermilk."[251]

A moment of truth was at hand, or so it seemed. But the FBI rushed to ask the Tenth Circuit Court of Appeals to review Judge Kimball's order, hoping to receive more favorable treatment.

CHAPTER 15

OUT OF THE SHADOWS

I NEVER SAW IT COMING until the whistleblower stepped out of the shadows to solve the mystery. A stunning revelation was at hand. It would eclipse our dilemma of who in our expanding cast of characters was or was not a government informant. We were about to hear from yet another undercover operative who believed that the Oklahoma City bombing was manufactured terror, made in Washington, DC, by the FBI.

It was 2011. I was again delving into the mystery of the surveillance videotapes that first hooked me on the bombing case. The prisoner depositions had never happened, and the moment of truth had been a mirage. The Tenth Circuit Court of Appeals had reversed Judge Kimball's order approving the videotaped depositions. Was it a close legal question? A hidden hand? We would never know, and the judge and the public would never get to watch Terry Nichols or David Hammer tell his story. We had to find a course correction.

The defeat was crushing. I thought hard about admitting the folly of the past five years and packing it in. I had answered Jannie Coverdale's call for help on instinct as if I was still at *America's*

Most Wanted—but I wasn't. It was only me chasing this mystery. Was I crazy?

That chaotic moment became my salvation. I bailed out of LA, leaving behind the whimsy of television executives, the frothy Starbucks meeting circuit, and the endless hours stuck in freeway traffic. I'd had my fill of television and started my life again in the tiny mountain village of Three Rivers, California, where I became an accidental innkeeper and writer in residence.

I opened the door to a house on the Kaweah River, downstream from Sequoia National Park in the majestic Sierra Nevada mountain range. That's where, in 2008, I launched Rio Sierra Riverhouse as a boutique riverside hotel. Travelers from around the globe and all walks of life lodged at Rio on their once-in-a-lifetime journeys to the Giant Forest and General Sherman, the world's most enormous tree. Around a campfire by the rushing river, guests roasted s'mores and marveled at stories of my travels to death row, Jesse's quest for justice for Kenneth, and Hammer's book *Deadly Secrets*, which I was editing. Their curious questions told me that my investigation was more than an obsession.

I knew that scenes from the journey would continue to haunt me: Kenneth's bloody handprint reaching for his prison cell's panic button, Jesse and his sister videotaping their brother's tortured corpse. I knew Jesse and Roger would never quit, and I couldn't either. We resolved to press one more FOIA lawsuit. Roger proposed targeting hidden CIA records to expose Andreas Strassmeir's possible role as a government informant. As a former TV producer, I believed the hidden surveillance videotapes would reveal the truth about the bombing. Jesse filed a two-pronged FOIA lawsuit, and we were back in the fight.

Thinking about those videos still boggles my mind. The blast happened in a moment, leaving a trail of disputed reality for the next thirty years. In what was then a city of about 450,000 souls, we have only been able to locate one eyewitness to the bomb exploding.

An Oklahoma City police report released to Jesse in 2009 by the FBI documented that sighting.[252] The witness—name redacted—traveled by bus with his pregnant fiancée to St. Joseph's Cathedral across Fourth Street from the Murrah Building. Just before 9:00 a.m., one of Oklahoma City's oldest churches was minutes away from the blast that would raise its roof off steel pillars, send pipes from the church organ raining down onto the pews below, and shatter its stained-glass windows. For a few more minutes, though, all was well.

While waiting for the church office to open, the couple ran an errand in the neighborhood. On their way back, probably on Fourth Street—facing the south side of the Murrah Building, not the north side, where the Ryder truck parked—the witness heard what he believed was an alarm, causing him to turn and look. "He was looking directly at the Murrah Building when suddenly he saw a fireball erupt from the upper floors of the building," according to the police report.

The witness and his fiancée "were both knocked down by the blast, which he believed to have come from somewhere in the upper part of the building, specifically stating the sixth floor or above," according to the police report.

A fireball exploding in the upper floors? The sole eyewitness account aligns with claims of a second explosion inside the Murrah Building, such as J.D. Cash reported in the *Gazette*, or David Hammer related in *Deadly Secrets*.

The witness struggled to stand and began to cross the street toward the Murrah Building. A white foreign-made car, possibly a Jaguar, traveling at high speed nearly struck him. He thought it strange that the vehicle was approaching the explosion, not heading away from it. He got a good look at the driver: a white male, possibly of Middle Eastern descent, thirty-five to forty-five years old, clean-shaven with dark-colored wavy hair combed straight back.

The witness's account, given to police the morning after the attack, raised issues that would perplex independent researchers for the next three decades. Did Timothy McVeigh's truck bomb alone destroy the Murrah Building? Did someone plant explosive charges inside? Was there one blast or two? Did McVeigh deliver the bomb alone? Or did he have accomplices?

Above all, the unnamed witness's account launched the maddening question: What really happened on April 19, 1995? The federal agent who initiated the interview and accompanied the Oklahoma City police officer worked for the ATF, part of a massive FBI-led task force collecting leads on the bombing. Was this sensational witness statement fed into the multiagency investigation? Were there other such leads that slipped through the cracks?

When I lobbied for the videotapes in 2008 as the target of our subsequent FOIA lawsuit, I convinced myself that eyewitnesses were the last hope of solving a nearly impenetrable mystery. I also knew that the FBI had another kind of "eyewitness" testimony that it had never allowed the public to see—as many as twenty surveillance video cameras, some with an even better view of the apocalyptic blast than the human witness had.[253] Our FOIA lawsuit would demand the release of those videos.

⅄

"Somebody's keeping them in the attic as a trophy or in case they need them," FBI whistleblower Frederic Whitehurst assured me when I checked in with him about our FOIA prospects.[254] Whitehurst had been a witness for the defense in the McVeigh trial, exposing unethical evidence-handling practices in the FBI's crime lab.[255] He had also won a million-dollar settlement after the FBI fired him following his allegations. Whitehurst's opinion was a confidence booster. A big worry was that Jesse would fight and win the FOIA case only to find that the videotapes had disappeared. Whitehurst's opinion underscored how risky such concealment would be with a federal judge watching.

All you had to do was read a newspaper or watch TV news in 1995 to get a good idea of the story recorded on the secret videotapes, capturing multiple bombers and multiple vehicles. On April 25, 1995, a week after the bombing, *The New York Times* quoted Weldon Kennedy, the FBI's case commander, saying investigators were examining the videos for images of "the bombers," plural. This captured-on-tape story was not going to be about lone-wolf terror.

Agent Kennedy's intel matched preliminary hearing testimony on April 27, 1995, by FBI agent Jon Hersley.[256] Under cross-examination, he admitted that the FBI had video capturing a prime view of the bomb truck and the bombers. That camera perched on an unspecified upper floor of the twenty-four-story Regency Tower apartments, a half block from the Murrah Building. It scanned Fifth Street, from the parking lot on one side to the Murrah Building on the other. Agent Hersley testified that

FBI investigators were still trying to identify and locate "other subjects," besides Timothy McVeigh.

Two days later, on April 29, an Associated Press story reported on a videotape showing a "mystery" vehicle, believed to have been used in the getaway, visible in the same frame of surveillance video with the Ryder truck, presumably parked outside the Murrah Building.[257]

Curiously, this story reported that someone had switched Timothy McVeigh's Arizona license plate from his yellow Mercury to the mystery vehicle. In news reports that followed, McVeigh's license plate, if mentioned at all, was only reported as missing.

This story's unnamed federal law enforcement source refused to describe the vehicle. Ten days after the bombing, with the global manhunt for John Doe 2 in high gear, why not describe this presumed getaway vehicle? Or better still, why not show the public a clip from the video, zeroing in on Timothy McVeigh's Arizona license plate LZC646?

Another head-scratcher was the mid-May *Houston Chronicle* story about the videotape from Trooper Hanger's dashcam during the McVeigh arrest.[258] No one ever answered the crucial question: Why didn't the supposedly intact and unedited video that Trooper Hanger turned over at McVeigh's preliminary hearing contain footage of the brown truck, suspected as being John Doe 2's getaway vehicle, seemingly convoying with McVeigh on his escape route. According to the news story, Trooper Hanger's dashcam videotaped the truck, and the FBI enhanced the video by linking it to McVeigh associate Stephen Colbern through its license plate. Where was that footage?

Later that year, in October 1995, the news team at KFOR TV in Oklahoma City, an NBC affiliate, continued its hot pursuit of the videotapes. Their producers had a source who claimed to have seen some of the surveillance video. Based on the source's account, KFOR produced a computer-generated reenactment of the final moments before the blast at the Murrah Building.[259] Leaving no doubt that John Doe 2 was there, the reenactment showed Timothy McVeigh exiting the truck while John Doe 2 stayed behind, then got out and walked away in the same direction as McVeigh.

Also, in October 1995, the cap on the year's steady stream of news reports on the bombing videotapes came from the Associated Press. On October 28, the wire service reported that surveillance video had captured a "shadowy figure in the passenger seat" of the bomb truck as it delivered its deadly payload. "There's a shape in there, but they can't see a face," a source reported. A glimpse of John Doe 2, soon to be dismissed by the Justice Department as phantom imaginings by eyewitnesses, was captured on videotape.

Our new FOIA case would build on the 1995 evidence to include information that had surfaced later, notably the Secret Service log referencing the surveillance videotape in FBI custody of "suspects," plural, exiting the bomb truck, and Jesse's discovery of the attempted million-dollar sale of the surveillance videotapes to NBC.[260] That attempt occurred in October 1995, when KFOR aired its reenactment news package. The FBI had investigated an agent in its Los Angeles field office but failed to learn who tried to sell the videotape.

Though I didn't learn about it until much later from researcher Richard Booth, the FBI's Danny Coulson dropped proof of the bombing videotapes on his book tour for *No Heroes*, Coulson's 1999 FBI memoir. "[We] had videotape of the truck being pulled up a couple minutes before nine," and "we had him [McVeigh] on videotape," Coulson said in a video clip that seemed to leave no room for debate.

We thought we had the high ground in our FOIA quest until September 2009, when the FBI released some of the hundreds of unseen videos it admitted it possessed to Jesse. The limited release covered only four locations, none including the best that might show the front of the Murrah Building looking onto Fifth Street, where the Ryder truck was parked.

Something else was wrong: The videotapes the FBI turned over went blank during the critical moments leading up to the blast.[261] "Four cameras in four different locations going blank at basically the same time on the morning of April 19, 1995?" Jesse wondered. He scoffed at official explanations that the cameras had run out of tape. "The interesting thing is they spring back on after 9:02," he said. "The absence of footage from these crucial time intervals is evidence that there is something there that the FBI doesn't want anybody to see." Jesse and the FBI had reached a standoff that only a trial would settle.

⅄

Meanwhile, Jesse was confronting potentially fatal setbacks on the CIA side of our FOIA case. Initially, his document demands produced the CIA's admission that it had fifty-two documents connecting the CIA or Andreas Strassmeir to the bombing case and that the CIA's National Geospatial-Intelligence Agency also had satellite images. There was a catch, however. The CIA invoked its right to keep those materials secret. "They said to release these documents would pose a grave threat to the security of the United States of America," Jesse said in a 2010 radio interview.[262]

The involvement of this little-known CIA division, which Roger Charles had heard of through his Pentagon background, led to another discovery. The CIA confirmed that it had a spy satellite over Oklahoma City.[263] "In my opinion, they were looking for that truck," Jesse told me. "Remember, Roger's theory was that the truck had a transponder on it. Even then, those satellites were good enough to read a license plate."

Judge Kimball backed the CIA when it asserted its right to a national security exemption from releasing the materials.[264] "But what he did, and I think he did this intentionally, is he wrote his opinion to let me know and the public know that there was a foreign connection to the Oklahoma City bombing," Jesse told the radio interviewer. "He goes through it, and he discusses the CIA's assistance in helping prosecute Tim McVeigh and Terry Nichols. And he talks about the contacts with foreign informants, foreign witnesses."[265]

Jesse called Judge Kimball's ruling, which ended the CIA side of our FOIA case, "the King's *X*." For our search party of three, everything was now riding on the surveillance videotapes—or so we thought.

⅄

"You've got all the pieces to the puzzle, but you just haven't put them together," John Matthews said when he called Jesse to offer his help in July 2011. Someone was finally about to make sense of a creepy voyeuristic vibe that hung over our investigation. Everywhere we looked, it seemed that someone was spying on someone else. PATCON, short for Patriot Conspiracy, was mainly a mystery to Jesse until John Matthews's phone call. It was on

Jesse's radar screen only because of random mentions in secret files flowing to him from the FBI in his FOIA lawsuits.

Dubbed the FBI's secret war on the "Patriot" Movement by analyst J. M. Berger,[266] PATCON's actual parameters are unknown. Publicly released documents depict an FBI infiltration program running from 1990 to 1993 targeting three radical anti-government groups: Civilian Materiel Assistance, the Texas Light Infantry militia, and the American Pistol and Rifle Association.[267] However, whistleblower John Matthews told Jesse that he infiltrated twenty-three radical right-wing groups for the FBI while serving as a PATCON operative from 1991 to 1998.

"It's bigger than you know and uglier than you can imagine," Matthews told Jesse on the phone. "I want to come see you and tell you about it."

Out of curiosity, Matthews had recently run a computer search on himself and discovered, to his horror, that the FBI had failed to redact his name in paperwork released in Jesse's FOIA lawsuit. "All those years, I've been a good boy and kept my mouth shut," he told *Newsweek* later. "Then you release my name? What kind of shit is that?"[268]

When Matthews visited Salt Lake City on July 24, 2011, he shared some of the highlights of his PATCON mission with Jesse. Following his Marine Corps service during the Vietnam War and a paramilitary adventure in Nicaragua on behalf of the CIA as part of Iran-Contra, Matthews had reconnected in 1991 with Tom Posey, a high-profile Marine veteran he had followed to Nicaragua a decade earlier.[269]

By then, Posey was bitter after a public fall from political grace, though he was still actively leading the Civilian Materiel Assistance paramilitary group. According to Matthews, Posey made him an alarming pitch. Would Matthews help steal a store of automatic weapons from the Browns Ferry nuclear plant in Alabama to sell on the black market? Posey also revealed that as part of the getaway, he planned to bomb the nuclear plant's control room.[270]

Within days, Matthews had reported Posey to the FBI and accepted a job offer to spy on him for $500 a week. That assignment led to Posey's 1993 arrest and eventual imprisonment, though only for an illegal sale of night vision goggles, not for the alleged plot against the nuclear plant. Afterward, Matthews soldiered on as a PATCON informant for five more years.

From his home base in Arizona, in the run-up to the Oklahoma City bombing and afterward, Matthews answered pages and went on the road to conduct surveillance at gun shows, biker bars, and paramilitary compounds. He traveled anywhere militia leaders, skinheads, and white supremacists gathered, constantly reporting to his FBI handler and friend Donald Jarrett in Phoenix, Arizona.

The work was stressful and dangerous, testing the bravery and cunning of the Third Marine Division veteran. "John was rough as a cob," Jesse told me. "His grammar was terrible, and he couldn't spell. But if you were to assume that John was not very intelligent, you would be very wrong. Many of the groups he infiltrated were extremely violent and would have shot him immediately if exposed. But he possessed the nimble presence of mind to persuade anyone he was not a fed."

In 1998, at the end of his PATCON tour, the FBI presented Matthews with a service plaque that read: "John W. Matthews: In appreciation and recognition for your outstanding efforts in assisting the FBI to combat domestic terrorism throughout the United States: March 28, 1991–May 30, 1998."[271] Thirteen years later, however, the man who visited Jesse was far removed from honorifics. The past haunted John Matthews. He told Jesse about the "AWOL bag" he kept by his door, containing ID, keys, a change of clothes, and a gun if he needed to make a fast getaway.

Something deeper than anger at being outed was bothering him. As he and Jesse talked, Matthews revealed his disillusionment about PATCON. "It seemed like the FBI was more interested in inciting violence than preventing it," Matthews said. He had signed on believing his mission was to monitor the Ku Klux Klan and neo-Nazi groups on the far-right fringe. However, Matthews came to believe that inciting violence was the fundamental mission of PATCON. He quit but couldn't shake off what he had seen and done. He wanted to expose PATCON and had sensational information to offer Jesse.

While conducting surveillance at a Texas Light Infantry militia training camp in San Saba, Texas, in 1994, Matthews said he observed Timothy McVeigh and Andreas Strassmeir together.[272] According to Matthews, they were training to learn how to convert flare guns into grenade launchers.[273] Matthews recalled about Strassmeir: "It stuck in my mind because he was German."[274]

The Texas Light Infantry was the same militia group whose members told J.D. Cash they followed Strassmeir entering a federal building at night and suspected he was an undercover ATF agent.[275] If Matthews's sighting was accurate, it was the third time witnesses in Jesse's investigation had put McVeigh and Strassmeir together, along with the Junction City party scene of 1992 and the Lady Godiva nightclub outing in Tulsa eleven days before the bombing.

After McVeigh's 1995 arrest, Matthews told Jesse he was shocked to recognize the suspected bomber on TV as the man he vividly remembered from San Saba.[276]

Matthews hurried to phone his FBI handler with the surprising news. Instead, Jarrett surprised Matthews by replying, "We know, John."[277] Matthews took this to mean the FBI had McVeigh under surveillance a year before the Oklahoma City bombing.

In another crucial disclosure, Matthews told Jesse that the Aryan Republican Army was an FBI front group created by the bureau to incite radical neo-Nazi violence. This disclosure was a breakthrough for Jesse's investigation. Through Peter Langan, he was so close to connecting the ARA to the bombing. What if that link led back to the FBI?

Matthews told Jesse that he believed the Oklahoma City bomb plot was a PATCON operation. However, he said he did not personally work on it, a claim Jesse would come to doubt as he learned more about Matthews's PATCON spying in the Kingman, Arizona, area where McVeigh stayed before the bombing.

As their meeting ended, John Matthews had one request: "I want my story told before I die," he told Jesse.[278] Matthews said he was terminally ill from exposure to Agent Orange in Vietnam. He was seeking closure in his life and maybe also for the man whose crusade for justice he had followed to Salt Lake City. Jesse knew just the journalist for the job of telling Matthews's story. AP's John Solomon was now a *Newsweek* editor, and Matthews was a guaranteed cover story.

Roger Charles answered the phone in Arlington, Virginia, with his reporter's notebook ready. "This guy is the real fucking deal,"[279] Jesse declared, launching another memorable series of entries in Roger's forty-two notebooks on the bombing case. Some notes may need more detail, but we can't ask for clarification. Tragically,

Roger Charles suffered a heart attack and died in 2022. The notes he left behind offer a precious glimpse of important news the public would, once again, miss learning when *Newsweek*'s cover story went disastrously sideways in November 2011.

On July 27, 2011, three days after the meeting in Salt Lake City, Jesse was working the *Newsweek* angle. "I told John Solomon about the meeting with Matthews," Jesse told Roger. "He expects blowback from the FBI, and Solomon could help. [Matthews is] a classic old jarhead from northern California on the Russian River."

On July 29, Jesse told Roger: "Matthews sent me two 302s, unredacted, about the plan [to bomb] the Browns Ferry plant."

On an August 12 conference call, the story grew exponentially bigger when Matthews claimed: "[President] Clinton was briefed every day on my work... I dealt with ATF and CID [the Army's Criminal Investigation Division]...did briefings...arranged a meeting of the ARA with [Aryan Nations leader Richard] Butler up in Idaho."

By its nature, PATCON's surveillance created a record of itself. "The FBI photographed every place I was at," Matthews recounted on the same call. "The FBI identified everybody there. They also taped meetings."

The story was underway. "A *Newsweek* reporter contacted [author Mark Hamm] for an interview about McVeigh and the ARA," Jesse told Roger on August 16. "John Matthews said Richard Lee Guthrie's gang was a knock-off the FBI started."

In a follow-up call that same day, Jesse elaborated: "*Newsweek* is doing a story on PATCON and Elohim City and Strassmeir, Ruby Ridge, McVeigh, Richard Lee Guthrie and OKBOMB." It was everything Jesse could have hoped for.

"*Newsweek* has been contacting [Matthews's] handlers," Jesse told Roger on August 18. "A guy down in Arizona had nothing but good to say." A day later, Solomon called Roger to report that Matthews's credibility was "looking better and better."

On August 22, the name Roger Moore surprisingly popped up in Roger's notebook. John Matthews "did a counterfeit deal in Florida with Roger Moore as Bob Miller," Roger's *Newsweek* sources told him.

By late August, Roger's sources reported that part of the story would be about the plot against the Browns Ferry nuclear plant, and part would be about Matthews's sighting of McVeigh at the Texas Light Infantry training camp. "They seemed to have talked to the FBI guy in charge of the investigation of TLI who confirmed McVeigh was there," Roger noted on August 30, 2011.

Newsweek's editor Tina Brown was "in love with the story," Roger's sources at the magazine told him on September 6.

The last pieces were falling together. That same day, Roger noted that the Tennessee Valley Authority confirmed the plot against the Browns Ferry plant.

As the reporting net closed around Andreas Strassmeir on September 7, Jesse told Roger that *Newsweek*'s reporter "listened to [a phone message to Jesse from Strassmeir's lawyer] Kirk Lyons and described him as one scared guy.

On September 8, in the biggest reporting score yet, "*Newsweek* placed Strassmeir as an informant with PATCON," Roger noted.

With John Solomon as the story's editor, this confirmation was compelling. Known for his impeccable law enforcement sources, Solomon could be trusted to thoroughly vet such a significant disclosure.

On September 16, the story's scope widened again to touch another national scandal. "The gun store in Fast and Furious was also used to move guns to PATCON," Jesse told Roger. Jesse was referring not to the movie franchise but to an actual ATF undercover operation in the early 2000s in which the Lone Wolf gun store in Phoenix played a central role. "John Matthews has been in the store many times," Jesse added.

From 2009 to 2011, the failed undercover "gunwalking" operation allowed the sale of illegal guns to so-called "straw purchasers" in hopes of tracking weapons embedded with microchips to Mexican drug cartel members. But when a drug gang ambushed a border patrol agent, killing him in a firefight involving Fast and Furious guns, congressional hearings ensued, bringing a 2012 contempt of Congress vote against Attorney General Eric Holder for refusing to disclose details about Fast and Furious.

On September 19, 2011, Roger noted that *Newsweek*'s Ross Schneiderman had spent two and a half hours on the phone interviewing Andreas Strassmeir. Jesse told Roger that Strassmeir "lied like a rug" in that call, adding: "Strassmeir did say, 'I don't guess we'll ever find out about OKCB.' Arrogant prick. What a shithead."

A blockbuster news story was in the bank, poised to expose a sweeping rogue federal surveillance program with tentacles reaching into two national catastrophes, the Oklahoma City bombing and Fast and Furious.

On the sidelines, Jesse and Roger felt good about the story. On September 25, Jesse called Roger with a riddle. "Guess who Posey's liaison to the CIA was for Iran-Contra?"

"Roger Moore," Roger answered.

"How the hell did you guess him?" Jesse marveled, which Roger duly recorded in his notebook.

Among the shrinking ranks of our search party, Roger must have felt rumblings of the excruciating reversal coming next most keenly. It was a carbon copy of the Carol Howe story crashing and burning at ABC News in 1997.

Warning signs surfaced on November 18. "I just got off the phone with Ross Schneiderman," Jesse told Roger. "He's fighting hard to keep McVeigh and the TLI stuff in, but it may not make it."

On November 21, 2011, the day of publication, Roger noted a call from John Solomon to say the story, headlined "I Was an Undercover White Supremacist" by R.M. Schneiderman, made the cover with "some nuggets taken out." Solomon told Roger he had "appealed to [*Newsweek* editor] Tina [Brown] on McVeigh and Strassmeir." Solomon had yet to see the final copy.

The appeal failed spectacularly. On the eve of publication, reportedly under pressure from the Justice Department, an executive edit gutted all mention of McVeigh and Strassmeir (and thus the Oklahoma City bombing), along with details concerning Matthews's PATCON activities. What remained was a human-interest piece exposing Matthews while keeping a tight lid on just how wide-ranging PATCON had been when he worked on it.

Jesse and Roger had watched the story develop step-by-step, making *Newsweek*'s denial that government pressure had driven the edit hard to believe. Roger struck back, leaking the uncut version to his blogger associate Mike Vanderboegh, formerly the creator of *The John Doe Times*, now the purveyor of the *Sipsey Street Irregulars*.

Vanderboegh's commentary concluded: "But at least, gentle readers, you know now the extent of *Newsweek*'s perfidy in hiding the truth that threatens both the comfortable bureaucratic existence of the FBI and the reputations of people such as Eric

Holder and Janet Napolitano—both of whom were knee deep in PATCON and the cover-up of the true circumstances behind the deaths of [168] men, women and children in Oklahoma City on April 19 1995."[280]

John Matthews was right when he said we had all the pieces to the bombing puzzle. Armed with his intel that the FBI created the Aryan Republican Army as a front group, we could finally fit the puzzle together. If John Matthews was right, the Oklahoma City bombing was a PATCON plot allowed to go too far, unleashing neo-Nazi violence on hundreds of innocent citizens.

We knew a terrible secret. What could we do about it?

⅄

Whistleblowers, the prized truth-tellers of our society, have suffered frighteningly harsh treatment from the federal government in the bombing case. When Hoppy Heidelberg complained that prosecutors were hiding evidence of John Doe 2 and withholding witnesses from the McVeigh grand jury, the presiding federal judge expelled Heidelberg, threatened him with jail if he violated grand jury secrets, and ignored his plea for a new grand jury.

When government informant Carol Howe tried to go public about her spy mission at Elohim City, the Justice Department retaliated by prosecuting her on flimsy criminal terrorism charges that a jury swiftly rejected. Then, when she volunteered to take the witness stand in the McVeigh trial and tell her spy story there under oath, the presiding judge barred her, calling her testimony irrelevant.

The next whistleblower in the bombing case would be John Matthews, furious after the watered-down *Newsweek* story. Matthews told Jesse *Newsweek* had put a target on his back, exposing him as an informant in the violent world he had infiltrated while thwarting his goal of exposing PATCON. Jesse asked if Matthews would consider testifying at the FOIA videotape trial. From the witness stand, he would have absolute immunity. Matthews jumped at the chance. It would be his last opportunity to tell his story on the record.

For Jesse, Matthews would be a star witness to the government's motive to hide the bombing videotapes from the public. We had long believed that the "others unknown," caught on video, might be accomplices, informants, or federal agents. We still did. However, Matthews's account of PATCON's routine videotaping of its surveillance targets added another possibility. What if a PATCON camera surveilling Timothy McVeigh had shot the bombing, producing video evidence the FBI could not allow the public to see because it would reveal its source?

John Matthews continued to fill in gaps for Jesse and Roger in his account of his PATCON years. Without ever admitting that he was part of a PATCON Oklahoma City undercover operation, Matthews revealed that in Arizona, he conducted PATCON surveillance on both Aryan Republican Army coleader Peter Langan and alleged Timothy McVeigh associate Stephen Colbern. Matthews's surveillance of McVeigh and Strassmeir in Texas made four persons of interest in the bombing case on whom Matthews had spied. It was quite a coincidence if they weren't connected.

On July 1, 2012, Jesse reported that Matthews said he saw Stephen Colbern "all over the place" in Arizona and confirmed that "McVeigh, Strassmeir, and Colbern" were "all involved with PATCON," according to Roger's notebook. In a third reference to Colbern, Matthews told Roger: "No one fucked with this boy Colbern there in Arizona."

Matthews knew that the illegal weapon sales he had witnessed while serving in PATCON were a scandal waiting to happen. He had more details to share. "Let's think over the years I work[ed] on the groups on how many cases of sporterized...AK47s and SKS's were sold to groups, and case after case of ammo for them all with the blessings of the FBI and ATF with no paperwork," Matthews wrote in an email on January 13, 2013.

About the Lone Wolf gun store, at the center of the Fast and Furious scandal, Matthews added this in the same email: "Also let's not forget the AR15's they were made full auto from the Lone Wolf Gun store back in the 90's by a guy brought in by the FBI for me to put in place. Those guns went to bikers who were sell[ing] drugs on the border. Those drugs were [believed] to be coming in from China."

A month later, on February 18, 2013, Matthews told Roger that PATCON "had a place in Winslow [Arizona] to take drugs out of tractors [from China] and give to biker gangs to sell."

Returning to his claim that the White House ran PATCON, Matthews recalled a slight that still offended him. He told Jesse his handler, Donald Jarrett, and high-ranking FBI officials had been invited to meet President Clinton without him. Jarrett, who was African American, regaled Matthews afterward with the story of President Clinton howling with laughter over the black handler supervising the white undercover operative on their joint mission to eradicate white supremacy from America.[281]

⅄

In July 2014, three years after the publication of the *Newsweek* story, Jesse was back in federal court seeking public disclosure of the bombing videotapes with the support of an FBI whistleblower. John Matthews would be Jesse's closer, a dramatic final witness to the federal government's motive to hide video evidence of PATCON helping McVeigh or shadowing him, or both when he blew up the Murrah Building.

In 1997, Carol Howe's bid to reveal that the government ignored her warnings of the bombing triggered extraordinary pressure from the Department of Justice. Could the judicial system protect John Matthews, another informant with knowledge of government secrets about the bomb plot? As a former insider on the McVeigh defense team, Roger knew firsthand how real the threat to Matthews was.

On April 15, 1997, in the early stages of that trial, Roger had written a memo to defense attorney Stephen Jones about the pressure the FBI was applying to exclude witnesses favorable to McVeigh from testifying.[282] The information came from J.D. Cash following an FBI interview at the *McCurtain Gazette*. FBI Agent Rick Ojeda told J.D. that "his assignment was to blunt efforts by Stephen Jones to drag Dennis Mahon in[to] the McVeigh trial." According to J.D., "Ojeda said two FBI agents had worked on the same task relative to Andreas Strassmeir, and three had been assigned to work to prevent [Jones] from dragging Carol Howe into the McVeigh trial."

It was a bright red flag. The FBI had detailed seven agents to shut down three potential witnesses who had information known to be material to the bombing case. None of those witnesses made it into the McVeigh trial. Seventeen years later, John Matthews knew the risk he was taking in the videotape trial. Jesse explained that he had no authority to subpoena Matthews in a FOIA case and would not have done so even if he could. Testifying would have to be Matthews's choice because he wanted to tell his story.

Still, heading into the trial, Jesse knew that Matthews had long been concerned about his safety. The first signs of pressure on the whistleblower came before the *Newsweek* story in November 2011. "The FBI came to visit and offered me more work down the road if I kept my mouth shut," Matthews told Roger.[283] Days after the story's publication, someone ransacked his daughter's home. She "had rent money, seven hundred dollars, and prescription drugs right out in the open, and they ignored it.... [T]hey didn't get what they were looking for, even though they did get the lockbox," Matthews told Roger.[284]

A few days later, a distressed Matthews emailed *Newsweek* reporter Ross Schneiderman that someone had hacked his computer and wiped it clean. "Something is going on," Matthews wrote. "This story is getting way out of hand.... The real story needs to be told. That way the BS stops. Rumors get folks killed. I know now, anyone I ever work for or looked at, is looking at me very hard now. All worry on what I may say or what they did."[285] The following year, in July 2012, Matthews told Roger: "I've had two visits from the FBI to my house. I don't want a third visit."

In the run-up to the videotape trial, knowing of Matthews's concern for his security in the Salt Lake City courtroom, Jesse had requested a court order allowing Matthews to testify by video conference from an undisclosed location. On July 15, 2014, Jesse emailed Matthews the judge's approval: "Judge said...I do not have to disclose the location to the FBI. You will testify at noon on Wednesday. Last witness." As far as Jesse knew, his closer was holding firm. Then everything fell apart.

"My house phone quit working Friday," Matthews emailed Roger and Jesse on July 16. "My internet is down too," Matthews told Roger, saying that he suspected the FBI was behind the disruption because he decided to testify. Even more alarming to Matthews was that AT&T found that someone had installed a wiretap on his phone line. For the next two critical weeks, Jesse couldn't reach Matthews.

When the FOIA trial opened on July 28, 2014, with his star witness incommunicado, Jesse found that the legal ground in the case had shifted seismically. For years, the FBI had argued that its search for the crime scene videotapes had been adequate but that it couldn't find them. Now, however, the FBI claimed that there were no videotapes of the Murrah Building crime scene. Testifying for the FBI nearly twenty years after the bombing, retired Special Agent Jon Hersley claimed he misspoke at Timothy McVeigh's preliminary hearing. Eight days after the bombing, Hersley had testified that he saw a video of the Ryder truck heading toward the Murrah Building. Now he said there was no such video.

Countering Agent Hersley were Jesse's witnesses, Jannie Coverdale, who lived in the Regency Tower apartments, where a key surveillance camera was thrown into doubt by Hersley's testimony, and retired Oklahoma City police officer Donald Browning. A first responder at the Murrah Building, Browning testified that he watched FBI agents climb an extension ladder and remove cameras, wiring and all, from the outside of the Murrah Building the day of the bombing, as if to conceal that cameras had once been there.

Other vital witnesses included former Trooper Charles Hanger on the integrity of the dashcam video from Timothy McVeigh's arrest; retired FBI Agent Stephen Brannan on the investigation into the million-dollar attempted bombing video sale to NBC; and FBI personnel on the computer searches conducted for the

FOIA request. After several days of testimony by these and other witnesses, it was time for Jesse's closer.

Finally, on July 29, the day before John Matthews's scheduled testimony, Roger got a call back from Matthews. When it came, Roger captured the whistleblower's sensational claim of witness intimidation by the FBI in real time in his bombing investigation *Notebook No. 41*.

"I was asked to stand down," Matthews told Roger. "They were supposed to tell Jesse Trentadue. The judge knows. The prosecution knows. The agency told me to stand down. The bureau was very clear. They threatened my disability pension and VA health coverage. Told [me] to take a trip for a week."[286]

In a declaration that Jesse submitted to the court, he recounted Matthews telling him that FBI Agent Adam Quirk had called him several times. The agent told Matthews, "It would be best for everyone if he did not testify," and told him to "take a vacation," making a subpoena impossible. If asked questions about PATCON, Matthews said, Agent Quirk told him he should answer, "I don't recall."[287]

When Matthews withdrew from the trial, his words to Roger were practically a plea. "They'll take my pension and my medical disability," the retired Marine said. "I don't want to be just another homeless vet living under a bridge."

While Jesse gathered evidence for a scheduled hearing on the witness tampering matter, Matthews initially agreed to testify. But later, by email, he told Jesse that he had spoken with his handler, Donald Jarrett. Based on that conversation, Matthews said he had decided not to testify.[288] In the email, contradicting his previous accounts, he also stated for the first time that neither he nor his family had been threatened or otherwise encouraged not to testify.

Jesse's witness, who had once told him about the bag he kept by his door in case danger required a fast getaway, had gone permanently AWOL. John Matthews's devastating flip-flop would leave the videotape case in legal limbo. Before issuing his ruling in that case, which concluded on July 31, 2014, US District Judge Clark Waddoups would investigate formal witness-tampering charges filed by Jesse against the Department of Justice.

In those contentious proceedings, which are still pending, the judge bluntly rejected the DOJ's attempt to have Jesse's and Roger's sworn statements to the witness intimidation dismissed as a conspiracy theory. Instead, the judge took the rare step of appointing a special master to oversee a full investigation. "At this point, it is beyond Trentadue's burden," Judge Waddoups told government attorney Kathryn Wyer at a hearing on August 25, 2014: "Now it is an issue for the court because the integrity of the court process has now been put at issue," the judge declared, signaling his consciousness of the gravity of the spiraling matter.

Eleven years later, the tangled question of whether the FBI silenced the whistleblower has become a mystery wrapped inside the Oklahoma City bombing case. Under a gag order imposed by the judge, John Matthews has never publicly spoken again about PATCON or his silencing. The same gag order prohibits Jesse from talking about the case. The lawsuit for access to the bombing videotapes remains stalled behind the witness-tampering investigation. And the American public still does not know the true story of the nation's worst domestic terror attack.

When Judge Waddoups bluntly chastised the FBI in the 2014 hearing, he told its lawyer: "The FBI is fond of arguing, well, these are all conspiracy theories. The best answer to a conspiracy theory is transparency."[289] But where is that answer, and when will the American public finally receive it? Time is not on the side of men in their seventies who've threatened to expose PATCON. Every day that passes without a witness tampering ruling favors those inside the Department of Justice who are still hiding secrets about the bombing.

Jesse can't speak. Neither can John Matthews. But as a journalist on the case for almost twenty years, I can speak before it's too late. I'm breaking the conspiracy of silence now. The Oklahoma City bombing wasn't lone-wolf terror. It was a rogue spy story. As promised, John Matthews helped us put the last pieces of our investigative puzzle together when he revealed PATCON. We had seen glimpses of shadowy, dangerous forces during our investigation. The whistleblower's PATCON revelations told us that we didn't imagine them.

From his eight years on the job as a PATCON operative, Matthews exposed the playbook on FBI-manufactured right-wing terror plots of the 1990s. To Jesse and Roger, he described a sweeping FBI spy program that morphed into a vast criminal enterprise. According to Matthews, PATCON operations included illegal weapon and ammunition sales, gunwalking, and even, seemingly, international drug smuggling. No whiff of such FBI corruption has ever leaked out, making it easy to understand why, if John Matthews told the truth, the Department of Justice would have exerted maximum pressure on *Newsweek* to keep PATCON out of its pages.

For the same reason, it is easy to understand why the DOJ would have fought tooth and nail to keep Matthews off the witness stand in the videotape trial. Matthews confirmed to Jesse repeatedly that the FBI formed the Aryan Republican Army as a front group to incite violence. If true, and if, as mounting evidence suggests, the ARA played a role in the bombing, the FBI was heavily accountable for the deaths, injuries, and damage of April 19, 1995.

Journalist John Solomon's confirmation that Andreas Strassmeir served as a PATCON operative adds to the weight of accountability. It aligns with Roger Charles's 2006 intel from his CIA source that Strassmeir was "a German government asset whose information was shared with the FBI." *Newsweek*'s reporting spotlighted troubling questions. Suppose it was true that Strassmeir was the FBI's PATCON operative. Who managed him while he reportedly spearheaded the bomb plot, advocated blowing up federal buildings, and went on scouting missions to Oklahoma City? Who was looking out for the innocent men, women, and children in the Murrah Building that terrible day?

In the spring of 1996, British journalist Ambrose Evans-Pritchard was on the trail of those questions a few months after Andreas Strassmeir slipped out of the US and flew home to Germany. In a series of interviews with Evans-Pritchard, Strassmeir spoke vicariously and seemingly with deep knowledge about the bombing, based on a "very reliable source" who Evans-Pritchard took to be Strassmeir himself. "I sensed that he was in deep anguish about the tragedy and wished to get some of it off his chest without violating any secret protocol he may have signed," Evans-Pritchard wrote in his 1997 book, *The Secret Life of Bill Clinton*.

"The different agencies weren't cooperating," Strassmeir told Evans-Pritchard. "In fact, they were working *against* each other. You even had a situation where one branch of the FBI was investigating and not sharing anything with another branch of the FBI."

But the ATF was the agency that most incited Strassmeir's scorn. "The ATF had an informant inside this operation," Strassmeir said. "They had advance warning, and they bungled it. What they should have done is make an arrest while the bomb was still being made instead of waiting til the last moment for a publicity stunt."

"Either you are a mass murderer, or you are an undercover agent," Evans-Pritchard told Strassmeir to push his subject into a disclosure. "So who was it then?" Evans-Pritchard challenged. "The ATF? The Bureau? Who were you working for?"

Strassmeir prepared to bail. "Look, I can't talk any longer."

Evans-Pritchard pressed on: "There comes a time in every botched operation when the informant has to speak out to save his own skin, and that's now, Andreas."

The reporter had finally hit home. "How can he?" Strassmeir shouted into the phone. "What happens if it comes out that the plant was a provocateur?"

"A provocateur?" Evans-Pritchard asked.

"What if he talked and manipulated the others into it? What then? The country couldn't handle it. The relatives of the victims are going to go crazy. He's going to be held responsible for the murder of 168 people."

Strassmeir had tiptoed to the edge but went no further. Reflecting on those interviews, Evans-Pritchard conjectured that "Strassmeir was a shared asset, on loan to the US government, but ultimately answering to German intelligence."

When British journalist Jon Ronson interviewed Strassmeir five years later, his position had hardened. Asked if he was ever an agent for any US agency, Strassmeir replied, "No, never."[290]

Remarkably, for many years, except for those two British interviews, Andreas Strassmeir did not face further questioning by US news media or bombing investigators, even though the victims who would go crazy were on the other side of the Atlantic Ocean.

Now you know. The Oklahoma City bombing is a scandalous spy story, disguised as lone-wolf terror, hidden by a conspiracy of silence, buried alive in maximum-security prisons, exposed by an FBI whistleblower, bottled up again by witness-tampering claims and gag orders, but still leaking out in unverified transatlantic fragments from a mystery man with inside knowledge of the bomb plot.

What would it take to make this scandal right?

Subpoenas.

CHAPTER 16

THE FULL WEIGHT

> Mulder: There's classified government information I've been trying to access, but someone has been blocking my attempts to get at it.
>
> Scully: Who? I don't understand.
>
> Mulder: Someone at a higher level of power. The only reason I've been allowed to continue with my work is because I've made connections in Congress.
>
> Scully: And they're afraid of what, that you'll leak this information?

So, I wasn't alone. FBI Agents Mulder and Scully chased classified government information from the first episode of *The X-Files*. Sure, their investigations were fiction while mine was real, but it feels like we've been sleuthing in parallel universes. There's Mulder, buried in his file-filled office, earnestly pursuing an unpopular agenda. I know that place. I've been there.

From the start, press coverage of the Oklahoma City bombing didn't add up. What to make of all those eyewitnesses, the missing surveillance footage, a phantom leg dressed in a terrorist-style boot, no less?

Mulder would have been all over it, but I turned off the news, focusing on my TV series in development until Jannie Coverdale's phone call a decade later urging me to come to Oklahoma City. This grieving grandmother's plea reignited the investigative reporting I'd done at *America's Most Wanted* and inspired an absolute commitment to pursue accountability for the bombing and its inexplicable cover-up by the FBI.

What began as a solo effort has grown into team coverage as many of the people you've met in this book mobilized to reveal the truth and bring closure to victims' families by sharing their firsthand knowledge, FOIA lawsuits, and deep dive research. My reporting evolved into collaborative journalism, our investigation.

⅄

Like Agent Mulder, we had some connections in Congress, notably Representative Dana Rohrabacher and Senate investigator Michael Hubbard. Still, the hearings that Hubbard's boss, Senator Orrin Hatch, the powerful chairman of the Judiciary Committee, repeatedly promised in the Kenneth Trentadue case never happened. We believe those hearings were a casualty of the hidden hand of rogue officials in the Justice Department, determined to bury the connection between Kenneth's murder and the FBI's botched sting operation in Oklahoma City.

Over the past three decades, the FBI has recruited a burgeoning army of citizen informers. Their assignments often involved them in morally compromising acts of betraying friends, family, or business associates. Meanwhile, their FBI managers seemingly gave them broad leeway or even encouraged them to incite their targets to commit crimes. Abuses of federal surveillance powers metastasized.

"[I]n the decade since 9/11, the FBI has built the largest network of spies ever to exist in the United States—with ten times as many informants on the streets today, as there were during the infamous Cointelpro operations under FBI Director J. Edgar Hoover," journalist Trevor Aaronson reported in his 2013 book *The Terror Factory*. Aaronson focused on surveillance abuses against Muslims in the era following 9/11. During that time, armed with a $3 billion annual budget to prevent the next 9/11, the FBI transformed itself from the world's premier investigative body into "something of a domestic CIA," as Aaronson put it.[291]

According to the watchdog group Open the Books, from 2012 to 2018, the FBI spent roughly $42 million annually on a private informant network numbering an estimated 15,000 citizen spies on any given day.[292] In 2017 and 2018, the FBI authorized its loosely regulated informant force to commit 9,600 crimes.[293] Predictably, disaster sometimes ensued when informants committed crimes with approval or, as some investigators suspect happened in the Boston Marathon bombing, when they went rogue.

Harking back chillingly to the Oklahoma City bombing, the Boston terror attack also took place on Patriots' Day, observed on April 15, 2013, in Boston. Muslim brothers Tamerlan and Dzhokhar Tsarnaev, born in Russia and Kyrgyzstan, planted backpack pressure-cooker bombs near the finish line of the city's annual marathon. The blasts killed three, maimed seventeen others who lost limbs and injured hundreds more, leaving what a prosecutor described as a "river of blood" on Boston's famed Boylston Street.[294] While on the loose, the terrorists shot and killed a Massachusetts Institute of Technology campus police officer. They severely wounded two more police officers in a firefight that left Tamerlan mortally injured a few days before Dzhokhar's capture.

Probing Dzhokhar Tsarnaev's prosecution in her book *Mayhem*, journalist Michele R. McPhee uncovered evidence that Tamerlan, the older brother, may have been an FBI informant.[295] Federal officials were tight-lipped about that in a Capitol Hill standoff that featured some of the same personalities involved in the Oklahoma City bombing case. One was Janet Napolitano, who had become secretary of homeland security. In April 2013, she faced congressional quizzing as to why Tamerlan Tsarnaev, who was on two terrorist watchlists, had been allowed to pass through Customs and return to the US after spending six months in a Chechen terrorist hotbed in Russia. Napolitano tried to explain away the lapse by citing a "spelling error," but Congress wanted to know more. Three months later, before being summoned to testify again, Napolitano resigned.[296]

Soon after, FBI Director Robert Mueller resigned his post too, placing himself out of reach of congressional inquiry after refusing to brief the House Homeland Security Committee on the Boston bombing in a closed-door session. "To this day, no one from the FBI with direct knowledge about Tamerlan's relationship to the Bureau has testified,"[297] McPhee wrote.

Weary of the FBI's stonewalling, Representative Dana Rohrabacher, who had blasted the Justice Department for obstructing his investigation into the Oklahoma City bombing, looked elsewhere for answers. Rohrabacher led a congressional delegation to Russia to meet with its Federal Security Service about the information it shared on Tamerlan Tsarnaev with the FBI. Though the trip didn't solve the mystery of Tamerlan's possible informant status, Representative William Keating told McPhee: "The Russians were more cooperative than the FBI."[298]

Senator Charles Grassley was frustrated too. "Ignoring my questions does not make them go away," he wrote to FBI Director

Mueller, a sentiment Grassley would later repeat in Congress. "They need to be answered fully and completely and in good faith."[299] But they weren't.

⅄

Seven years later, in 2020, the right-wing extremist plot to kidnap Michigan's Governor Gretchen Whitmer put another FBI informant operation in the spotlight. Once the prosecutions played out, the Whitmer case became an eye-opening learning laboratory for everything that could go wrong when FBI undercover operatives run amok. The story created a sensation when it broke a month before the presidential election. It had all the hallmarks of a scripted television drama showcasing the rise of far-right domestic terror. The liberal governor, who issued a strict stay-at-home mandate during the Covid pandemic, was glamorous. The weapons-enthralled suspects—a lethal blend of radicals and misfits, half belonging to a group calling itself the Wolverine Watchmen—were menacing. So was their nighttime scout of the governor's vacation home, featuring a stop along the way to inspect a bridge where they might plant explosives.

However, the picture changed as the trials played out and defense attorneys ferreted information about the FBI's part in the plot. Besides the perpetrators, the conspiracy was loaded with twelve undercover FBI informants and two FBI agents, almost a one-to-one ratio of undercover operatives to suspects.

As more information leaked, risking the collapse of prosecutions and extreme embarrassment for the bureau, the FBI stepped in to silence one of the key informants. A militia leader and convicted felon paid nearly $20,000 by the FBI for his work on the case, the informant played such a prominent role that some in the plot believed he was in charge, not the men prosecutors named as ringleaders.[300]

Not daring to allow this undercover informant to take the witness stand, the FBI charged him with illegal possession of a firearm and then ensured his silence by approving his plea deal. Still, the kidnap case continued to unravel. The final trial in 2023 ended in acquittals for those three defendants, who argued that the FBI entrapped them illegally. By then, nine men had been convicted in the plot through three other trials or guilty pleas. Five received sentences ranging from a maximum of sixteen to twenty years in prison. In May 2024, Barry Croft Jr. and Adam Fox, portrayed by prosecutors as ringleaders, requested new trials. In his brief, Croft called the charges against him a "farce" stemming from a plot "orchestrated [by] the FBI and its tightly controlled informants."

On the other end of the political spectrum, Trevor Aaronson's 2023 podcast *Alphabet Boys* featured the case of convicted violent felon Michael "Mickey" Windecker. The FBI paid him $20,000 to infiltrate Black Lives Matter in Denver during the social justice riots of 2020 after the killing of George Floyd. Windecker was white, wore military fatigues, drove a silver hearse with a trunk full of semiautomatic weapons, and bragged of having served in the French Foreign Legion. It wasn't the most convincing cover story, but it worked.[301]

Sounding like an Andreas Strassmeir clone, as portrayed by informant Carol Howe, Windecker told a Black Lives Matter leader: "I can teach you how to shoot a gun, to hand-to-hand combat, all the way up to like blowing up fucking buildings and guerilla warfare tactics and sabotage." The revelation of Windecker's informant exploits eventually led Senator Ron Wyden on the

Senate Intelligence Committee to tell the *Guardian*, "The FBI owes the public a full accounting of its actions, including how anyone responsible for attempting to entrap and discredit racial justice activists will be held accountable."[302]

The *Guardian* sought out former Senator Gary Hart, the last surviving member of the landmark 1975 Senate Church Committee investigation. That probe led to new curbs on surveillance activities by federal intelligence agencies, including the FBI. "The Denver story and other recent stories indicate that in some ways oversight may have become lax," Hart said. "Maybe—and I don't know this for sure—but maybe the FBI is slipping back into the old patterns." FBI whistleblower John Matthews's disclosures to Jesse Trentadue about PATCON provide compelling support for that view.

⅄

Following the 2021 Capitol riot, another informant controversy slowly gathered momentum, beginning with the revelation that at least two FBI informants were embedded with the crowd on January 6.[303] Suspicion swirled of a heavier presence of FBI undercover operatives at the Capitol that day, but few answers materialized. In 2023, an FBI supervisor admitted to Congress that he "lost track of" the number of FBI informants at the riot.[304]

Also in 2023, Representative Thomas Massie grilled Attorney General Merrick Garland. "How many agents or assets of the government were present on January 5 and January 6, and agitating in the crowd to go into the Capitol, and how many went into the Capitol?" Massie asked. When Garland replied that he did not know the answer to either question, the exasperated congressman shot back: "I think you may have just perjured yourself."[305]

In December 2024, when the Justice Department's Inspector General Michael Horowitz released his long-delayed report on the riot, those on both sides claimed validation for their positions.

According to the watchdog report, the FBI had twenty-six undercover informants on the ground at the riot, and most of them engaged in illegal activity by entering the Capitol or restricted areas during the mayhem. [306]

"For those keeping score at home, this was labeled a dangerous conspiracy theory months ago," Vice President-elect J.D. Vance posted on *X*.

On the other hand, the watchdog report concluded that the bureau did not have undercover FBI agents, as opposed to informants, on the ground, that it only sent three of the twenty-six informants to the Capitol, with the rest going on their own, and that it did not instruct any of them to break the law.

Outgoing FBI Director Christopher Wray had previously gone on the record emphatically dismissing the idea that January 6 was an "inside job" orchestrated by the FBI to make President Trump look bad. "This is not violence orchestrated by FBI sources or agents," Wray told Congress in November 2023.

Still, coming ahead of the imminent return to the White House of President Trump, the central figure in the January 6 riot, the release of the inspector general's report drew rapt attention from political observers.

Prominent sports and political commentator Stephen A. Smith broke from his usual liberal viewpoint and torched Democrats for their insurrection narrative. "My big issue is that I'm really, really sick and tired of every time I turn around, finding something else that the Democrats have lied about or downplayed or misrepresented along the way," Smith fumed on his December 14, 2024, podcast.

Meanwhile, Senator Charles Grassley signaled his intention to probe deeper into the controversy on Capitol Hill when he became chairman of the Senate Judiciary Committee in 2025. In a letter to Inspector General Horowitz, Grassley and Senator Ron Johnson pointedly asked whether informants from other Justice Department agencies "in addition to the FBI, were present on January 6, what their role was, and whether DOJ had knowledge of their attendance."

From the Oklahoma and Boston terror attacks to the kidnap plot against Michigan's governor, the social justice riots, and January 6, proven or suspected informant connections raise the specter of a hidden lethal spy world. Here, federal law enforcement handlers dispatch undercover operatives on missions that can spiral into real-life double crosses, revenge killings, and fatal silencings matching Agent Mulder's worst nightmares in *The X-Files*.

Though we don't know the details, our investigation suggests that is how and why Kenneth Trentadue died in cell 709A of the federal prison in Oklahoma City, as part of a cover-up of a rogue FBI informant operation. As inmate Alden Baker, who, incredibly, met the same fate, put it, "No one is exempt here in this prison, or any prison for that matter, to where if something wants to be done to you, it can be done."

Another high-profile hanging in federal custody took the life of sexual predator Jeffrey Epstein in 2019 in the New York City federal facility where he was awaiting trial on sex trafficking charges. Epstein was also suspected as an FBI informant following a controversial lenient 2008 federal plea deal. What better place to silence an inmate with damaging information about the FBI than in federal custody, where Richard Guthrie, Alden Baker, and Kenneth Trentadue all died in suspicious deaths declared suicides by hanging?

Besides the three prisoners, the other mystery deaths uncovered by our investigation are equally suspicious. Hero cop Terrance Yeakey. The Muellers and their eight-year-old daughter, Sarah. Twenty-three-year-old Shawn-Tea Farrens. All these otherwise unconnected victims—the prisoners, the police officer, the regular citizens—had a brush with the Oklahoma City bombing case. Did they know too much for the comfort of someone inside the government who was watching them?

Early in our investigation, Timothy McVeigh's prosecutor, Joseph Hartzler, reportedly tracked down ABC producer Don Thrasher at home and warned him that if he got in the way of the bombing case, Hartzler would "bring down the entire weight of the federal government" on him. That threat was figurative and did not deter the producer. Other instances we uncovered were alarming.

With every escalation in the effort to conceal the failed sting operation in Oklahoma City, someone felt the government's full weight bear down on them. Citizen activists Glenn and Kathy Wilburn felt it. Whistleblowers Hoppy Heidelberg, Carol Howe, and John Matthews did as well. Journalists Roger Charles and J.D. Cash felt the weight. Jesse Trentadue felt the weight when he was threatened with federal indictment for being on a "campaign to discredit the federal government" while protesting its weak effort to investigate his brother's death.[307] Spying eyes somewhere inside the DOJ always seemed to be watching and, when necessary, taking action to keep the real story of the bombing secret.

⅄

Attorneys general, FBI directors, and Justice Department managers will come and go. We need them. They are the guardians of our law and order who shoulder the full weight of the federal government as well as imposing it. Most of them will excel at serving the public and keeping us safe, as did the two retired FBI bombing case officials who sounded the alarm in 2004, calling on the bureau to reopen the compromised investigation. When Justice Department leaders fall short, however, their enormous powers can muzzle the watchdog news media that are trained to bark. If they don't, who will?

From 2020 to 2024, Merrick Garland dedicated his term as United States Attorney General to combat white supremacy, designating it as the gravest menace facing our nation. But as the Justice Department prosecutor who personally supervised Oklahoma City's bombing cases, didn't he know about the FBI's PATCON program and the neo-Nazi terrorism it recklessly manufactured? In the years that followed, on his way to becoming the nation's top law enforcement officer, didn't he come to understand the menace of America's creeping surveillance crisis?

Will Garland's legacy be seen as an attorney general who stood with Justice Department secret keepers, not with those laboring to unlock the secrets? America's existential crisis wasn't white supremacy. It was the abuse of the enormous power within our justice system. Jesse often quotes Supreme Court Justice Louis Brandeis for the lesson of our investigation:

> Decency, security and liberty alike demand that government officials shall be subjected to the same rules of conduct that are commands to the citizen. In a government

> of laws, [the] existence of the government will be in peril if it fails to observe the law scrupulously. Our government is the potent, the omnipresent teacher. For good or for ill, it teaches the whole people by its example. Crime is contagious. If the government becomes a lawbreaker, it breeds contempt for the law and invites every man to become a law unto himself.[308]

An ardent advocate for privacy rights, Justice Brandeis wrote this dissenting opinion in a 5–4 Supreme Court vote in a 1928 surveillance case. The decision helped make telephone wiretapping an accepted police practice. Over the years, Jesse has repeatedly cited this passage in court pleadings about his brother's murder and the Oklahoma City bombing.

Curiously enough, Timothy McVeigh also quoted from it after receiving the death penalty on August 14, 1997. "I wish to use the words of Justice Brandeis," McVeigh said in the courtroom. "He wrote, 'Our government is the potent, the omnipresent teacher. For good or ill, it teaches the whole people by its example.' That's all I have."[309]

Coming from McVeigh, the quotation struck most people as cryptic and obscure. David Hammer told Jesse from death row that McVeigh had taken the Brandeis quote from Jesse, and maybe he did. We know that McVeigh was greatly interested in the Kenneth Trentadue case, even before meeting Hammer. What seems most telling at this juncture is how the two men, fiercely opposed to government overreach, found common ground quoting Justice Brandeis.

McVeigh saw overreach in Ruby Ridge and Waco. Jesse saw it in cell 709A of the Federal Transfer Center. One man delivered his opposition with a bomb. The other, a lawyer, offered his opposition in court. And there, in that judicial arena, with Justice Brandeis as our guide, our investigation will press on. We will rely on the Freedom of Information Act to continue our search for the bombing videotapes, the still-hidden informant connections to the bombing, and Kenneth Trentadue's murderers, no matter how slowly the wheels of justice turn.

Many of those in our investigation have moved around or through the justice system long ago. Michael Fortier, the star witness against Timothy McVeigh, was released from prison and taken into witness protection in 2006.

Peter Langan, serving life in prison for the Aryan Republican Army gang's bank robbery spree, changed his name to Donna Langan and completed his gender identity transition. Langan was the first federal prison inmate to receive sex-reassignment surgery.

The rest of the ARA gang—Michael Brescia, Kevin McCarthy, Scott Stedeford, and Mark Thomas—had returned to life on the outside by 2022 when Stedeford became the last to make parole. As the only gang member besides Langan who refused to cooperate with prosecutors, Stedeford served hard time. Shawn Kenny, who helped Langan and Richard Guthrie form the ARA and later helped the FBI capture Guthrie, was never charged in the bank robbery case. Kenny was last known to serve in the US Army in Bosnia.

Cleared John Doe 2 suspect Steven Colbern reinvented himself as a UFO expert after his 1997 parole on federal weapons charges. He continues to deny any involvement in the bombing. Trooper Hanger's dashcam video—the one the *Houston Chronicle* reported showing Colbern's pickup truck pulled over with

Timothy McVeigh's Mercury Marquis—has never been released in full or explained by authorities.

Dennis Mahon, not suspected by the FBI in the Oklahoma City bomb plot, mailed a package bomb to Scottsdale, Arizona's Office of Diversity in 2004. The bomb exploded and severely injured the director and a secretary. That same year, at a white supremacist event called Aryan Fest, Mahon said on stage in front of hundreds of people that he "knew Tim Tuttle quite well."[310] After Mahon's arrest for the package bombing, an informant the ATF planted as his cellmate reported that Mahon divulged that he was "the third man in the Oklahoma City bombing."[311] He is serving a forty-year sentence in the federal prison in Terre Haute, Indiana, where Timothy McVeigh and David Hammer both died.

⅄

Andreas Strassmeir, who slipped out of the US across the Mexican border in January 1996, soon began an odd practice of occasionally dispensing insider information about the bombing scenario to journalists. When Ambrose Evans-Pritchard interviewed him in Germany that spring, Strassmeir posed this rhetorical question: "It's obvious that it was a government 'op' that went wrong, isn't it?"[312]

He understood the players: "The ATF had something going with McVeigh. They were watching him, of course they were.... I am told they thought it would be better to put a bigger bomb in there. The bigger, the better. It would make them more guilty.... McVeigh knew he was delivering a bomb, but he had no idea what was in that truck. He just wanted to shake things up a little, you know, make a gesture."

Strassmeir had intel on what went wrong: "The bomb was never meant to explode. They were going to arrest McVeigh at the site with the bomb in hand, but he didn't come at the right time.... Maybe he changed the time. You never know with people who are so unreliable."

He knew the inner workings: "The truck had a transmitter, so they could track it with a radio-receiving device. I don't know how they could have lost contact. I think there was misinformation that the operation had been canceled."

That transmitter reference caught Roger Charles's attention, causing him to wonder in *Soldier of Fortune* how Strassmeir knew something so exclusive, which only leaked out several years later in an oblique reference in a *Washington Post* report.

Still, in a 1997 interview with Germany's *Der Spiegel* magazine, Strassmeir again denied any involvement in the bombing. Jesse Trentadue wasn't convinced. Some years later, in 2006, Jesse presented Strassmeir, through a friend, with a privacy waiver that would open access to records held by US intelligence agencies. After the friend said she was sure Strassmeir would sign the waiver, he refused, thus keeping a lid on secrets shared by or about him with the US government.

In 2013, Mark Potok of the Southern Poverty Law Center checked in on Strassmeir for a newsletter item. Far from his former role as Elohim City's paramilitary trainer, Strassmeir was in business with a partner in Germany selling "historically accurate" miniature figurines from Nordic, Roman, Germanic and Native American cultures.

A decade later, though, Strassmeir was schooling another journalist on the bombing. Striking his confident insider pose, he added fresh detail in an interview with American journalist

Ken Silva. "My most likely scenario—which matches all the circumstantial evidence—is that McVeigh was supposed to drive the Ryder van under the building in the garage, but it didn't fit," Strassmeir said.[313] "And so he parked outside while the ATF was waiting inside to arrest him. They were waiting in the garage, but they [McVeigh and John Doe 2] didn't come to the garage."

Strange but true: On the thirtieth anniversary of the Oklahoma City bombing, in 2025, history would still record the official story of the tragedy as lone-wolf terror by Timothy McVeigh. Andreas Strassmeir knows better. So do we. So did rogue grand juror Hoppy Heidelberg, the only citizen witness to the colossal sleight of hand that ushered John Doe 2 out of the sight of the American public.

In early 1996, a few months after the grand jury vote to indict Timothy McVeigh, Terry Nichols, and the "Others Unknown" for the bombing, the ex-juror said for the record: "It is likely John Doe No.2 is a government agent or informant. And if this is true, then the government wouldn't want that to come out."

⅄

As this journey concludes, I return to the tribe of news junkies I belong to more proudly now than ever. On or off the job as a journalist, I'm always a news junkie, and this odyssey satisfied that irresistible craving and more. Following Jesse Trentadue on his crusade for justice took me places far beyond the pages or screens that make up my everyday world of puzzling over what really happens in the news. I got to step into the story with someone as driven to chase the truth as Agent Mulder, and uniquely equipped to find it.

This was Jesse Trentadue's guerrilla war with the FBI, but I got to go along. Isn't that what news junkies live for—the story? It's not just words on a page or soundbites on a screen. News junkies live for the story that plays in the theater of their mind after subjecting someone else's narrative to tough questions, second-guessing, and further research. The more perplexing, dangerous, marquee, or mysterious the story, the better the ride.

When Jesse told me about Kenneth's bloody handprint by the panic button, the anonymous tipster, and the three suspicious jail cell hangings, I could see the story. When he recounted sneaking a tape recorder into a prison in a pouch of chewing tobacco to interview an inmate witness to Kenneth's murder, I knew we were going places. Soon, as Jesse's "stealth reporter," thanks to his ingenuity, I could bypass prison lockdowns and meet Terry Nichols, David Hammer, and the Aryan Republican Army's coleader Peter Langan face-to-face. For a news junkie, this was grand opera.

Once J.D. Cash connected Kenneth's murder to the bombing through the bizarre case of mistaken identity with the ARA's Richard Guthrie, the genie was out of the bottle. We were in pursuit of a megaton story. The Washington, DC, cover-up brought the full weight of the federal government down on people. When it did, grand juror Hoppy Heidelberg, informants Carol Howe and John Matthews, journalist Roger Charles, and others bravely spoke truth to power. They breathed life into a story that Justice Department insiders were moving heaven and earth to kill.

Lightning isn't supposed to strike twice, but it did in my career. The phone call from Jannie Coverdale was as imperative as the letter I received all those years ago from the condemned prisoner. The miscarriage of justice we uncovered in the bombing case while pursuing Kenneth's murder was as grievous as the death-row innocence case in Chicago. Neo-Nazi terror suspects walked free in Oklahoma. Justice was denied for the bombing victims to save face and careers at the FBI.

After considering the evidence, what story do you believe about one of America's darkest days? The official one, now regarded as history? That Timothy McVeigh built and delivered the bomb that killed 168 victims in Oklahoma City by himself? Or the story this investigation has uncovered of a neo-Nazi plot manufactured by the FBI that unwittingly helped trigger America's worst domestic terror attack?

We're confident that a federal court will one day order the FBI to show the American public the real story, caught on videotape. One day, congressional investigators will use their subpoena power to unlock the surveillance secrets of the bombing case. Or an attorney general will appoint a special prosecutor. Our investigation has delivered the evidence to bring on those reckonings, and we believe it will.

Those of you who have followed the twisting course of our investigation are probably news junkies like the author. You know we're at a crossroads moment as a nation. Confidence in our government institutions and news media is at a crisis-low level. Until Congress and the courts rise to the occasion on the bombing case, until our news media reclaim our trust or surrender to emerging media, it falls to us, the news junkies of America, to be the scouts on a new frontier.

It's critical thinking, what we do anyway because we can't resist it. But now, critical thinking can rescue us at this bewildering moment without authorities we trust. That sound you can practically hear across America today is the sound of curious minds posting on X, hitting each other up with links, following, sharing, and liking information. That swelling sound is the hum of the truth rising from people who believe, as I do, that the story of what really happens in America belongs to all of us, not locked away in secret government vaults. Every untold story someone shares wins another life. We are the human chain that keeps those stories alive until reckoning and justice come.

Mulder was right. The truth is out there. Pass the word.

Rio Sierra Riverhouse
Three Rivers, California
January 2025

DOCUMENTS APPENDIX

Oklahoma City Police Department Report April 20, 1995, from an Eyewitness Who Saw a "Fireball Erupt from the Upper Floors" of the Murrah Building

Standard Continuation Page

Reported Date: 04/20/95 Time: 09:00 Case: 95-036389 Page: 2
Code: 21-701.7 SS Crime: MUR/BOMB Class:

b6
b7C

AS [redacted] WAS WAITING FOR THE CHURCH TO OPEN HE RECEIVED A PAGE ON HIS PAGER AND BEGAN LOOKING FOR A PAY TELEPHONE. [redacted] THEN REALIZED THAT HE DIDN'T HAVE ANY CHANGE TO MAKE THE CALL AND DECIDED THAT HE WOULD WALK TO THE SOUTHWESTERN BELL TELEPHONE COMPANY TO USE THE TELEPHONE AND STARTED WALKING IN THAT DIRECTION. [redacted] THEN REALIZED HE HAD NOT BROUGHT HIS CALLING CARD WITH HIM AND WOULD BE UNABLE TO PLACE THE CALL AND TURNED WHEN HE THEN HEARD WHAT HE STATED WAS A SECOND ALARM TO THE NORTH OF HIS LOCATION. [redacted] BELIEVED THIS TO BE AN ALARM ON A BUSINESS AND THAT IT DID NOT SOUND LIKE A CAR ALARM. [redacted] STATED THAT HE WAS LOOKING DIRECTLY AT THE MURRAH BUILDING WHEN SUDDENLY HE SAW A FIREBALL ERUPT FROM THE UPPER FLOORS OF THE BUILDING. [redacted] AND [redacted] WERE BOTH KNOCKED DOWN BY THE BLAST WHICH HE BELIEVED TO HAVE COME FROM SOMEWHERE IN THE UPPER PART OF THE BUILDING SPECIFICALLY STATING THE 6TH FLOOR OR ABOVE.

[redacted] THEN STARTED ACROSS THE STREET TOWARDS THE BUILDING AND WAS CROSSING THE STREET TO THE MURRAH BUILDING WHEN SUDDENLY A VEHICLE SPED DOWN THE STREET ALMOST STRIKING HIM. [redacted] OBSERVED THE VEHICLE TO BE TRAVELING SOUTH AT A HIGH RATE OF SPEED AND PASSED BY HIM THEN TRAVELED ONE BLOCK SOUTH AND THEN TURNED EAST IN THE NEXT BLOCK. [redacted] BELIEVED THIS TO BE STRANGE AS THE VEHICLE WAS TRAVELING TOWARDS AND THEN BY THE AREA OF THE EXPLOSION INSTEAD OF AWAY. [redacted] STATED HE OBTAINED A GOOD LOOK AT THE DRIVER AS THE VEHICLE SPED BY AND DESCRIBED HIM AS FOLLOWS: W/M 35-45 CLEAN SHAVEN, NEAT IN APPEARANCE, WEARING A WHITE SHIRT, HAVING DARK COLORED WAVY HAIR COMBED STRAIGHT BACK. [redacted] DESCRIBED THE VEHICLE AS A WHITE IN COLOR MEDIUM SIZED VEHICLE OF FOREIGN MAKE. [redacted] FURTHER BELIEVED THE VEHICLE TO POSSIBLY BE A JAGUAR AND RELATED HE LIKES CARS AND WAS ALMOST SURE THAT IT WAS A JAGUAR.

b6
b7C

IN REFERENCE TO THE SUBJECT DRIVING THE VEHICLE, [redacted] STATED HE IS FROM CHICAGO ORIGINALLY AND THAT IN HIS NEIGHBORHOOD PEOPLE FROM THE MIDEAST RAN SEVERAL GROCERY STORES IN THE AREA AND THAT HE IS FAMILIAR WITH THEIR APPEARANCE. HE STATED THAT HE BELIEVED THE DRIVER TO BE OF EASTERN DESCENT.

DISPOSITION AND SUMMARY

[redacted] SEEMED POLITE AND COOPERATIVE DURING THE INTERVIEW BUT NOT OVERLY HELPFULL. [redacted] DID ADMIT TO HAVING WATCHED TELEVISION COVERAGE OF THE INCIDENT PRIOR TO THE INTERVIEW AND IT IS THE INVESTIGATORS OPINION THAT HE WAS VERY SURE OF THE MAKE OF THE VEHICLE BUT SOMEWHAT LESS CONFIDENT OF THE RACE OF THE DRIVER.

b6
b7C

END OF REPORT
INSP. [redacted]
O.C.P.D.
H-2

b6
b7C

Standard Trailer - Continuation

Reporting Officer: [redacted] Number: 000166 Date: 04/20/95 Time: 09:07
Typed by: [redacted] Number: 166 Date: 04/20/95 Time: 09:07
Approving Officer: Number: Date: Time:

00[illegible] 10

Informant Carol Howe's Debriefing Statement April 21, 1995, Pointing to the Ward Brothers of Elohim City as Resembling John Doe 1 and John Doe 2

174A-OC-56120
JRB/csc

1

The following investigation was conducted by Special Agent (SA) JAMES R. BLANCHARD, II, and SA ANGIE FINLEY, Alcohol, Tobacco and Firearms (ATF), on April 21, 1995:

SA BLANCHARD and SA ANGIE FINLEY, ATF, talked with SA FINLEY's confidential source "CAROL". CAROL stated she believes in 1994, she saw an individual resembling the composite of UNSUB #1 in a white separatist paramilitary camp called "Elohm City" (phonetic) (EC). This camp is located around Stillwell, Oklahoma. CAROL knows this person as "PETE." CAROL has seen an individual named "TONY" resembling the composite of UNSUB #2. TONY is PETE's brother, and is not well liked at EC. TONY would do as his brother directed, however.

When CAROL saw the television pictures of TIMOTHY JAMES MCVEIGH, she said MCVEIGH doesn't look like "PETE." CAROL recalled that she did see a person who looked like MCVEIGH in a photograph in a photo album she saw at a 1994 Klan Rally.

CAROL began going to EC around June of 1994. She learned about EC when she called a racist hotline in May, 1994. CAROL met the hotline operator/owner DENNIS MEHAUN (phonetic) who would visit EC to engage in paramilitary training. CAROL began firearms training at EC.

CAROL learned that EC is operated by BOB LAMAR. EC's "Chaplain" is ZERA PATTERSON. EC's Security Officer is ANDY STRASMEYER, an illegal alien from Germany, who is a former West German Infantry Officer.

STRASMEYER speaks English fluently, but has a German accent. STRASMEYER has talked frequently about direct action against the U.S. Government. He is trained in weaponry and has discussed assassinations, bombings and mass shootings. STRASMEYER frequently talks about direct action against the U.S. Federal Government. CAROL has not seen PETE ever training at EC, but is friends with STRASMEYER.

CAROL has heard frequent anti-Federal government philosophy. CAROL described EC residents as being ultra-militant white separatists. Many of the younger members practice Odinism, the worship of the Norse God Odin. There is much required reading at the compound such as <u>Mien Kamph</u>, <u>The Silent Brotherhood</u> and <u>The Turner Diaries</u>. <u>The Turner Diaries</u> is a book which described the idea of driving a delivery truck loaded with explosives into the delivery area of a Federal building and detonating it at 9:30 a.m.

174A-OC-56120-E-427

Informant Carol Howe's FBI Debriefing Statement April 21, 1995, that Dennis Mahon Discussed Bombing Federal Installations, Including the Murrah Building

174A-OC-56120

2

Many EC residents have sympathies to DAVID KORESH and even have a Branch Davidian flag hanging in the EC church. CAROL has heard a lot of discussion of hatred toward the U.S. Government for the WACO raid, and that EC could be the government's next victim. Although some EC members have suggested that they should strike the government first, CAROL has heard of no specific plans for vengeance.

EC receives funds from a Neurosurgeon, Dr. PETER LIPRON, who resides in Lawton, Oklahoma. LIPRON has associated with MEHAUN and various "militia" movements in Oklahoma. LIPRON has purchased communication equipment and medical supplies for EC.

MEHAUN has talked with CAROL about targeting federal installations for destruction through bombings, such as the IRS Building, the Tulsa Federal Building and the Oklahoma City Federal Building. MEHAUN has also discussed a plan for destroying power lines from Oklahoma City to Catousa, Oklahoma, during the hottest time of the summer. MEHAUN reasons this will create a panic, and without air conditioning, mass race riots would begin.

MEHAUN resides at 1448 N. College, Tulsa, Oklahoma. MEHAUN and STRASMEYER has taken three trips to Oklahoma City in November, 1994, December, 1994, and February, 1995. CAROL only accompanied the group once, in December, 1994. CAROL remembered visiting a church on the NW or NE 10th. They also visited the "Jesus is Lord" salvage yard on Northwest 10th operated by JOE CECIL.

EC has computer equipment, food, agricultural resources, two fishponds, reservoirs, livestock and weapons. CAROL said EC has 308 rifles, MAC 90s, mini-14s, and various fully automatic weapons. STRASMEYER once bragged about having an M-60 automatic machine gun, but later denied it.

April 18th is the anniversary of the WACO raid and April 19th is HITLER's birthday. CAROL said EC residents are very conscious of these dates.

CAROL attempted to use ATF equipment to make a consensually recorded telephone call to MEHAN on April 21, 1995, but was unsuccessful in reaching him. SA FINLEY supervised CAROL in these attempts.

Jennifer McVeigh's Affidavit from a May 2, 1995, FBI Interview Admitting She Laundered Bank Robbery Money for Timothy McVeigh

JM holding a garage sale at the residence. My brother and I had a conversation in the kitchen, as I believe there were other persons present at the residence in connection with the sale. At that time he advised me as follows:

He had been involved in a bank robbery but did not provide any further details concerning this robbery. He advised me that he had not actually participated in the robbery itself, but was somehow involved in the planning or setting up of this robbery. Although he did not identify the participants by name, he stated that "they" had committed the robbery. His purpose for relating this information to me was to request that I exchange some of my own money for what I recall to be approximately three (3) $100 bills. He explained that this money was from the bank robbery and he wished to circulate this money through me. To the best of my recollection, I then gave my brother what I recall to be approximately $300.00 of my personal cash, in exchange for three (3) $100 bills, which I deposited within the next several days in an account at the Unit #1 Federal Credit Union, Lockport, New York. I cannot recall if this money was deposited into a checking or savings account. I do recall that the deposit amount was for more than what had been provided to me by my brother. I believe the total deposit may have been for approximately $500.00.

I observed at that time that my brother had on his person an undetermined quantity of $100 bills, of which he JM

5

FBI Report May 4, 1995, on a Search of Bank Robbery Files for Methods of Operations 'Believed to Have Been Used by Subject MCVEIGH and His Associates'

174A-OC-56120 Lead Control #04467
TPR:tpr

The following investigation was conducted on May 4, 1995, at San Francisco, California, by Special Agent (SA) THOMAS P. RAVENELLE:

Reference Bureau teletypes to all field offices dated 4/27/95, and 5/1/95.

Referenced Bureau teletypes directed all field offices to review bank robbery files and compare methods of operations (mo's) to mo's outlined in the teletype dated 4/27/95, which are believed to have been used by subject MCVEIGH and his associates.

San Francisco reviewed bank robbery files dating back to 1/1/94, and only located five bank robberies wherein a hoax explosive device was used and all five of these bank robberies occurred between September and December of 1994. PAUL ROBERT FRANKS was arrested for the five robberies, and during the subsequent interview he admitted to acting alone. FRANKS advised that his robberies only began after his wife left him for her lesbian lover. FRANKS has been convicted and is to be sentenced soon. He received approximately sixty to seventy thousand dollars as a result of these robberies.

The San Francisco case agent for these five bank robberies was involved in the interview of FRANKS and that agent is confident that FRANKS acted alone and is in no way connected to the subjects of the Oklahoma City bombing or any militia group. FRANKS' bank robberies occurred in and around Santa Cruz and San Jose, California, and he has been a long time resident of Santa Cruz.

San Francisco was unable to find any other bank robberies with a similar mo as described in the referenced teletype.

E-4206

174A-OC-56120-E-4206

FBI Director's January 4, 1996, Teletype Revealing that a Southern Poverty Law Center Source Reported Timothy McVeigh's April 17, 1995, Call to Elohim City

PAGE THREE DE RUCNFB 0051 UNCLAS E F T O

ATTORNEY WHO REPRESENTS RADICALLY CONSERVATIVE INDIVIDUALS/ MOVEMENTS AND IS THE [redacted] OF [redacted] WHO REPRESENTS THE C.A.U.S.E. FOUNDATION, WHICH HAS AN AFFILIATION.

IN EARLY 1995, CW [redacted] AND [redacted] AT THEIR [redacted], PROPERTY AND SAW SEVERAL PLASTIC FOLDERS CONTAINING AUDIO TAPES LABELED "LEARNING SPANISH". [redacted] TOLD CW THAT HE WAS LEARNING SPANISH AND THAT IT WAS IMPORTANT TO KNOW OTHER LANGUAGES.

WHILE THERE IS NO EVIDENCE TO DIRECTLY LINK [redacted] TO THE BOMBROB INCIDENTS, IT WOULD APPEAR POSSIBLE THAT [redacted] COULD HAVE KNOWLEDGE AND/OR CONSPIRATORIAL INPUT INTO SUCH CRIMINAL ACTIVITY.

INFORMATION HAS ALSO BEEN RECEIVED THROUGH THE SOUTHERN POVERTY LAW CENTER (SPLC) THAT ONE [redacted], AKA [redacted] TELEPHONE CALL FROM TIMOTHY MCVEIGH, ON OR ABOUT 4/17/95, TWO DAYS PRIOR TO THE OKBOMB ATTACK, WHEN [redacted], PER A SOURCE OF THE SPLC, WAS IN THE WHITE SUPREMACIST COMPOUND AT [redacted], OK. [redacted] ALLEGEDLY HAS HAD A LENGTHY RELATIONSHIP WITH TIMOTHY MCVEIGH, ONE OF TWO INDICTED OKBOMB DEFENDANTS. THE SOURCE OF THE SPLC

b7D-1 b6-1 b7c 1

b6-2 b7c-2

3

FBI Director's January 4, 1996, Teletype Reporting that Andreas Strassmeir Was in North Carolina Planning to "Leave the U.S. Via Mexico, in the Near Future"

PAGE FOUR DE RUCNFB 0051 UNCLAS E F T O

b6-2 ADVISED THAT [redacted] IS CURRENTLY RESIDING WITH [redacted] IN b6-1

b7c-2 [redacted] NC, AND PLANS TO LEAVE THE U.S. VIA MEXICO, IN b7c-1

THE NEAR FUTURE. THE SOURCE FURTHER ADVISED THAT HE/SHE HAS LEARNED THAT [redacted] FOR AN UNKNOWN REASON.

PRIOR OKBOMB INVESTIGATION DETERMINED THAT MCVEIGH HAD PLACED A TELEPHONE CALL TO ELOHIM CITY ON 4/5/95, A DAY THAT HE WAS BELIEVED TO HAVE BEEN ATTEMPTING TO RECRUIT A SECOND CONSPIRATOR TO ASSIST IN THE OKBOMB ATTACK. THE OKBOMB COMMAND POST IS ATTEMPTING TO VERIFY THE VERSION OF EVENTS AS SET FORTH BY THE SOURCE AND TO DEVELOP FURTHER INFORMATION.

THE ABOVE IS PROVIDED FOR INFORMATIONAL PURPOSES.

BT

#0051

NNNN

4

Lady Godiva Nightclub Owner's September 22, 1996, FBI Statement Placing Two Ryder Trucks in Tulsa April 8, 1995, When Witnesses Said Timothy McVeigh Visited

FD-302 (Rev. 10-6-95)

-1-

FEDERAL BUREAU OF INVESTIGATION

Date of transcription 9/23/96

Floyd Ratcliff, white male, owner of Lady Godiva's, 1850 South Sheridian, Tulsa, Oklahoma, telephone number (918) 836-8536 was advised the official identity of the interviewing agent and the purpose of the interview. Ratcliff was advised he was being interviewed regarding the bombing of the Alfred P. Murrah Federal Building, Oklahoma City, Oklahoma which occurred April 19, 1995. Ratcliff was advised that he would be requested to furnish any information he had regarding Timothy McVeigh and Michael Fortier.

Ratcliff had contacted FBI Task Force Agent (TFA) Thomas E. Lee on September 20, 1996, at approximately 3:00 p.m., concerning possible information relating to the Federal Building Bombing in Oklahoma City in April of 1995. Ratcliff requested a meeting for Sunday, September 22, 1996, at his cabin on Grand Lake, Ketchen, Oklahoma. TFA Lee contacted Ratcliff at the cabin at approximately 1:00 p.m., on September 22, 1996. Ratcliff furnished the following information:

Ratcliff advised he is the owner of an exotic night club called Lady Godiva's, which is located at 1850 South Sheridian, Tulsa, Oklahoma. Lady Godiva's is strip/joint night club. Ratcliff advised he has a video recorder viewing the dressing room of the female employees of Lady Godiva's. The video recorder is used for security of the dancers and their property. On April 8, 1995, at approximately 11:00 p.m., a fight occurred between two (2) dancers. One dancer by the name of Tari was hit by an opening of the door by another dancer who was new from Arkansas. Ratcliff advised he kept the tape to show the dancers what can happen and how to keep the group a tight working unit.

Shortly after the altercation, the dancer from Arkansas was removed by Ratcliff's security people. Upon being placed in the parking lot the Arkansas dancer was yelling and screaming, she ripped her clothes off and went to one (1) of two (2) Ryder trucks in the parking lot and urinated on the wheels.

Investigation on 9/22/96 at Wichita, Kansas

File # 174A-OC-56120 -D - 16036 Date dictated 9/23/96

by TFA Thomas E. Lee:tel TEL

Lady Godiva Nightclub Owner's September 22, 1996, Account of Staff Placing Timothy McVeigh and Michael Fortier in Tulsa on April 8, 1995

FD-302a (Rev. 10-6-95)

174A-OC-56120-D

Continuation of FD-302 of Floyd Ratcliff, On 9/22/96, Page 2

Ratcliff advised his bartender, Joe Partridge, took the video recorded of the fight in the female dressing area to Arkansas to show to a group of club owners. They watched the video tape in its entirety. One of the club owners has a friend, Bruce Dirks, who works for NBC on a contract basis. With the information concerning the Ryder trucks and the statement made to Tari, Bruce Dirks started an investigation. Ratcliff advised he was later contacted by his bartender Joe and informed about an audio portion of the tape and a statement. Dirks has shown several photographs in which Timothy McVeigh and Michael Fortier were identified as being in the club on April 8, 1995. Ratcliff advised Dirks has shown the photographs to Ashley and Susie who identified McVeigh and Fortier. Dirks has shown the group of photographs to Dale, the doorman, who has a photographic memory and he identified McVeigh and Fortier.

Upon viewing the video tape, it was noted that at approximately 9:00 p.m., a dancer identified as Tari, real name Pam Neouk, was talking with another dancer Shawn-Te, real name Shawn Tea Farrens. On the audio portion, the statement was made by Tari that one of the two individuals had stated, "I'am a pretty smart man, after April they will always remember him and he would be rich". At approximately 9:11 p.m., Tari talks with Shawn-Te trying to get her to join the two (2) at their table because they wanted a girl to party with. Shawn-Te refuses at first, but joins them later. Ratcliff advised at approximately 1:00 a.m., Tari was in the dressing room and collapses on the floor. Tari was taken to the office and didn't awake until approximately 3:00 a.m. Ratcliff advised he thinks the two (2) males placed something in her drink.

Ratcliff advised the date this event occurred was determined because the Tulsa Police Department arrested another Lady Godiva's dancer for traffic warrants that evening. The dancers name is Susie unknown last name. Ratcliff advised since this incident, Tari has moved to Dallas, Texas, and is believed still there. Shawn-Tea Farrens was found dead in her apartment in Tulsa, Oklahoma just recently. Ratcliff advised he thought the Tulsa Police Department is working the death as a homicide. Shawn-Tie Farrens funeral is scheduled for Tuesday, September 24, 1996, at 10:00 a.m. at Butlers, located at 3rd and Lewis Street in Tulsa, Oklahoma. Ratcliff advised his security people advised there were two (2) Ryder trucks in the parking lot, one (1) new and one (1) old and unmarked, on April 8, 1995.

FBI Director's August 23, 1996, Teletype Linking an April 5, 1995, Phone Call from Timothy McVeigh to Elohim City and Movements by ARA Gang Members

PAGE TWO DE RUCNFB 0141 UNCLAS E F T O

THAT [redacted] HAD RESIDED IN ELOHIM CITY, OKLAHOMA FOR MANY YEARS AND HIS WIFE'S FATHER IN LAW WAS SAID TO HAVE BEEN A FORMER HEAD OF SECURITY AT ELOHIM CITY.

INFORMATION HAS BEEN DEVELOPED THAT [redacted] [redacted] WERE AT THE HOME OF [redacted] ELOHIM CITY, OKLAHOMA ON 4/5/95 WHEN OKBOMB SUBJECT, TIMOTHY MCVEIGH, PLACED A TELEPHONE CALL TO [redacted] RESIDENCE. ON 4/16/95, A TELEPHONE CALL WAS PLACED FROM [redacted] RESIDENCE TO [redacted] RESIDENCE IN PHILADELPHIA DIVISION. BOMBROB SUBJECTS [redacted] LEFT [redacted] RESIDENCE ON 4/16/95 ENROUTE TO PITTSBURGH, KANSAS WHERE THEY JOINED [redacted] AND GUTHRIE. [redacted] DID NOT ACCOMPANY [redacted] AND [redacted] BUT RATHER RETURNED DIRECTLY TO THE PHILADELPHIA DIVISION.

b7C

b7C

GUTHRIE'S INTERVIEW BY THE FBI PROVIDED SIGNIFICANT INSIGHT OF THE ACTIVITIES OF THE ARA. MUCH OF THE INFORMATION PROVIDED BY GUTHRIE HAS BEEN CORROBORATED BY [redacted] AS AN EXAMPLE, [redacted] GUTHRIE BOTH ADMITTED TO PAYING [redacted] MONEY DERIVED FROM BANK ROBBERIES AND IDENTIFIED [redacted] AS AN ACCOMPLICE IN CERTAIN BANK ROBBERIES.

b7C

ON 6/6/96, [redacted] CONSENTED TO WEARING A BODY RECORDER AND TRANSMITTER WHILE MEETING WITH [redacted] WHO VISITED [redacted] AT

Terry Nichols's May 26, 2005, FBI Interview Claiming John Doe 2 Was Someone Whose 'Name Had Not Been Mentioned' During the Bombing Investigation

To: Counterterrorism From: Denver
Re: 266A-DN-6. .68, 06/24/2005

On May 13, 2005, FBI Denver provided a [redacted] additional information regarding Nichols to [redacted] b7

Referral/Consult

On May 16, 2005, FBI Denver forwarded copies of the Denver-generated serials to FBI Oklahoma City and Detroit.

On May 26, 2005, FBI Denver interviewed Nichols. Nichols declined to identify John Doe #2. Nichols advised John Doe #2's name had not been mentioned during the investigation and, as a result, he feared for his and his family's well being should it become public. Nichols provided a wiring diagram of the truck bomb. FBI Denver advised Nichols no significant, useable forensic evidence was recovered from the explosives. Nichols discussed general correspondence between Nichols and [redacted] Nichols repeated his fear if the unidentified co-conspirator was identified his (Nichols'). family would be "harmed." b6 b7C

DTOU asked FBI Denver if the present time would be appropriate to allow Congressman Rohrabacher to interview Nichols. DTOU further advised Denver the interview was to focus only on a IT nexus to the Oklahoma City Bombing. Additionally, only Congressman Rohrabacher, possibly one of his Congressional Aide, one FBI Denver SA, and possibly a former OKBOMB Case Agent, were to attend the interview. Denver advised DTOU this time would be an appropriate occasion for the Congressman to interview Nichols. CTD was to identify potential interview dates with Congressman Rohrabacher and advise Denver to ensure coordination with ADX. DTOU expressed concern regarding John Doe #2's name surfacing during the Congressman's interview. After the one Denver SA departed ADX. [redacted] Referral/Consult

DAD Lewis advised FBI Denver he wanted Nichols re-interviewed on May 27, 2005, by two FBI SAs, during which time the Agents were to advise Nichols that unless he provided new,

SELECTED BIBLIOGRAPHY

Aaronson, Trevor. *The Terror Factory: Inside the FBI's Manufactured War on Terrorism.* IG Publishing, 2013.

Accountability Utah. "Utahn's Brother Tortured & Murdered by Federal Government." July 17, 2005.

Associated Press. "Report: Satellite Used After OKC Bombing." December 15, 2005.

Bacharach, Phil. "Dead in His Cell." *Oklahoma Gazette,* August 1997.

Belew, Kathleen. *Bring the War Home: The White Power Movement and Paramilitary America.* Harvard, 2018.

Berger, J. M. "PATCON: The FBI's Secret War Against the 'Patriot' Movement, and How Infiltration Tactics Relate to Radicalizing Influences." *New America Foundation National Security Studies Program Policy Paper,* May 2012.

Blade, Leslie, and Gregory Flannery. "Queen City Terror." *Cincinnati CityBeat,* September 8, 2004.

Booth, Richard. "All-Points Bulletin: Timothy McVeigh and the Brown Pickup Truck." Substack, June 17, 2023.

Bowers, Rodney, and Michael Whiteley. "'Cover' Blown: Moore." *Arkansas Democrat-Gazette,* June 22, 1995.

Boylan, Jeanne. *Portraits of Guilt: The Woman Who Profiles the Faces of America's Deadliest Criminals.* Simon & Schuster, 2000.

Cash, J.D. "Agents Probe OKC Bombing Links to Bank Robberies." *McCurtain Daily Gazette,* July 16, 1996.

———. "Canadians Air Club Film." *McCurtain Daily Gazette,* October 23, 1996.

———. "FBI Say Strassmeir Was Government 'Operative.'" *McCurtain Daily Gazette*, July 14, 1996.

———. "Federal Agents Probing New Links to OKC Bombing." *McCurtain Daily Gazette*, December 12, 1996.

———. "In the Matter of Kenneth Michael Trentadue." *McCurtain Daily Gazette*, May 1, 2003.

———. "Informant Who Warned of Bombing Now Fears for Her Life." *McCurtain Daily Gazette*, February 11, 1997.

———. "Mahon: McVeigh Planned Bank Heists, Wanted to Be 'Patriot Hero.'" *McCurtain Daily Gazette*, April 1, 1997.

———. "Mystery Surrounds German's Link to Bombing." *McCurtain Daily Gazette*, February 4, 1996.

———. "Receipt Shows Head of FBI Anti-Terrorism Task Force in OKC Hours Before Blast." *McCurtain Daily Gazette*, January 21, 2002.

———. "Secondary Explosion Revealed in Murrah Blast: Were High Explosives Removed from Floor Above Day Care Center?" *McCurtain Daily Gazette*, May 4, 1995.

———. "Snell 'Cased' Murrah Building." *McCurtain Sunday Gazette*, March 24, 1996.

———. "Star Witness in OKC Bombing Trials Implicated in Earlier Plot." *McCurtain Daily Gazette*, May 6, 2003.

———. "Strassmeir Helped Fortify, Arm Elohim City Bunkers." *McCurtain Daily Gazette*, April 13, 1997.

———. "The Rev. Robert Millar Identified as FBI Informant." *McCurtain Daily Gazette*, July 1, 1997.

———. "Under Review Pt. 1." *Soldier of Fortune*, July 2002.

———. "Under Review Pt. 2." *Soldier of Fortune*, August 2002.

———. "Under Review Pt. 3." *Soldier of Fortune*, September 2002.

Cash, J.D., and Roger Charles. "Company Boy." *Soldier of Fortune*, September 2001.

———. "Federal Judge Rules It's a Fact: McVeigh Was Monitored by Informants in Wider Conspiracy." *McCurtain Daily Gazette*, March 30, 2006.

———. "Former DOJ Officials Claim OKC Bombing Cover-Up Began in D.C." *McCurtain Daily Gazette*, July 15, 2005.

———. "Morris Dees Had Informant at Elohim City Before OKC Bombing." *McCurtain Daily Gazette*, December 14, 2003.

———. "OKC: From Bank Robbers to Bombers?" *Soldier of Fortune*, October 2001.

———. "Rarely Used Spy Satellite Monitored Elohim City." *McCurtain Daily Gazette*, December 20, 2005.

———. "Southern Poverty Law Center Tracked Bomb Plot Around the Globe." *McCurtain Daily Gazette*, July 31, 2005.

Cash, J.D., and Jeff Holladay. "Hunt for 'John Doe No. 2' Intensifies; Did FBI Blow Another Lead?" *McCurtain Daily Gazette*, June 30, 1996.

———. "Investigation Clearly Suggests Prior Knowledge of OKC Bombing." *McCurtain Daily Gazette*, May 14, 1996.

———. "Startling New Evidence: At Least 4 People Directly Involved in Bombing." *McCurtain Daily Gazette*, January 23, 1996.

———. "The Final Moments Before the Oklahoma City Bombing." *McCurtain Daily Gazette*, January 24, 1996.

Cash, J.D. et al. *Deathtrap Oklahoma City: Were Innocent Victims Used as Bait?* Peoples Network,1997.

Charles, Roger. "OKC's Unanswered Questions." *Soldier of Fortune*, July 2001.

———. "Prior Warning: Pt. 1." *Soldier of Fortune*, November 1997.

———. "Prior Warning: Pt. 2." *Soldier of Fortune*, December 1997.

Coulson, Danny O., and Elaine Shannon. *No Heroes: Inside the FBI's Secret Counter-Terror Force*. Simon & Schuster, 1999.

Dees, Morris. *Gathering Storm: America's Militia Threat*. HarperCollins, 1996.

Evans-Pritchard, Ambrose. "Case Against Oklahoma Bomb Suspect Collapses." *Sunday Telegraph*, February 2, 1997.

———. *The Secret Life of Bill Clinton: The Unreported Stories*. Regnery Publishing, 1997.

Final Report on the Bombing of the Alfred P. Murrah Federal Building April 19, 1995. Oklahoma Bombing Investigation Committee, 2001.

Fischer, Mary A. "A Case of Homicide?" *GQ*, September 1996.

———. "Cover-Up in Cell 709A." *GQ*, December 1997.

Gumbel, Andrew, and Roger Charles. *Oklahoma City: What the Investigation Missed—and Why It Still Matters*. William Morrow, 2012.

Hamm, Mark S. *In Bad Company: America's Terrorist Underground*. Northeastern University Press, 2002.

Hammer, David Paul. *Deadly Secrets*. AuthorHouse, 2010.

Hammer, David Paul, and Jeffery William Paul. *Secrets Worth Dying For*. 1st Books Library, 2004.

Hoffman, David. "The Death of Terrance Yeakey." *Washington Weekly*, April 21, 1997.

———. *The Oklahoma City Bombing and the Politics of Terror*. Feral House, 1998.

Jones, Stephen, and Peter Israel. *Others Unknown: Timothy McVeigh and the Oklahoma City Bombing Conspiracy*. PublicAffairs, 2001.

Lake, Thomas. "Why Did This Cop Turn Up Dead?" CNN, March 3, 2023.

McPhee, Michele R., *Mayhem: Unanswered Questions About the Tsarnaev Brothers, the US Government and the Boston Marathon Bombing.* Steerforth Press, 2020.

Michel, Lou and Dan Herbeck. *American Terrorist: Timothy McVeigh & the Oklahoma City Bombing.* Harper Collins, 2001.

Moore, Michele Marie. *Oklahoma City: Day One*. The Harvest Trust, 1996.

New York Times. "Excerpts from Timothy McVeigh Letter." July 1, 1998.

Noble, Kerry. *Tabernacle of Hate*. Voyager, 1998.

Painting, Wendy. *Aberration in the Heartland of the Real: The Secret Lives of Timothy McVeigh.* TrineDay, 2016.

Queary, Paul. "Tape Shows Shadowy Passenger in Bomb Truck." Associated Press, October 28, 1995.

Ridgeway, James. "In Search of John Doe No. 2: The Story the Feds Never Told About the Oklahoma City Bombing." *Mother Jones*, August 2007.

Roberts, Craig. *The Medusa File II: The Politics of Terror and the Oklahoma City Bombing.* Consolidated Press, 2017.

Rohrabacher, Rep. Dana. "The Oklahoma City Bombing: Was There a Foreign Connection?" *Oversight and Investigations Subcommittee of the House International Relations Committee,* December 26, 2006.

Sanders, Kathy. *After Oklahoma City: A Grieving Grandmother Uncovers Shocking Truths About the Bombing...And Herself.* Master Strategies Publishing, 2005.

———. *Now You See Me: How I Forgave the Unforgivable.* FaithWords, 2014.

Schneiderman, R. M. "I Was an Undercover White Supremacist." *Newsweek*, November 28, 2011.

Serrano, Richard A. *One of Ours: Timothy McVeigh and the Oklahoma City Bombing. W.W. Norton*, 1998.

Smith, Brent L., Kelly R. Damphousse, and Paxton Roberts. *Pre-Incident Indicators of Terrorist Incidents: The Identification of Behavioral, Geographic, and Temporal Patterns of Preparatory Conduct*. Terrorism Research Center at Fulbright College, March 2006.

Sniffen, Michael J. "Source: Tape Captures Possible 2nd Getaway Car." Associated Press, April 29, 1995.

Solomon, John. "Document: Oklahoma City Bombing Was Taped." Associated Press, April 19, 2004.

———. "Documents Suggest McVeigh Had an Accomplice." Associated Press, April 20, 2004.

———. "Ex-FBI Agents Call for New McVeigh Probe." Associated Press, February 25, 2004.

———. "FBI Destroyed Possible McVeigh Evidence." Associated Press, February 26, 2004.

———. "FBI Suspected McVeigh Link to Robbers." Associated Press, February 25, 2004.

———. "FBI Tied McVeigh to Supremacist Plotter." Associated Press, February 12, 2003.

———. "Government Had Information Suggesting Oklahoma City Attack in Weeks Before McVeigh Struck." Associated Press, February 11, 2003.

———. "Internal Probes Found Problems in Oklahoma Office." Associated Press, May 17, 2001.

———. "Memos: FBI Tried to Avoid Trentadue Death Hearings." Associated Press, May 29, 2003.

———. "Nichols Says FBI Withheld Documents." Associated Press, March 10, 2004.

Talley, Tim. "Attorney: OKC Bombing Tapes Edited." Associated Press, September 28, 2009.

Thrasher, Don, and Roger Charles. "The Families Want to Know." *20/20*, ABC News, 1997.

Thomasson, Dan and Peter Copeland,"Third Suspect Identified in Bombing," *Houston Chronicle,* May12,1995.

Toobin, Jeffrey. *Timothy McVeigh and the Rise of Right-Wing Extremism.* Simon & Schuster, 2023.

Wirges, Gene. "Triple Murders a Mystery." *Common Sense American,* July 12, 1996.

Wright, Stuart. *Patriots, Politics, and the OKC Bombing*. New York: Cambridge University Press, 2007.

ENDNOTES

Chapter 1: Trail of Death

1 Paul Queary, "Tape Shows a Shadowy Passenger in Bomb Truck," Associated Press, October 28, 1995.

2 FBI Insert E-4206, Lead Control #04462, May 4, 1995.

3 Photos and video taken of Kenneth Trentadue's body as it was returned to the family depict a beating. Medical Examiner Dr. Fred Jordan said "anyone who saw those photos would have to conclude that Kenneth Trentadue's death was not simply a suicide by hanging." https://kenneth-trentadue.com/.

4 *United States v. Kehoe,* Memorandum Opinion, August 2008, 7–11; see also David Paul Hammer and Jeffery William Paul, *Secrets Worth Dying For* (Bloomington, IN: 1st Books Library, 2004), 210–11.

5 Gene Wirges, "Triple Murders a Mystery," *The Common Sense American* (July 12, 1996).

6 Brent L. Smith, Kelly R. Damphousse, and Paxton Roberts, *Pre-Incident Indicators of Terrorist Incidents: The Identification of Behavioral, Geographic, and Temporal Patterns of Preparatory Conduct,* Terrorism Research Center at Fulbright College, University of Arkansas, March 2006, 14, https://www.ojp.gov/ncjrs/virtual-library/abstracts/pre-incident-indicators-terrorist-incidents-identification.

7 Thomas Lake, "Why Did This Cop Turn Up Dead?" CNN, March 3, 2023, https://www.cnn.com/interactive/2023/03/us/oklahoma-city-bombing-yeakey-death-cec-cnnphotos/.

8 Craig Roberts, *The Medusa File II: The Politics of Terror and the Oklahoma City Bombing* (Consolidated Press, 2017), 285–317.

9 David Hoffman, "The Death of Terrance Yeakey," *Washington Weekly,* April 21, 1997.

10 Ibid. The piece reproduces a letter Yeakey wrote where he asks why and how so many fully riot-geared federal agents had arrived at the scene within minutes, noting that it takes five to ten minutes for a tactical team to get suited up, in addition to the travel time required. The same detail is recounted in CNN's Thomas Lake story.

11 Affidavit of Matthew J. Moning, June 9, 2004, 4.

12 James Ridgeway, "Dead Men Don't Talk," *Village Voice,* July 23, 1996.

13 FBI 302 report D-16036, interview with Floyd Ratcliff on September 22, 1996.

14 Ibid., 2.

15 FBI 302 report D2-2617, interview with Lea McGown April 26, 1995. McGown said McVeigh backed a Ryder truck into the Dreamland parking lot on Sunday April 16 when she sent her son, Eric McGown, to tell McVeigh to move the truck to the front of the motel. FBI 302 report D-8151, interview with Lea McGown May 7, 1995. McGown said the Ryder truck on the motel grounds on the 16th did not have the word "Ryder" on the back doors, was faded yellow in color, and had no printing visible. FBI 302 report D-2609, interview with Eric McGown April 25, 1995; FBI 302 report D-2605, interview with David King April 27, 1995; McVeigh trial testimony of Herta King May 27, 1997; Terry Nichols federal trial testimony of Renda Truong December 2, 1997. All said McVeigh was at the Dreamland with a Ryder truck on Easter Sunday.

16 Estate of Kenneth Michael Trentadue et al. v. U.S.A., U.S. Court of Appeals for the Tenth Circuit, Appeal Brief, September 21, 2002, 36.

17 Mary A. Fischer, "Cover-Up in Cell 709A," *GQ*, December 1997, 277, https://kennethtrentadue.com/pdf/Mary_Fischer_2_Dec_1997-OCR.pdf.

18 John Parker, "Report Supports Suicide as Cause of Inmate's Death," *The Oklahoman*, July 15, 1998.

19 Report of Dr. E. Paul France, PhD, BCFE, April 14, 1999.

20 Mary A. Fischer, "A Case of Homicide?" *GQ*, September 1996, https://kennethtrentadue.com/pdf/Mary_Fischer_1_Sep_1996.pdf.

21 Fischer, "Cover-up in Cell 709A," 277.

22 *Trentadue et al. v. USA*, Deposition of Alden Gillis Baker on November 13, 1998.

23 *Trentadue et al. v. USA*, Appeal Brief, 76.

Chapter 2: The Phantom

24 Michele Marie Moore, *Oklahoma City: Day One* (Eagar, AZ: The Harvest Trust, 1996).

25 "Experts Say Blast Bears Hallmarks of Mideast Terrorism," *Baltimore Sun*, April 20, 1995.

26 FBI 302 report D-71, interview with Manuel Acosta and Claudia Rossavik April 19, 1995, for the witness accounts. The APB, see David Hoffman, *The Oklahoma City Bombing and the Politics of Terror* (Venice, CA: Feral House, 1998), 178.

27 Hoffman, 436, note 414: "David Hall, interview with author. Hall said the APB was canceled by an FBI agent named Webster."

28 Terry Nichols federal trial testimony of Charles Hanger on November 5, 1997.

29 Initially, Fortier said on CNN that "Timothy McVeigh is an innocent man." Danny Coulson writes in his book that Fortier's compliance came after "my remark about the gurney and the lethal injection had taken a little of the starch out of him."

30 FBI Insert E-8507, October 27, 1995; FBI Insert E-8508, October 27, 1995.

31 Dan Thomasson and Peter Copeland, "Third Suspect Identified in Bombing," *Houston Chronicle*, May 12, 1995.

32 FBI 302 report D-4461 interview with Linda Willoughby, manager of the Mail Room, May 12, 1995. This FBI 302 report has as an attachment an ATF interview in which it was recorded that Willoughby "ID'd a photograph of Colbern to ATF" and further told ATF that "McVeigh authorized both Colbern and Michael Fortier to pick up his mail."

33 Andrew Gumbel and Roger G. Charles, *Oklahoma City: What the Investigation Missed—and Why It Still Matters* (New York: William Morrow, 2012), 216.

34 Richard Booth, "All-Points Bulletin: Timothy McVeigh and the Brown Pickup Truck," Substack, June 17, 2023, https://richardbooth.substack.com/p/all-points-bulletin-timothy-mcveigh.

35 Author's phone call to Peter Copeland.

36 David Johnston, "Leg in the Oklahoma City Rubble Was That of a Black Woman," *New York Times*, August 31, 1995, https://www.nytimes.com/1995/08/31/us/leg-in-the-oklahoma-city-rubble-was-that-of-a-black-woman.html.

37 Jon Rappoport, "Interview with OKC Grand Jury Member Hoppy Heidelberg."

38 *A Noble Lie*, Free Mind Films, 2012. Interview with Hoppy Heidelberg.

39 Lawrence Myers, "OKC Grand Juror Claims 'Cover-up,'" *Media Bypass*, November 1995.

40 Hoppy Heidelberg letter to US District Court Judge David L. Russell on October 5, 1995. See also: Nolan Clay and Randy Ellis, "Fired Grand Juror Complains 'John Doe 2' Evidence Withheld," *The Oklahoman*, October 27, 1995, https://www.oklahoman.com/story/news/1995/10/27/fired-grand-juror-complains-john-doe-2-evidence-withheld/62375273007/.

Chapter 3: The Call

41 John Solomon, "Internal Probes Found Problems in Oklahoma Office," Associated Press, May 17, 2001.

42 "McVeigh Executed: Eyes Open in Death; Time of Death Called at 8:14 AM," Associated Press, June 11, 2001

43 *Final Report on the Bombing of the Alfred P. Murrah Federal Building April 19, 1995,* Oklahoma Bombing Investigation Committee, 2001.

44 Ibid., 449.

45 Ibid., 331.

46 *Executive Summary of Evidence Regarding the Murder of Kenneth Michael Trentadue and Cover-up of That Crime,* Exhibits 47–49. The *Executive Summary* exhibits are online: https://kennethtrentadue.com/pdf/EXECUTIVE_SUMMARY_KMT-EXHIBITS.pdf.

47 Phil Bacharach, "Dead in His Cell," *Oklahoma Gazette,* August 1997.

48 Ibid.

49 Michael Hubbard interview with author, April 2024.

50 Sen. Orrin Hatch at Senate Judiciary Committee Oversight Hearing on May 1, 1997, https://www.youtube.com/watch?v=Tt0yyZT-BBY.

51 *Trentadue Chronology,* March 25, 1997. Jesse Trentadue notes that "the Civil Rights Division attorneys conducting the Grand Jury and the FBI hold a meeting to discuss the possibility of indicting me for 'obstruction [of justice] or fraud.... The consensus of those present at that meeting is not to open a separate investigation of me because I would have to be notified that I was a 'target.'"

52 *Trentadue Chronology,* January 16, 1997.

53 *Trentadue Chronology,* May 29, 1997.

54 *Trentadue Chronology,* July 1, 1997.

55 *Trentadue Chronology,* July 3, 1997.

56 *Trentadue Mission,* a collection of Justice Department emails obtained by Jesse Trentadue through discovery in the family's civil lawsuit; shared with author.

57 Letter from Jesse Trentadue to Sen. Patrick Leahy, chairman of the Senate Judiciary Committee, December 19, 2008; shared with author.

Chapter 4: The Outsider

58 "Talk of the Town: Oklahoma Scoops," *New Yorker,* March 17, 1997. Regarding press ignoring the seismographic evidence, see J.D. Cash, "Relatives of OKC Bombing Victims Seek Probe of Cause," *McCurtain Gazette,* June 18, 1995.

59 Ibid., Cash.

60 "The Families Want to Know," *20/20,* ABC News, January 17, 1997, covers the fire department threat, the bomb squad, and the absent ATF agents. Regarding authorities trying to track a transponder signal, see

Roger Charles, "OKC's Unanswered Questions," *Soldier of Fortune*, July 2001, 68–69.

61 "The Families Want to Know," *20/20*, ABC News, interview with Bruce Shaw in 1997. Shaw's testimony was also included in the *Final Report on the Bombing of the Alfred P. Murrah Federal Building April 19, 1995*, Oklahoma Bombing Investigation Committee, 2001, 270–271.

62 David Johnston, "New Suspect Is Ruled Out in Bombing," *New York Times*, June 15, 1995, https://www.nytimes.com/1995/06/15/us/new-suspect-is-ruled-out-in-bombing.html.

63 Jo Thomas, "Suspect's Sketch in Oklahoma Case Called an Error," *New York Times*, January 30, 1997, https://www.nytimes.com/1997/01/30/us/suspect-s-sketch-in-oklahoma-case-called-an-error.html.

64 Data compiled by researcher Richard Booth, sourced from FBI 302 reports, Nichols and McVeigh trial transcripts, grand jury testimony, news clippings, and witness interviews conducted for various documentary films.

65 Kerry Noble, *Tabernacle of Hate: Why They Bombed Oklahoma City* (Bristol, UK: Voyager, 1998), 133.

66 Noble, 134.

67 Stuart Wright, *Patriots, Politics, and the OKC Bombing* (Cambridge, UK: Cambridge University Press, 2007), 91.

68 Kathleen Belew, *Bring the War Home: The White Power Movement and Paramilitary America*, (Cambridge, MA: Harvard University Press, 2018), 172.

69 Julie DelCour, "Role in Bombing Denied," *Tulsa World*, February 6, 1996.

70 Noble, 9.

71 Andrew Gumbel and Roger G. Charles, *Oklahoma City: What the Investigation Missed—and Why It Still Matters* (New York: William Morrow, 2012), 20.

72 Ibid., 29–30.

73 Morris Dees, *Gathering Storm: America's Militia Threat* (New York: HarperCollins, 1996), 162–63.

74 Roger Charles interview, 2018; shared with author.

Chapter 5: Marine Landing

75 Thrasher pitch memo, from Roger Charles's notes; shared with author 2017.

76 Jeffrey Toobin, *Homegrown: Timothy McVeigh and the Rise of Right-Wing Extremism* (New York: Simon & Schuster, 2023), 220.

77 The John Doe 1 descriptions were provided by Elliott's Body Shop witnesses Eldon Elliott, Vicki Beemer, and Tom Kessinger. Descriptions compiled from the following FBI 302 reports: D-1347 interview with Eldon Elliott, April 19, 1995; D-1348 interview with Eldon Elliott, April 20, 1995; D-1349 interview with Vicki Beemer, April 20, 1995; D-1197 interview with Tom Kessinger, April 19, 1995. Additional details on height and weight of JD1 were sourced from FBI 302 D-14259 interview with Tom Kessinger by Raymond Rozycki, April 20, 1995, where Kessinger described JD1 as "175–185 lbs" and 5'10" and FBI 302 D-1348 interview with Eldon Elliott, April 20, 1995 where Elliott described JD1 as "180 –185 lbs" and 5'10".

78 Ibid., D-14259 Kessinger and D-1348 Elliott, D-1349 Beemer.

79 Statement by FBI Special Agent in Charge Weldon Kennedy, April 20, 1995. The statement transcript notes that JD1 was "5'10"–5'11" and 180–185 pounds.

80 FBI 302 D-1200 interview with Tom Kessinger by Ronald Koziol, April 30, 1995.

81 Ibid.

82 FBI 302 D-6107 interview with Eldon Elliott by Jon Hersley, June 8, 1995.

83 Jeanne Boylan, *Portraits of Guilt: The Woman Who Profiles the Faces of America's Deadliest Criminals* (New York: Simon & Schuster, 2000), 233.

84 Ramos interview detailed in FBI Insert E-1507.

85 Ibid.

86 McVeigh Federal Trial Exhibit: McDonald's security camera footage. The footage has a 3:57 p.m. time stamp, and McVeigh is recorded wearing light-colored pants, and a long-sleeved shirt with collar over a T-shirt.

87 Transcript, Preliminary Hearing, *US v. Timothy McVeigh*, April 27, 1995, 123.

88 Kessinger's description of John Doe 2 here comes from FBI 302 D-14803, ARTIST COMPOSITE FOR UNSUB #2, Tom Kessinger interview by Raymond Rozycki, April 20, 1995. Rozycki's notes on his FBI Facial Identification Fact Sheet recorded Kessinger's descriptions of "muscular, large chest, thick neck" with "dark hair trimmed square" and a weight of up to 200 pounds.

89 FBI 302 D-1198 interview with Tom Kessinger by Ronald Koziol, April 27, 1995.

90 Ibid.

91 Ambrose Evans-Pritchard, *The Secret Life of Bill Clinton: The Unreported Stories* (Washington, DC: Regnery Publishing, 1997), 13.

Chapter 6: My Blonde Nazi

92 *Roger Charles' Reporter's Notebook #4*, covering the period of January 14 through February 20, 1997; shared with author 2018.

93 *US v. Viefhaus*, Appellate Brief, February 16, 1999. Judge Briscoe read into the record verbatim Viefhaus's answering machine message, see: https://casetext.com/case/us-v-viefhaus.

94 J.D. Cash with Jeff Holladay, "Hunt for 'John Doe No. 2' Intensifies; Did FBI Blow Another Lead?" *McCurtain Daily Gazette*, June 30, 1996. Cash reports that Morris Dees said McVeigh visited Elohim City "more than a dozen times" and his own source reported numerous visits by McVeigh. This was later reported by NPR as "more than 20 times." See: Michele Norris and Robert Siegel, *All Things Considered*, National Public Radio, May 7, 2004.

95 Terry Nichols's federal trial testimony of Carol Howe on December 10, 1997.

96 Charles, *Reporter's Notebook #4*.

97 David Dishneau, "Prosecutor No Stranger to Adversity," Associated Press, June 17, 1995.

98 Ambrose Evans-Pritchard, "Case Against Oklahoma Bomb Suspect Collapses," *Sunday Telegraph*, February 2, 1997. Evans-Pritchard reported that on Wednesday, January 29, 1997—"the day before Brescia's arrest"—the [DOJ] "announced that John Doe #2 had never existed."

99 FBI Insert E-427, Carol Howe debriefing by SA James Blanchard (FBI) and SA Angie Finley (ATF) on April 21, 1995.

100 Andrew Gumbel and Roger G. Charles, *Oklahoma City: What the Investigation Missed—and Why It Still Matters* (New York: William Morrow, 2012). See endnote on the Ward brothers' Oregon arrests and curious FBI bailout, 460–61.

Chapter 7: Truth to Power

101 *Roger Charles' Reporter's Notebook #4*, covering the period of January 14 through February 20, 1997; shared with author 2018.

102 Stephen Jones and Peter Israel, *Others Unknown: Timothy McVeigh and the Oklahoma City Bombing Conspiracy* (New York: PublicAffairs, 2001), 220.

103 Roger Charles interview with author, 2017.

104 John Solomon and Aaron Mehta, "Memo Suggests FBI Had Mole Inside ABC News in 1990s," Website of the Center for Public Integrity, April 5, 2011, https://publicintegrity.org/accountability/memo-suggests-fbi-had-mole-inside-abc-news-in-1990s/.

105 Ibid. "Obviously any reporter who is simultaneously working for a media outlet and giving info to the government has a conflict of interest, said Jill Olmsted, who taught journalistic ethics in her role as journalism division director for American University's School of Communication," https://www.american.edu/soc/faculty/jolmste.cfm.

106 Keach Hagey, "CBS's Isham: I Was No FBI Informant," *Politico*, April 5, 2011, https://www.politico.com/story/2011/04/cbss-isham-i-was-no-fbi-informant-052616.

107 David Harper, "Howe's Facts Differ from Government's," *Tulsa World*, July 28, 1997.

108 David Harper, "Howe Acquitted in Bomb Case," *Tulsa World*, August 2, 1997.

109 Andrew Gumbel and Roger G. Charles, *Oklahoma City: What the Investigation Missed—and Why It Still Matters* (New York: William Morrow, 2012), 97–98.

110 J.D. Cash, "Mystery Surrounds German's Link to Bombing," *McCurtain Daily Gazette*, February 4, 1996.

111 J.D. Cash, "FBI Says Strassmeir Was Government 'Operative,'" *McCurtain Sunday Gazette*, July 14, 1996.

112 Gene Wirges, "Triple Murders a Mystery," *The Common Sense American* 2, no. 8 (July 12, 1996). Wirges quotes Mueller from a November 1995 interview, writing that "he believed one or both (Strassmeir or Brescia) might be connected with his home's burglary, or even ATF." Regarding Mueller thinking Strassmeir or Brescia might "assassinate" him see Smith, Damphousse, and Roberts, *Pre-Incident Indicators of Terrorist Incidents: The Identification of Behavioral, Geographic, and Temporal Patterns of Preparatory Conduct,* 14, https://www.ojp.gov/ncjrs/virtual-library/abstracts/pre-incident-indicators-terrorist-incidents-identification.

Chapter 8: Blind Justice

113 Peter Slover, "McVeigh Admitted Bombing, Memos Say; His Attorney Disputes Documents' Credibility," *Dallas Morning News*, March 1, 1997.

114 "McVeigh Considered Dallas as Target, Magazine Reports Defense Attorneys Say Internet Article Corrupts Jury System," *Dallas Morning News*, March 13, 1997.

115 Roger Charles interview with author, 2019.

116 J.D. Cash, "Mahon: McVeigh Planned Bank Heists, Wanted to Be 'Patriot Hero,'" *McCurtain Daily Gazette*, April 1, 1997.

117 Sworn statement of John David Cash III, March 26, 1996.

118 "Tim McVeigh's New Friends," *George*, May 1997.

119 Jack Douglas Jr., "Jury Seated in Oklahoma Bombing Trial," *Ft. Worth Star-Telegram*, April 23, 1997.
120 Julie DelCour, "A Question of Justice," *Tulsa World*, April 19, 2015.
121 "McVeigh Jury May Be Selected Today," *Atlanta Journal Constitution*, April 22, 1997.
122 McVeigh trial testimony of Lori Fortier, April 29, 1997.
123 Stephen Jones and Peter Israel, *Others Unknown: Timothy McVeigh and the Oklahoma City Bombing Conspiracy* (New York: PublicAffairs, 2001), 315–17.
124 Ibid., 316–17.
125 McVeigh trial testimony of John Jeffrey Davis, May 22, 1995.
126 J.D. Cash, "Mysterious John Doe 2 Is Apparent Defense Cornerstone," *McCurtain Daily Gazette*, May 23, 1997.
127 J.D. Cash, "Witness Changes Testimony, Says Memory Faulty," *McCurtain Sunday Gazette*, May 25, 1997.
128 Andrew Gumbel and Roger G. Charles, *Oklahoma City: What the Investigation Missed—and Why It Still Matters* (New York: William Morrow, 2012), 308–9.
129 *United States v. Timothy McVeigh*, Proffer for Testimony of Carol E. Howe, 1.
130 Jones and Israel, 337.
131 J.D. Cash, "Defense Rests in Trial After Ruling Cuts Key Testimony," *McCurtain Daily Gazette*, May 29, 1997.
132 Helen Kennedy, "Death Penalty for Killer of 168," *Daily News*, June 14, 1997.

Chapter 9: Labyrinth

133 Andrew Gumbel and Roger G. Charles, *Oklahoma City: What the Investigation Missed—and Why It Still Matters* (New York: William Morrow, 2012), 337.
134 David Paul Hammer, interviews with author.
135 Mary A. Fischer, "A Case of Homicide?" *GQ*, September 1996, 310.
136 "Utahn's Brother Tortured & Murdered by Federal Government," Accountability Utah, July 17, 2005, https://www.accountabilityutah.org/IssuesAlerts/LegAlerts/2005/trentadue071705.htm. Accountability Utah published entries from Jesse Trentadue's investigative diary, which he shared with them in 2005. The opening pages of the report detail the crime scene videotape.
137 *Trentadue Chronology*; shared with author August 21, 1995.

138 *Estate of Kenneth Trentadue v. United States,* testimony of Roger Groover on November 16, 2000.

139 *Trentadue Chronology,* October 5, 1997. FBI attorney Kathleen Timmons reported the results of her viewing the Groover tape in a memorandum for "superiors within the FBI," to include "FBI Director Louis Freeh." In addition to a potential perjury issue, Timmons noted "serious issues" included mishandling of the corpse and mishandling of the crime scene.

140 Ibid. On this date Timmons wrote another memo, where she expressed fear that a specific BOP employee could face criminal charges due to "lack of efforts to resuscitate the victim." Timmons reported that the video confirmed no CPR was administered. A BOP employee had told federal investigators that he did perform CPR and signed affidavits attesting to this. The employee that Timmons feared might face perjury charges also testified before the federal grand jury that he administered CPR.

141 *Trentadue Chronology*. Jesse's investigative diary notes that on June 8, 1999, Norman Perle's oral report to the OIG investigators was that "the camera was working on the date in question, 8/21/95," and that "there is specific evidence of tampering [with the Groover videotape] and the testing confirms that visual and audio material was removed (obliterated)."After Perle's analysis, the OIG then retained former FBI Crime Lab supervisor Bruce Koenig, then working in private practice, who rendered for them an opinion that "the tape had not been erased."

142 *Executive Summary of Evidence Regarding the Murder of Kenneth Michael Trentadue and Cover-up of that Crime,* 15–16.

143 *Trentadue Chronology,* April 2, 1998. Jesse Trentadue notes how the Polaroid crime scene "photographs were never shown to either the grand jury or to the Oklahoma County District Attorney's Office's investigators" and that the photos "show blood spatter in cell 709A."

144 Ibid. Rita M. Sampson was assistant general counsel for the FBI's Civil Litigation Unit in Washington, DC. FBI agent Tom Linn learned from Sampson that the FBI had obtained the photographs from "BOP Regional Headquarters in Dallas, Texas in August of 1996."

145 *Trentadue Chronology,* January 17, 1998.

146 *Trentadue Chronology,* January 23, 1998.

147 *Trentadue Chronology,* July 10, 1998. This entry details fabric expert J. Douglas Perkins's findings: "he could not tear the sheet into strips and fashion a ligature because of a heavy hem; that in several places someone had used scissors or a knife to partially cut and then tear this sheet into strips; and that the noose portion of the ligature had not been cut."

Perkins's findings were given to both the Oklahoma County District Attorney's investigators and the Office of the Inspector General.

148 Ibid.

149 Jesse Trentadue interview with author, 2024.

150 *Trentadue Chronology*, November 13, 2000. This entry details evidence developed for trial, including a photograph Jesse Trentadue's investigative diary describes as showing that "the mark left by the ligature" that strangled Kenneth Trentadue "matched a plastic handcuff of the type used by guards at the FTC." (https://kennethtrentadue.com/ligature.html).).

151 Ed Godfrey, "$1.1 Million Awarded Over Trentadue Death," *Daily Oklahoman*, May 2, 2001.

152 Jesse Trentadue obtained via FOIA copies of Sen. Orrin Hatch's five questions and FBI Director Robert Mueller's written responses following Mueller's appearance before the Senate Judiciary Committee on July 23, 2003. Provided to author 2023.

Chapter 10: The Crossing

153 Rob Warden and Margaret Roberts, "Will We Execute an Innocent Man?," *Chicago Lawyer*, July 1982.

154 "The Death Penalty on Trial," *Newsweek*, June 11, 2000.

155 Roger Charles, "Prior Warning Pt. 1," *Soldier of Fortune*, November 1997, 72.

156 FBI teletype January 4, 1996, from Director Louis Freeh to OKBOMB Command Post and many field offices; pp. 3–4 reference an "SPLC informant" at Elohim City and details relating to Strassmeir.

157 Andrew Gumbel and Roger G. Charles, *Oklahoma City: What the Investigation Missed—and Why It Still Matters* (New York: William Morrow, 2012), Bob Ricks interviews by Gumbel in 2010 and 2011.

158 J.D. Cash, "Last Words—Last Lies," *Soldier of Fortune*, July 2001.

159 Roger Charles, "OKC's Unanswered Questions," *Soldier of Fortune*, July 2001.

160 Ibid.

161 Gumbel and Charles, endnote, 370

162 J.D. Cash and Roger Charles, "OKC: From Bank Robbers to Bombers?" *Soldier of Fortune*, October 2001, 60.

163 J.D. Cash and Roger Charles, "Company Boy," *Soldier of Fortune*, September 2001, 33.

164 Ibid.

165 J.D. Cash and Roger Charles, "OKC: From Bank Robbers to Bombers?" *Soldier of Fortune*, October 2001, 63.

166 J.D. Cash, "Under Review Pt.1," *Soldier of Fortune*, July 2002, 68.

167 J.D. Cash, "Under Review Pt. 2," *Soldier of Fortune*, August 2002, 52.

168 Ibid., 55.

169 J.D. Cash, "Under Review Pt. 3," *Soldier of Fortune*, September, 2002, 68. Cash notes that "Kennedy's travel records reflect a meeting with a Sedona FBI supervisor and the local police at Camp Verde."

170 J.D. Cash, "Star Witness in OKC Bombing Trials Implicated in Earlier Plot," *McCurtain Gazette*, May 6, 2003.

171 Ibid.

172 J.D. Cash, "Receipt Shows Head of FBI Anti-Terrorism Task Force in OKC Hours Before Blast," *McCurtain Daily Gazette*, January 21, 2002; "FBI Document Raises Questions About Prior Knowledge in OKC Bombing," News Radio 1000 AM KTOK in OKC, January 17, 2002. Receipt: https://libertarianinstitute.org/documents/img-FBI-Coulson-Danny-Hotel_receipt_04_19_95-OKC.jpg. Cash wrote that Coulson and FBI official Larry Potts's travel records were "missing" for those crucial periods of time, which could confirm the accuracy of Coulson's arrival time.

173 Danny Coulson and Elaine Shannon, *No Heroes: Inside the FBI's Secret Counter-Terror Force* (New York: Simon & Schuster, 1999), 1. Coulson's memoir opens with him recounting the morning of April 19, 1995. Coulson writes, "We were finishing up breakfast with some old friends in Fort Worth when we heard the first news bulletin, something about a big explosion up in Oklahoma."

174 David Willman and Ronald J. Ostrow, "Investigators Believe Bombing Was the Work of 4 or 5 People," *Los Angeles Times*, April 28, 1995. A passage in the *Times* piece relates that "FBI agents are investigating whether those responsible for the Oklahoma City explosion may have financed their activities with the proceeds from a bank-robbing spree across the Midwest." See also David Johnston, "Bomb Investigators Explore Terrorist Link to Unsolved Robberies," *New York Times*, April 27, 1995.

175 J.D. Cash, "In the Matter of Kenneth Michael Trentadue," *McCurtain Gazette*, May 1, 2003.

176 Lee Hancock and David Jackson, "McVeigh's Sister Was Burning Papers, Authorities Report Possible Bank Robbery Tie Probed," *Dallas Morning News*, May 6, 1995.

177 David Paul Hammer, *Deadly Secrets* (Bloomington, IN: AuthorHouse, 2010), 189.

178 Ibid., 188–89.

Chapter 11: Heavily Redacted

179 Stephen Jones and Peter Israel, *Others Unknown: Timothy McVeigh and the Oklahoma City Bombing Conspiracy* (New York: PublicAffairs, 2001), 166–170.

180 Letter from Terry L. Nichols to US Attorney General John Ashcroft, September 3, 2004.

181 Second Declaration of Terry Lynn Nichols, November 21, 2007, 2–3.

182 Ibid., 4.

183 Author interview with Jesse Trentadue.

184 US Secret Service Timeline, 79, https://libertarianinstitute.org/documents/1995_05_01-US_Secret_Service_Timeline-excerpt_re_video_tapes.pdf.

185 John Solomon, "Documents Suggest McVeigh Had an Accomplice," Associated Press, April 20, 2004.

186 Gregory Flannery and Leslie Blade, "Queen City Terror," *Cincinnati CityBeat*, September 8, 2004, https://www.citybeat.com/news/cover-story-queen-city-terror-12174597.

187 J.D. Cash and Roger Charles, "Morris Dees Had Informant at Elohim City Before OKC Bombing," *McCurtain Daily Gazette*, December 14, 2003. See also FBI teletype January 4, 1996, from Director Louis Freeh to OKBOMB Command Post and many field offices, 3–4, which detail an "SPLC informant" at Elohim City.

188 Ibid. Dees quote, cited by Cash from a press conference in Durant, Oklahoma, at Southeastern Oklahoma State University.

189 FBI teletype from director to FBI Philadelphia re: BOMBROB, August 23, 1996, pp. 2–3.

190 John Solomon, "Ex-FBI Agents Call for New McVeigh Probe," Associated Press, February 25, 2004.

191 John Solomon, "Surprise FBI Review of McVeigh Case Faces Tantalizing but Contradictory Evidence," Associated Press, February 28, 2004.

192 Judy L. Thomas, "Oklahoma City Bombing: New Evidence Renews Conspiracy Debate," *Kansas City Star*, January 15, 2006. This piece summarizes the 2004 FOIA suit as it existed in 2006: "In 2004, Jesse Trentadue filed two Freedom of Information Act requests, asking the FBI to produce documents he thought contained information that held clues to his brother's death. Last May, the FBI acknowledged in court that it had located about 340 documents that may satisfy Trentadue's request."

193 Andrew Gumbel, "A Cover-Up Under Two Presidents: The Unsolved Mystery of the Oklahoma City Bombing," *Truthdig*, February 21, 2006, archived: https://web.archive.org/web/20150328190521/http://www.truthdig.com/report/item/20060221_oklahoma_city_bombing.

194 *Trentadue v. FBI*, Order by Judge Dale Kimball, May 5, 2005, 2–7.

195 Jesse Trentadue's 2004 Family Holiday Letter; shared with author.

196 Morris Dees was quoted at differing times saying, varyingly, that Timothy McVeigh visited Elohim City "a couple times" and up to "a dozen times." *The Denver Post* first reported Dees saying, "several times": Howard Pankratz, "Records Hint at Link with Elohim City," *Denver Post*, April 13, 1996. Reported as "up to a dozen times" two months later by the *McCurtain Daily Gazette*: J.D. Cash with Jeff Holladay, "Hunt for 'John Doe No. 2' Intensifies; Did FBI Blow Another Lead?" *McCurtain Gazette*, June 30, 1996. NPR would later report that McVeigh visited "up to 20 times"; see Michele Norris and Robert Siegel, *All Things Considered*, National Public Radio, May 7, 2004.

197 *Trentadue v. FBI*, Order by Judge Dale Kimball, May 5, 2005, 6. Judge Kimball gives the FBI just over one month—until June 15, 2005—to produce the unredacted documents.

198 Letter from Terry L. Nichols to Jesse C. Trentadue, September 25, 2006.

Chapter 12: The Insider

199 Transcript of press conference by Terry Nichols jury foreperson Niki Deutchman on January 7, 1998.

200 Kathy Sanders, *Now You See Me* (New York: FaithWords: 2014), 250, Kindle.

201 Rep. Dana Rohrabacher, "The Oklahoma City Bombing: Was There a Foreign Connection?" Oversight and Investigations Subcommittee of the House International Relations Committee, December 26, 2006, 10.

202 Ibid.

203 Jim Myers, "Official Continues Push for OKC Probe," *Tulsa World*, April 1, 2006.

204 *The Scott Horton Show*, episode 2632, interview with Roger Charles, December 4, 2012, https://www.youtube.com/watch?v=WOxOdSzJc78, starting at 01:23:55.

205 *Nichols Dossier*, "Key Players in OKC Bombing," November 18, 2006, 2.

206 Ibid.

207 Ibid.

208 Wendy Painting, *Aberration in the Heartland of the Real: The Secret Lives of Timothy McVeigh* (Walterville, OR: TrineDay, 2016), 346.

209 *Nichols Dossier* "Facts Regarding Roger Moore's Home Robbery," November 21, 2006, 5–6.

210 *Nichols Dossier*, "Events Leading up to the Oklahoma City Bombing," November 9, 2006, 7.

211 *Nichols Dossier*, "Facts Regarding Roger Moore's Home Robbery," November 21, 2006, 15.
212 Steven Jones defense team memo, notes on interview with Timothy McVeigh, December 12, 1995, 2.
213 *Nichols Dossier*, "Facts Regarding Roger Moore's Home Robbery," November 21, 2006, 21.
214 *Nichols Dossier*, "Timeline," November 11, 2006, 16.
215 *Nichols Dossier*, "Timeline," November 11, 2006, 17.
216 *Nichols Dossier*, "Facts Regarding Roger Moore's Home Robbery," November 21, 2006, 21.
217 Terry Nichols defense memo from Roland Leeds and Alliance Services to Michael Tigar, re: Roger Moore, October 10, 1996, 9.
218 Rodney Bowers and Michael Whiteley, "'Cover' Blown: Moore," *Arkansas Democrat-Gazette*, June 22, 1995.
219 *Nichols Dossier*, "Timeline," November 11, 2006, 17.
220 Ibid.
221 *Nichols Dossier*, "Key Players in OKC Bombing," November 18, 2006, 9.
222 Declaration of Terry Nichols, February 16, 2007, 12.
223 *Nichols Dossier*, "Facts Regarding the OKC Bombing," August 28, 2006, 5.
224 *Nichols Dossier*, "Letter from Terry Nichols to Jesse Trentadue," October 18, 2006.
225 *Nichols Dossier*, "Facts Regarding the OKC Bombing," August 28, 2006, 7.
226 *Nichols Dossier*, "Unlocking Moore's Cryptic Letter to McVeigh," November 15, 2006, 19.
227 *Trentadue v. FBI*, Complaint, February 9, 2024.
228 Jesse Trentadue interview with author, August 2024.
229 Declaration of Terry Nichols, February 16, 2007, 14.

Chapter 13: Death Row Secrets

230 David Paul Hammer, *Deadly Secrets* (Bloomington, IN: AuthorHouse, 2010), 21.
231 Ibid., 25.
232 "Excerpts from Timothy McVeigh Letter," *New York Times*, July 1, 1998, https://www.nytimes.com/1998/07/01/us/excerpts-from-timothy-mcveigh-letter.html.
233 Wendy S. Painting, *Aberration in the Heartland of the Real: The Secret Lives of Timothy McVeigh* (Walterville, OR: TrineDay, 2016), 46.
234 Stephen Jones and Peter Israel, *Others Unknown: Timothy McVeigh and the Oklahoma City Bombing Conspiracy* (New York: PublicAffairs, 2001), 31.
235 Hammer, *Deadly Secrets*, 33.

236 Ibid., 53.
237 Ibid., 54.
238 Declaration of David Paul Hammer, February 16, 2007.
239 Ibid., 2–3.
240 Ibid.
241 David Paul Hammer and Jeffery William Paul, *Secrets Worth Dying For* (Bloomington, IN: 1st Books Library, 2004), 177.
242 Hammer, *Deadly Secrets*, 72.
243 Ibid., 69–70.
244 Ibid.
245 Hammer, *Deadly Secrets*, 70.
246 Hammer, *Deadly Secrets*, 75.

Chapter 14: Blood of Oklahoma

247 John Solomon, "Government Had Information Suggesting Oklahoma City Attack in Weeks Before McVeigh Struck," Associated Press, February 11, 2003.
248 Mark S. Hamm, *In Bad Company* (Boston: Northeastern University Press, 2002), 29.
249 Ibid., 293.
250 Ibid.
251 Letter from Jesse Trentadue to FBI Director William Mueller, September 21, 2007.

Chapter 15: Out of the Shadows

252 FBI documents released to Jesse Trentadue through FOIA on May 28, 2009, were introduced as Exhibit 34 in Trentadue's 2014 FOIA trial. The OKC PD report detailing the lone witness appears on pp. 9–10.
253 *Hoffman v. DOJ*, US District Court for the Western District of Oklahoma, Order, December 15, 1999. Judge Wayne Alley documents in this order that the FBI had at least twenty-two video recordings at its Oklahoma City field office and one videotape located at FBI headquarters. The recordings with the best views would be the Regency Tower apartments video and the Murrah Building's own surveillance cameras. Regarding the Murrah Building's own cameras, see Declaration of Bradford Cooley, February 1, 2010; Declaration of Don Browning, February 16, 2010.
254 Frederic Whitehurst interview with author, 2018.
255 Frederic Whitehurst's testimony at the McVeigh federal trial on May 27, 1997. See also: DOJ Office of the Inspector General (OIG) report "The FBI Laboratory: An Investigation into Laboratory Practices and

Alleged Misconduct in Explosives-Related and Other Cases," April 1997. Released just one month before Whitehurst's testimony, the OIG report deemed the crime lab's OKBOMB investigation had "serious flaws," used "unscientific" practices, and had made "unjustified" conclusions that "lacked scientific foundation."

256 *US v. Timothy McVeigh,* Preliminary Hearing Transcript, April 27, 1995, pp. 63 and 98 both identify the Regency Tower as the source for some of the FBI's still images and video that Hersley cited in his testimony, https://libertarianinstitute.org/documents/1995_04_27-Preliminary_Hearing_-_April27_1995-OCR-compressed.pdf.

257 Michael J. Sniffen, "Source: Tape Captures Possible 2nd Getaway Car," Associated Press, April 29, 1995. This astonishing report was brought to the author's attention by researcher Richard Booth and is one of several early reports providing tantalizing (and often conflicting) accounts about McVeigh's license plate and/or John Doe #2's getaway.

258 Dan Thomasson and Peter Copeland, "Third Suspect Identified in Bombing," *Houston Chronicle,* May 12, 1995. The story remains today the sole source of an incredibly specific and bold claim: that Stephen Colbern's license plate was on a vehicle traveling with Timothy McVeigh.

259 The KFOR news package was part dramatization ("reenactment") and part computer generated, with reporter Brad Edwards narrating what was said to appear on the surveillance tapes. The piece aired in October 1995 on news channel 4, Oklahoma City's local NBC affiliate.

260 US Secret Service Timeline p. 79 refers to "suspects" exiting the truck, while p. 73 establishes the source as "security video." For the attempted sale of the video to *Dateline* NBC, see FBI Insert E-8508 October 27, 1995; FBI Insert E-8507 October 30 1995; Exhibit 50 in Jesse Trentadue's FOIA trial. Also a magazine piece on the attempted sale by Lawrence Myers: "A Closer Look," *Media Bypass,* December 1995, https://libertarianinstitute.org/documents/MAG-1995_December-Media_Bypass-A_Closer_Look_video_tapes.pdf.

261 Tim Talley, "Attorney: OKC Bombing Tapes Edited," Associated Press, September 28, 2009.

262 Scott Horton, "They Are Lying to You About the Oklahoma City Bombing: Scott Horton Interviews Jesse Trentadue," Antiwar Radio and KAOS 95.9 FM Radio in Austin, Texas, April 19, 2010.

263 J.D. Cash and Roger Charles, "Rarely Used Spy Satellite Monitored Elohim City," *McCurtain Gazette,* December 20, 2005; "Report: Satellite Used After OKC Bombing," Associated Press, December 15, 2005.

264 *Trentadue v. CIA,* Order and Memorandum Decision by Judge Waddoups, March 26, 2010.

265 Scott Horton interview with Jesse Trentadue, April 19, 2010.

266 J. M. Berger, "PATCON: The FBI's Secret War Against the 'Patriot' Movement, and How Infiltration Tactics Relate to Radicalizing Influences," *New America Foundation National Security Studies Program Policy Paper*, May 2012.

267 In the 600-plus pages of PATCON documents released by the FBI through FOIA, it can be discerned that investigations were carried out into at least three groups, as well as general investigations into the sale of stolen night-vision goggles and Stinger missiles. The fragmentary record serves to provide an incomplete picture.

268 R. M. Schneiderman, "I Was an Undercover White Supremacist," *Newsweek*, November 28, 2011.

269 Ibid.

270 Ibid.

271 *Roger Charles Reporter's Notebooks #40–41*. Entry on July 27, 2011. These notebooks cover the years 2011–2014, including many conversations with John Matthews and Jesse Trentadue; shared with author, 2018.

272 *Roger Charles Reporter's Notebook #40,* entry on July 9, 2011. Conversation with Jesse Trentadue.

273 *Roger Charles Reporter's Notebook #40,* entry on July 25, 2011. Conversation with Jesse Trentadue re: John Matthews's interview on July 24, 2011.

274 *Roger Charles Reporter's Notebook #40,* entry on August 12, 2011.

275 J.D. Cash, "Strassmeir Helped Fortify, Arm Elohim City Bunkers," *McCurtain Daily Gazette*, April 13, 1997.

276 *Roger Charles Reporter's Notebook #40,* entry on July 25, 2011.

277 Ibid.

278 Jesse Trentadue to author.

279 *Roger Charles Reporter's Notebook #40,* entry on July 25, 2011.

280 Mike Vanderboegh, "Reprise: Hiding Mass Murder Behind 'National Security'—What Newsweak & the FBI Didn't Want You to Know About PATCON and the OKC Bombing," *Sipsey Street Irregulars*, November 28, 2011, https://sipseystreetirregulars.blogspot.com/2011/11/reprise-hiding-mass-murder-behind.html. Note: Vanderboegh's incorrect figure ("176 victims") was corrected in the text to "[168] victims."

281 Jesse Trentadue to author.

282 Stephen Jones defense team memo from Roger Charles, about FBI and OSBI meeting with John Cash at *McCurtain Gazette*, April 15, 1997.

283 *Roger Charles Reporter's Notebook #41,* entry on May 30, 2013, notes of discussion between John Matthews and Roger Charles.

284 *Roger Charles Reporter's Notebook #40,* entry on November 27, 2011.

285 Email from John Matthews to Ross Schneiderman, Jesse Trentadue, and Roger Charles, November 27, 2011; shared with author.
286 *Roger Charles Reporter's Notebook #41,* entry on July 29, 2014.
287 *Trentadue v. FBI,* Plaintiff's Declaration re: Motion to Strike, August 25, 2014, 9.
288 Ibid., 11.
289 *Trentadue v. FBI,* Transcript of August 25, 2014, Motion Hearing, 21.
290 Jon Ronson, "The Secret Rulers of the World—Part 3: Timothy McVeigh, the Oklahoma Bomber," UK Channel 4, May 13, 2001.

Chapter 16: The Full Weight

291 Trevor Aaronson, *The Terror Factory* (New York: Ig Publishing, 2013), 16.
292 Adam Andrzejewski, "FBI And Other Agencies Paid Informants $548 Million in Recent Years with Many Committing Authorized Crimes," *Forbes,* November 18, 2021, details the $42 million annual figure. For the estimated 15,000 informants, see C. J. Ciaramella, "It's (Almost) Always the Feds: How the FBI Fabricates Schemes to Entrap Would-Be Radicals," *Reason,* October 2022.
293 Dell Cameron, "FBI Informants Committed Over 9,000 Crimes in Early Trump Years," Gizmodo, May 6, 2021, https://gizmodo.com/fbi-informants-committed-over-9-000-crimes-in-early-tru-1846840537.
294 Ann O'Neill, "Ladies and Gentlemen of the Jury, Listen with Your Eyes," CNN, May 20, 2015.
295 Michele R. McPhee, *Mayhem: Unanswered Questions about the Tsarnaev Brothers, the US Government and the Boston Marathon Bombing* (Hanover, NH: Steerforth, 2020).
296 McPhee, 221.
297 Ibid.
298 McPhee, 220.
299 McPhee, 141.
300 Trevor Aaronson and Eric L. VanDussen, "The FBI's Double Agent," The Intercept, March 6, 2024.
301 Ed Pilkington, "Fears of Renewed FBI Abuse of Power After Informant Infiltrated BLM Protests," *Guardian,* February 14, 2023.
302 Ibid.
303 Miranda Devine, "FBI Lost Count of How Many Paid Informants Were at Capitol on Jan. 6, and Later Performed Audit to Figure Out Exact Number: Ex-Official," *New York Post,* September 19, 2023; see also "FBI Informant Testifies for Proud Boys Defense That January 6 'Not Organized,'" *Guardian,* March 29, 2023.

304 Ibid., Devine.

305 Josh Christenson, "Rep. Thomas Massie Rips Merrick Garland Over Jan. 6 Informants: 'You May Have Just Perjured Yourself,'" *New York Post*, September 20, 2023.

306 "A Review of the Federal Bureau of Investigation's Handling of Its Confidential Human Sources and Intelligence Collection Efforts in the Lead Up to the January 6, 2021 Electoral Certification," U.S. Department of Justice Office of the Inspector General, December 2024, 5. https://oig.justice.gov/sites/default/files/reports/25-011.pdf

307 *Trentadue Chronology*, March 25, 1997.

308 *Olmstead v. United States*, 277 US 438 (1928).

309 Nolan Clay and Penny Owen, "McVeigh Slams Government at Sentencing He Quotes High Court Justice," *Oklahoman*, August 15, 1997.

310 Susy Buchanan and David Holthouse, "Barbecue Nations," *Phoenix New Times*, February 19, 2004.

311 ATF Report of Investigation, Logan Bombing, Report #308 SA Tristan Moreland September 3, 2009.

312 Ambrose Evans-Pritchard, *The Secret Life of Bill Clinton: The Unreported Stories* (Washington, DC: Regnery Publishing, 1997), 90–91.

313 Ken Silva, "EXCLUSIVE: Notorious 'Andy the German' Responds to TV Series Depicting Him as OKC Terrorist," Headline USA, May 22, 2023, https://headlineusa.com/exclusive-andy-responds-to-series/.

ACKNOWLEDGMENTS

THIS INVESTIGATION, spanning almost twenty years, has depended on many people's talent, kindness, and generosity.

First and foremost, Jesse Trentadue's relentless commitment to justice for his brother Kenneth set an example for us all. As a lawyer, brother, and fighter, Jesse led a dogged campaign that had to be chronicled. During the writing of this book, he was the encyclopedia of the case, sharing meticulous documentation and vivid recollections.

Researcher Richard Booth is the architect of the online Oklahoma City Bombing Archive, which collects a wealth of information and makes it available to all in the spirit of open-source research. Richard served as editorial copilot during the manuscript's production. Without him, there would be no *Blowback*.

Michael Linder, creator of *America's Most Wanted,* reached back in time with the author to reconnect with our phenomenal television triumph that was the catalyst for *Blowback*. Michael kept the story in view with uncanny clarity even when the author couldn't see it yet. His journalism, story editing, writing, and design elevated the book.

Thankfully, J.D. Cash was compelled to report the story that obsessed him. By publishing Cash's groundbreaking journalism, Bruce Willingham's *McCurtain Gazette* preserved the indelible trail of a critical American story nearly lost to history.

Roger Charles, whose investigative research skills approached wizardry, tragically died before this book could honor his work.

Blowback tells part of his story, but Roger lived it like the proud Marine he was.

Leslie Blade, Ambrose Evans-Pritchard, Mary Fischer, Mark Hamm, David Hoffman, Wendy Painting, Craig Roberts, Kathy Sanders, and John Solomon, among the authors and journalists around Jesse, have informed this book with compelling evidence that sometimes fell through the cracks of mainstream journalism.

As *Blowback* went through several iterations—a report, a memoir, an investigation—a loyal circle of readers provided invaluable feedback. Without Walton Beacham, Dianne Donovan, Patricia LaCroix, Phil Lerman, Dana Millikin, and Rob Warden, this book would still be a work in progress.

My agent, Jonathan Bronitsky, took on a book he knew would face political headwinds because he believed in it.

My editor Adam Bellow at Bombardier Books made the call that mattered most to publish *Blowback*. Managing editor Aleigha Koss at Post Hill Press patiently guided this first-time author into print.

My lawyer, Vincent Cox, always takes care of business, remembers the human side of the equation, and excels at gallows humor.

These people deserve special thanks for their assistance, inspiration, moral support, and reality checks over a long campaign: Phil Bacharach, Anthony Batson, Deborah Beacham, Didier Ciambra, Tamara Dutro, Dan Kavanaugh, Chuck LaCroix, Mahrya MacIntire, Allison Millner, Dane Millner, Lee Papa, Daphne Pinkerson, Craig Roberts, David Roberts, Robin Roberts, Michael Rodriguez, Deborah Ross, Guy Shalem, Rick Sherrow, and Tony Zanelotti.

Heartfelt thanks to my wise friend Jay West, who showed me how to do it, step-by-step.

–MR

PHOTOGRAPHY ACKNOWLEDGMENTS/ GRAPHIC INSERT

Page 1

Murrah Building Aftermath, AFP via Getty Images

Timothy McVeigh, photo by Ralf-Finn Hestoft, Getty Images

Page 3

Terry Nichols Trial; photo by Larry W. Smith, Getty Images

Page 4

Kenneth Trentadue Portrait, Kenneth Trentadue Collection

Jesse and Kenneth Trentadue, Kenneth Trentadue Collection

Jesse Trentadue Close-up, AP

Jesse Trentadue Examines Kenneth's Photo, AP

Page 5

J.D. Cash Portrait, photo by David Allen

Elohim City, photo by William Campbell, Getty Images

Andreas Strassmeir photo by Richard Sherrow

Page 6

Davidian Compound Burning, photo by Gregory Smith, Corbis via Getty Images

Davidian Compound Burned photo by J. David Ake, AFP via Getty Images

Page 7

McVeigh on Death Row, by Lou Michel, Getty Images

Terry Nichols by Larry W. Smith, Getty Images

Roger Moore, AP

Page 8

Spray-painted Message, *New York Daily News* Archive